Praise for *Boy's Passage*

"What I love about Brian Molitor's [...] miss" way for each of us to make the boys and young men in our families feel like grand-prize winners. You'll learn about the power of mentoring, blessing, and a rite-of-passage ceremony and hear of lives changed as a result. And whatever your family situation, you'll learn exactly how to create a positive plan for your son's development and for an incredibly significant day in his life, one on which he will be surrounded by a crowd of family and supportive fans. It will be a day that neither you, your son, nor anyone who attends will ever forget."

—From the Foreword by John Trent, marriage and family counselor and author of *The Light of Home* and *The Gift of the Blessing*

"Fathers everywhere should celebrate this significant book and what it will do for their families. The author has focused on a neglected area of fathering, highly significant in other cultures but sadly lacking in our own. I appreciate the tone of this book, which does not lay a guilt trip on fathers for what they have not done but lovingly encourages them into some practical ways to have a life-changing time of bonding with their sons. I highly recommend this book to fathers around the world."

—V. Gilbert Beers, Ph.D., best-selling author of over one hundred books for children, contributor to the *Life Application Bible* and the *TouchPoint Bible*

"With the manly sensitivity and spirituality that could only come from a father, Brian Molitor has given us a prescription that is both practical and needed. The seeds of a significant national movement are in this work."

—Jeff Wright, president of Urban Ministries

"A wonderful, motivational book to help a dad understand his God-given role in shaping his son, this book is far more than simply an excellent read. What you have in your hand is a complete strategic business plan. The goal is to help you understand the mission, the objectives, and the step-by-step tactics to ensure successful fatherhood.

The dividend is a happy, fulfilled, and godly son. What could possibly be more valuable?"

—Robert Wolgemuth, author of the notes in the best-selling *Devotional Bible for Dads*

"Filled with uplifting personal experiences, *Boy's Passage—Man's Journey* expresses the responsibility we have as parents to prepare our sons to be men of God. Brian Molitor not only gives insight into the necessity of this transition celebration but also provides ideas on ways to prepare for such an event. A great tool for understanding our role in the spiritual development of our young men."

—Kathleen B. Jackson, founder and publisher of the *Godly Business Woman* magazine

"If every parent adopted the creative ideas contained in this book, we would not have the crisis in male leadership we have today. I found myself in tears as I read this account of the importance of giving every son a rite of passage into adulthood. I realized the impact of my own lack of formal recognition of my entry into adulthood. Who knows what a difference a book like this could have made."

—Os Hillman, president of Marketplace Leaders, author of *TGIF: Today God Is First*

"To say that *Boy's Passage—Man's Journey* is absolutely captivating and inspiring is an understatement. Molitor's concept could truly make a difference for an untold number of lives."

—Tina Coonce, cofounder of TCT Television Network

BOY'S PASSAGE
MAN'S JOURNEY

BRIAN D. MOLITOR

Emerald
Books

P.O. BOX 635, LYNNWOOD, WA 98046

Emerald Books are distributed through YWAM Publishing. For a full list of titles, visit www.ywampublishing.com or call 1-800-922-2143.

Boy's Passage—Man's Journey
Copyright © 2004 by Brian D. Molitor

Published by Emerald Books
P.O. Box 635
Lynnwood, WA 98046

Fourth printing 2012

Library of Congress Cataloging-in-Publication Data
Molitor, Brian D., 1952–
  Boy's passage, man's journey / by Brian D. Molitor.— [Rev. and expanded ed.].
     p. cm.
  Rev. ed. of: A boy's passage. c2001.
  ISBN 1-932096-06-X
  1. Teenage boys—Religious life. 2. Initiation rites—Religious aspects—Christianity. 3. Maturation (Psychology)—Religious aspects—Christianity. I. Molitor, Brian D., 1952– Boy's passage. II. Title.
  BV4541.3.M64 2004
  248.8'421—dc22   2004004507

ISBN-13: 978-1-932096-06-4; ISBN-10:1-932096-06-X

All Scripture quotations, unless otherwise indicated, are taken from the Holy Bible, New International Version® NIV® Copyright © 1973, 1978, 1984 by International Bible Society. Used by permission of Zondervan Publishing House. All rights reserved. Scripture quotations marked NKJV are taken from the New King James Version. Copyright © 1982 by Thomas Nelson, Inc. Used by permission. All rights reserved. Scripture quotations marked KJV are taken from the King James Version.

Printed in the United States of America

This book is dedicated to the greatest man I have ever known,
my grandfather, Henry A. Molitor.

GRANDPA, YOU ALWAYS HAD TIME to teach the important things in life. At your side I learned how to catch a fish, how to hunt, and how to build the most marvelous creations out of wood.

The hours we spent together in northern Michigan are etched deeply in my mind. I still marvel at how you always knew just where to go to find a bluegill, bass, partridge, or white-tailed deer.

You took time with your grandchildren and made each of us feel as if we were the only kid in the world. When I made mistakes, you helped me fix them. You never yelled; instead you just had me try again. It was so clear that you lived for your children and grandchildren, not for yourself.

The scars on your body told of your sacrifice for your country in "the war to end all wars." Other people sometimes stared, but to me you were the most handsome man on earth. I took note that despite your pain, you never complained and you never gave up.

Grandpa, when your time on earth was through and God took you home, my heart shattered into a million pieces. It took years for that same God to put the pieces back together.

I still miss you more than you could ever know.

I have a family of my own now. I sure wish you could have gotten to know them.

My wife, Kathleen, is the best thing that ever happened to me this side of heaven. She sticks with me through all of life's ups and downs. She's beautiful, both outside and inside.

I have some children too. Christopher is my oldest. He's a son other dads dream of. He is strong, smart, and good-looking. Best of all, he loves God very deeply.

My next son, Steven, is a man after your own heart. Grandpa, he can make anything, fix anything, and work better than most men twice his age. His sense of humor keeps our family from taking life too seriously. I wouldn't trade him for anyone. God has a big plan for Steven.

Next comes Jenifer. God must have known that we couldn't handle three boys in a row. She is the most precious child you could ever imagine. She is tall and lovely. Her heart is so tender toward her mom and me. Jeni is love personified and ministers to me with her smile.

My youngest son is Daniel Elijah. Grandpa, he is made just like you. He is strong and gentle at the same time. He is still young enough to want to just sit on my lap and hear what his dad has to say. When we talk, I teach him about important things. Like how to catch a fish and how to hunt. And how to build things out of wood. At times, I tell him about his great-grandpa Henry and what it is like to become a man.

Thanks, Grandpa, for allowing God to use you in such a powerful way in my life.

CONTENTS

FOREWORD

AT AN NFL FOOTBALL GAME I attended here in Phoenix, a grand prize was awarded to one lucky contestant during halftime. For months people had stuffed entry forms into boxes at local grocery stores, and the seven finalists now stood on the field. Each had received a "key" to a new Cadillac Escalade that had every accessory imaginable. Each took a turn walking up to the sparkling new car. Each got close enough to open the door, sit behind the wheel, and put the key in the ignition to see whether it actually started the car.

With a good pair of binoculars I'd brought for the game, I could see a close-up of the face of each person who tried and failed to start the car. Expectation, hope, and excitement changed to deep dejection and disappointment in an instant; they were so close, yet so far from being able to drive that beautiful car into the future. I also had a close-up view of the one person who finally turned the key that worked. Incredible joy and anticipation beamed from his face. His family cheered in excitement, and I could see the unbridled happiness they felt as the winner slowly drove his new car out of the stadium.

What does winning or losing an Escalade in a contest have to do with raising confident, loved, affirmed, and empowered sons? Actually, quite a bit! For realize it or not, there is a way for a father to put a winning "key" to a positive, blessed future into his son's hand—a prize that doesn't depreciate over time. The key I'm talking about doesn't start a car, but it does start a boy or young man on the road to a positive, empowering future, even as it creates an unforgettable, joyful event.

Having been a marriage and family counselor for over twenty-five years, I have spoken with literally thousands of men who have grown up feeling like the grand-prize losers at that NFL football game. When it came to leaving home with tangible feelings of love, acceptance, and affirmation, not to mention a vision for the future and confidence in who they could become, these men either felt they were never entered in the drawing or, worse, felt that they were close enough to get behind the wheel but were missing the right key. That's a terrible legacy to leave with a young man who has to walk into the future feeling loss, not gain, discouragement, not excitement. Yet it happens every day when a young man leaves home without really feeling that he has his father's "blessing"—his love and acceptance.

What I love about Brian Molitor's book is that it outlines a "can't miss" way for each of us to make the boys and young men in our families feel like grand-prize winners. You'll learn about the power of mentoring, blessing, and a rite-of-passage ceremony and hear of lives changed as a result. And whatever your family situation, you'll learn exactly how to create a positive plan for your son's development and for an incredibly significant day in his life, one on which he will be surrounded by a crowd of family and supportive fans. It will be a day that neither you, your son, nor anyone who attends will ever forget.

So get ready to learn how to put that key to a special future into your son's, grandson's, or young friend's hand. The look of joy and fulfillment on his face when the "engine turns over" will become a priceless memory to you, a tremendous witness to others, and a priceless gift to him.

John Trent, Ph.D.
StrongFamilies.com
Author of *The Light of Home* and *The Gift of the Blessing*

A WORD TO WOMEN

I NEED TO SHARE MY HEART with you about this book. I wrote it primarily to light a fire under the men of our nations. Why? Because we men have so often left the important matters of spiritual instruction, childrearing, and mentoring our sons and daughters for someone else to handle. We have tried to hand this off to our wives, our mothers, and our children's teachers, but it has not worked. The problem with this approach is that no one else can pick up a man's God-given responsibilities. As a result, our wives have suffered, our children have suffered, and while we may try to hide it, we men have suffered. That is all about to change. As he said in the book of Malachi, God is turning the hearts of the fathers to their children and the hearts of the children to their fathers.

Therefore, as you read, please don't feel slighted or undervalued because the focus is on fathers. Neither is there any message here, hidden or overt, that boys are better, more special, or more highly valued than girls in any way. Believe me, if my daughter, Jenifer, had been born first, this book would be about a girl's passage. I am pleased to announce that my wife and I are in the process of completing a book on that subject in order to help parents and other mentors guide their girls into mature womanhood. While the focus of this book is primarily on sons, daughters will benefit equally from a solid plan of mentoring, intentional blessing, and rites of passage.

I ask you to read this book prayerfully and carefully. It will help you understand why the men in your life act the way they do. It also holds keys to your son's future as a mature man. It provides a plan to help our sons, grandsons, and neighbors' sons, and even your husbands, grow into their God-given callings as men. If you are raising your son without the support of his father, it will show you the positive steps you can take to help your son succeed.

Please join me in praying that men get the message that we must do more than just bring our sons into this world. We must also launch them into their manhood and walk with them every step of the way.

PREFACE

OUR WORLD TODAY IS FILLED with many crises. Wars, crime, moral decay, poverty, political and corporate scandal, drug abuse, and divorce are just a few of the seemingly insurmountable problems that steal our innocence and haunt our lives.

Many fight this trend toward societal disaster by whatever means they can. Every counselor, pastor, priest, politician, and parent who has ever taken a stand for righteousness helps hold the line of decency. Yet an honest review of the facts shows that while our society may win an occasional skirmish and even a battle or two, we are still losing the war.

Most people involved in this fight recognize that to reverse this negative trend we must address our problems' causes *before* they explode into crises. Failure to do so condemns us to years of just trying to suppress symptoms. Violence, rage, abuse, hopelessness, and breakdown of relationships are clearly seen in action, yet the root cause of these outward manifestations of human pain lies hidden deep within the soul.

My quest for answers to society's recurring problems began in earnest when my first son, Christopher, was born. As he grew, and as his brothers and sister followed, my wife, Kathleen, and I wanted to empower our children with hope, faith, and integrity; we wanted them to approach life by design and not by default. To do so, we recognized that we needed to strengthen them from the inside out.

Kathy and I acknowledged that the foundational answer to society's plight is first found in a personal relationship with God and in living according to the guiding principles found in the Bible. However, we also realized that entering into a relationship with God was just the first step of a fulfilled life. After that, a person's heart, character, and view of the world must continue to be formed or, better yet, transformed. Sadly, in our society today much of this work is being done after the fact. Rather than investing a dozen or so years preparing, mentoring, and encouraging our young people, we spend lifetimes trying to bring restoration, reconciliation, and healing to broken adults.

As my wife and I wrestled with these issues, we came to one simple conclusion: to reverse our society's downward spiral and to become victorious with the next generation, we had to impart a sure sense of identity to our children when they were still young. Kathy and I had particular interest in reaching young men as we saw Christopher approach adolescence and manhood.

It became clear that the heart of a man must receive instruction, love, affirmation, and mentoring at the proper time if we are to turn the tide of crises in our world. These are the same men who will start wars or stop them, commit crimes or solve them, build families or destroy them. We must not allow one more boy to drift into an uncertain future questioning his manhood. The stakes are too high, the potential losses too great.

I wrote this book to help us understand our sacred duty to raise our children to love God, their neighbors, and themselves so that our families and our nations may be healed. While the primary thrust of this book deals with young men, it also provides strategies for healing older men who lacked support in their early years. It will give you a strategy for doing your part and an assurance that others will do theirs.

The capstone of the strategy is a rite of passage for the boy or young man in your life. Back in 1997, as the rite-of-passage celebration for my first son came to a close, I mistakenly thought that I was done with the concept until son number two, Steven, came of age. Man, was I wrong! Before they left the gathering that night, many men asked for written instructions for putting together a rite of passage for their sons. Clearly, the hearts of those who attended burned with passion about the importance of this type of ceremony. As these few men spoke with others about what had happened, that wonderful fire spread rapidly, and parents from as far away as Nigeria and the United Kingdom began to host celebrations for their children.

By God's grace and promptings, my early attempts at creating a "how to" outline for rites of passage actually became the foundations for this book. It finally began to sink in that God was restoring rites of passage as an integral part of a strategy to combat all of the evil aligned against our sons. But that's not all. I am delighted to also be working on a book on the subject of a girl's passage. Not too long after the celebrations for Christopher and Steven, it was my daughter's turn. When Jenifer turned thirteen, her mother and I hosted a rite of passage for her that confirmed two things for us. First, the rite of passage is every bit as powerful for girls as it is for boys. Second, while the foundations are the same and both help our children transition to adulthood, each has unique aspects.

Over the years I have received more and more inquiries about celebrations and mentoring plans for both sons and daughters. To respond to them more effectively, in 2002 some associates and I created the Malachi Global Foundation. This nonprofit ministry is dedicated to the fulfillment of Malachi 4:6, wherein the hearts of fathers will turn to their children and the hearts of children will turn to their fathers. Through this foundation, we now host retreats around the world where men's hearts are healed and then turned toward the next generation. Each man who attends our retreats leaves with a complete plan to mentor, bless, and host rites of passage for the children in his life.

From people's response, it is clear that God wants to use this strategy to touch and redeem the next generation. As the word about rites of passage spreads, more and more pastors and youth ministers are finding ways to modify the concept for the boys and girls in their churches, especially those who are without fathers at home. The number of people who visit our website, www.malachiglobal.org, increases each month. Some are from nuclear families; some are grandparents raising their second families. Many are single mothers seeking information on how they can host celebrations for their sons, especially if they lack the support of the boy's father. As this continues, we will see a revival among our youth and a restoration of our families. Amazingly, wonderfully, this all begins with the simple turning of a father's heart to the next generation.

God bless you, strengthen you, and encourage you as together we begin to reclaim what we never should have lost in the first place—the hearts of our children.

PORTRAITS
OF PASSAGE

THE BIRTH OF A CHILD. Few moments in life hold as much wonder, excitement, and promise. Months of anticipation and anxiety are quickly eclipsed as the baby miraculously appears. The new daughter or son fills your home with marvelous warmth.

From that moment on, life is never the same for any member of the family. By perfect design, the child looks to you for everything he or she needs to survive and grow during the early years. But that soon changes.

Days rush by and turn into years. Your boy's once tiny frame fills with muscle, and his mind fills with dreams. Perilous bicycle trips around the block become business trips around the world. All too soon the baby is grown and begins to leave his own legacy for others to see.

Throughout the process, parents do their level best to equip their sons with all they need to succeed. Nutrition, tuition, transportation, lectures, and love—all have been liberally supplied. Surely this is sufficient for our young men to prosper.

Or is it?

If these basics are all a young male needs to succeed, then why are so many in our society struggling to find purpose, identity, and manhood itself? Why are so many men, young and old, depressed or anxious about life? What could possibly cause today's endless stream of horror stories involving crime, teen sex, drug and alcohol abuse, gangs, murder, and suicide?

Although "experts" have studied these questions, few seem to offer lasting answers, and the quality of young men's lives continues to disintegrate at an alarming rate. Since the tide has not turned, we have to reach one simple conclusion: we must be missing something. What is it? Do our sons need more government programs or more money thrown at them? How about better schools and stricter punishment to shape them up? Maybe peppier youth ministries or in-depth counseling sessions would forever change the hearts and lives of the young. Perhaps.

However, I am convinced that we can find more foundational and effective answers to our modern dilemma by looking at other societies, past and present, to discover a powerful secret of individual and national success. This secret is revealed as we study cultures that have long helped their sons to transition into mature manhood by design rather than by default. Let's begin our cultural journey by visiting a tribe of eastern Africa.

THE MAASAI: WALKING TOWARD DESTINY

Young Sidimo huddled against the cold night air. The small fire warmed his skin and comforted his soul. The weariness in his body could not prevent his mind from racing with thoughts of what dawn would bring. Tomorrow was his special day. The day he had waited for since he was old enough to understand its significance. In a few short hours he would follow the path his father and all other fathers of the Maasai tribe had walked for countless generations. Tomorrow, in the presence of the elders, Sidimo would become a man.

Thunder rolled far in the distance, and lightning crashed around the sacred mountain, *Oldoinyo le Engai,* the Mountain of God. Young Sidimo strained his eyes to catch a glimpse of the majestic peaks that rose high into the ebony sky. Deep in his soul, he prayed that Engai— the god of his people—would be pleased with him.

The East African veldt was alive with the sounds and smells he'd known from early childhood. Powerful emotions surged through Sidimo as he heard the roar of a mighty lion not far away. A strange mixture of fear and exhilaration flooded his mind as he remembered the first time he heard that terrible sound. As a child, he'd been sleeping in his family's hut when a great black-maned lion leaped over the thorn fence to grab one of his family's prized calves. Sidimo's father had fearlessly grabbed a spear and rushed outside to challenge the beast. At the sight of him, the lion dropped the calf and retreated into the night.

Go ahead and roar, Simba, thought Sidimo. *One day I will meet you with a spear of my own and you will flee. For when I pass the test tomorrow, I will become a man like my father!*

Sleep eluded Sidimo as his thoughts leaped about like nervous gazelles. This night was just as his father had told him it would be. Mysterious. Adventurous. Sobering. More exciting than any other night in his young life. This was the time when his past, present, and future all came together.

Sidimo thought of the items he'd left behind when he entered the jungle to begin his rite of passage. His father had instructed him to discard all the possessions associated with his childhood. The ornaments and trappings of a boy had to be abandoned if he truly wanted to become a man.

His father was so wise. Sidimo remembered the many hours he sat with him and the other elders to learn the ways of a man. For many generations the elders of the tribe had taught the younger members that honesty, courage, loyalty, and personal responsibility were virtues associated with true men. Some of the elders' teachings were deeply spiritual, and others dealt with the practical aspects of sexuality, marriage, and how to survive in the often harsh environment of eastern Africa.

As Sidimo stirred the fire with a small stick, he mused on the many preparations of the past two months. Last week he had raided a beehive and filled his cowhide container to the top with precious honey. The angry welts on his hands bore silent witness to the ferocity of the hive defenders. His mother had used the honey to make the traditional honey beer for the elders to drink after tomorrow's ceremony. Sidimo smiled as he thought about how even now the liquid was chilling in a calabash gourd safely inside his mother's hut.

He also thought about his attempts to outwit an ostrich in order to secure several wing feathers for the headdress that he would soon wear. Despite the fact that one kick from the giant bird could have ripped his belly open, Sidimo had completed his task and safely brought the plumes back to his village.

His mental inventory completed, Sidimo took momentary solace in the fact that all was finally ready for his transition into manhood. With great joy he visualized the new hut that had been constructed for his triumphant return from his circumcision ceremony. Sidimo was more than willing to endure a few moments of pain for a lifetime of honor.

In the next instant his thoughts raced forward, anticipating what would happen when dawn broke over the low hill in the east. *I will walk to the center of the village, where the elders will be waiting. I will then take my seat and sit straight as a spear,* thought Sidimo. *All of the other men of my village will surround me. My favorite uncle will take his position behind me to give me strength as the sharp blade cuts into my flesh. I will not cry out— I will not even blink at the sight of my blood as it spills on the ground, for if I were to "kick the knife" and show cowardice, my family would be disgraced. We would be spat upon, and no one would eat the food prepared for the celebration! That would be terrible! What if I...?*

"No!" shouted Sidimo.

He was startled by the sound of his voice as it shattered the stillness of the night. As quickly as they came, his doubts drifted away like smoke, and peace returned.

My name means "He is able." No, I will not cry out, and soon the pain will be over and my family will cheer. Only then will my mother be allowed to bring the milk she has collected so that both the knife and I may be cleansed. Then my relatives will say to me, "Get up, Sidimo! Get up! You are now a man!" But I will not move until they assemble to present many cattle to me so that I can begin my own herd.

Afterward my uncle will lead me to the safety of my mother's hut. There I will stay until I am healed. When I have regained my strength, I will proudly walk through the village to my new hut, where I will start a family of my own. It is there that someday I will share the ways of the Maasai with my own children. I will tell my sons of this night and of how their father became a man.

For the next few hours, Sidimo sat very still and gazed into the glowing pit until all that remained were a few scattered embers. He noted that the fire seemed unwilling to relinquish its last moments but finally surrendered to the inevitable.

Although it had served him well, Sidimo felt no sense of loss at the passing of the fire. Like his childhood, its time was over. Moments later the huge crimson ball burst forth in the east, signifying that the new day had finally arrived. As the warmth of the sun touched Sidimo's face, he rose and walked toward his destiny.

THE LAKOTA: VISION QUESTING FOR MANHOOD

Worlds away, a boy named White Fox sat alone in the darkness. He kept a silent and lonely vigil atop a mountain in the territory that is now called South Dakota. Chilling winds blew raven-colored hair across his weathered face. Clad only in a buckskin loincloth, this young member of the Lakota tribe sat in the stillness and waited. His thin frame was weakened from the hours he'd spent purifying his body in the sweat lodge and from his days of fasting before ascending the mountain. Normally hunger pains would have sent White Fox on a quest for food. Now, however, the ache in his belly served to remind him how important tonight was. He knew that what happened in the next few hours would set the course for the rest of his life. Tonight was special. This was the night of his vision quest. For generations the young men of his tribe had come to this place to earnestly seek the will of the Great Spirit for their lives.

White Fox could feel the strength of those who had come here before him as he called out to his creator. "Oh, Great Spirit," White Fox prayed as a wolf's eerie howl pierced the night, "come show me the vision for my life. Why have you given me breath? What is my purpose for being?" For now he heard no answers, only the sounds of the night.

The young man's heartfelt questions soon gave way to quiet reflections on his childhood. He vainly searched his memory for an image of his father, but none came. White Fox could recall only the story of how, when he was scarcely two seasons old, a band of renegades had raided his village. All of the braves fought valiantly against the invaders, but several were mortally wounded. While his father was defending his family, a lance pierced his side, and he died. White Fox was proud to know that the blood of his father, the great chief who willingly sacrificed his own life so that others could live, flowed in his veins. Tonight, however, the boy's heart ached for the strong touch of his father's hand upon his shoulder.

Brown eyes turned toward the heavens, White Fox spoke again. This time there was no shout, only a quiet, pleading whisper. "Great Spirit, why was he taken away? Who will fill this canyon that I feel deep in my heart?" Pain clawed at his chest, fighting to escape. Anger, rage, and bitterness lurked close by, waiting for an opportunity to scar his tender soul. However, they never got the chance.

Soon the boy's swirling thoughts found refuge in a pleasant place. Bittersweet tears welled up in his eyes as he thought of his mother's love for him. She had been the one to watch over him for more than a decade. Despite the hardships of fending for her family, she had made sure that White Fox learned how to become respected among the tribe.

Others had rallied around him as well. Throughout the years his father's friends had treated him as their own son. Early on these loving mentors showed White Fox how to ride the painted ponies that seemed to fly across the grasslands. He remembered the time one of the elders presented him with his first bow and a quiver of hand-painted arrows. Fondly he recalled the many evenings spent sitting silently near the watering holes with these quiet warriors, waiting for mule deer to appear. As they talked together, these men taught him about the ways of a warrior. They took time to teach him about the changes that he would experience on his journey to manhood. From these times of training, White Fox learned about the importance of a man's honor and the responsibilities of community leadership.

Suddenly the vision White Fox had been seeking exploded before him. A smile broke across his broad face. His vision came riding upon the words his mother had spoken to him many years ago. They flashed across his mind like lightning. "Someday," she had said, "you will take your father's place and lead others in our tribe."

"Great Spirit!" White Fox shouted as he leaped to his feet. "I now understand why you have given me breath. I am to walk in the ways of my father and the teachings of my mother. Now that he is gone, I am to take my father's place! At first light I will return to my lodge and tell my family of my vision. Tomorrow will be a most special day for me!"

With his life's vision tucked securely in his heart, White Fox was suddenly free to think beyond the moment. He pondered the needs of his tribe and the many ways in which he could help others around him. The time had come for him to walk as a man, just as his father before him had done.

THE ANCIENT ROMANS: HONORING A NEW CITIZEN

Centuries earlier another boy waited impatiently for the ceremony that would catapult him into manhood. Young Marcus stood on the balcony of his family's villa, which overlooked the seven hills on which Rome was built. A warm breeze carried the faint scent of the sea into his nostrils and reminded him of times past on the sandy Italian shores.

Carefully cultivated fields flanked the redbrick roads that snaked through the countryside. For years Marcus had watched these fields change with the seasons. Men who understood such things kept a continuous vigil over those fertile lands. They meticulously planted seed in spring, then carefully weeded and pruned and watered during the summer. Finally, in the fall, the precious crops were harvested and transformed into the life-giving bread that sustained the Roman people.

From his vantage point Marcus could see the city in all its splendor. The boy's eyes soon locked onto the soldiers of the Praetorian Guard as they paraded through the narrow streets. These were special men of the emperor's garrison who had proven themselves worthy to guard the very heart of the empire, Rome itself.

To the north, Marcus saw groups of politicians filing into the great forum for another round of heated debates about matters of state. He was proud to know that his father was among them.

Marcus continued to scan the vast city and wondered at what men had been able to build. He marveled at the extensive aqueducts that brought water to Rome's many public baths. In the marketplace he saw hundreds of street vendors noisily trying to entice citizens and slaves alike to buy their wares. Fish from the sea, cattle from the fields, and household goods made of bronze, wood, and clay were sold throughout the day. The air was filled with the sounds and colors and dust of the many visitors who came from the four corners of the earth just to experience this great city.

Marcus rarely tired of watching the hustle of his city. Today, how-ever, was different, and he quickly withdrew to the quiet of his room. He could scarcely believe what the next twenty-four hours would bring.

This was the month of March, and tomorrow the festival of Bacchus would begin. This meant that the special coming-of-age cere-monies would be held for every citizen's son who had reached his four-teenth birthday during the previous year. Tomorrow Marcus would go with his family to the great forum and assemble with countless others who knew the value of this rite of passage.

As part of the ceremony, Marcus would discard his boyish neck charms and the clothing of a child. He would also go with his father to the barber and be shaved for the first time. Following that he would be registered as a citizen of Rome. Once accepted as a citizen, Marcus would enjoy all the privileges and responsibilities that accompanied such an honor. At the end of the public ceremony, Marcus and his peers would offer sacred honey cakes on the altar of Bacchus.

Later in the day many people would gather in his father's home for more celebration and to acknowledge his transition into manhood. The grand occasion would last for nearly a week, and there would be much eating and drinking. During that time his father's friends would visit, bringing Marcus wonderful gifts.

This young soon-to-be-man marveled that such an occasion would be held in *his* honor. However, even more wonderful than the party or the many gifts was the realization that from that day forward, everyone would treat him differently. They would no longer see him as a child but rather as a man.

Tomorrow I will become a man, Marcus thought as his mind's eye flooded with pictures of the soon-coming event. *Then I will accompany my father when he goes into the city. I will walk beside him and even hear his speeches at the great assembly.*

Marcus knew that his father, a senator, was to address the assembly that day about the growing problems facing their empire. More than once his father's calm demeanor and sage advice had been instrumental in forming a consensus among the politicians gathered at the forum. Even the great emperor Augustus took note of what his father had to say.

The boy's thoughts were gently interrupted by the quiet voice of Demetrius, his father's most trusted servant. "Marcus, it's time for your lessons."

Marcus tried to calculate how many times he had heard those words over the years. On most mornings he had met with Demetrius to learn about history, geometry, geography, astronomy, boxing, wrestling, music, and philosophy. Recently Marcus had begun to study public speaking in preparation for his future. He wanted to become a senator, just like his father.

Over the years Demetrius taught Marcus about spiritual things as well. The boy recalled the hushed tones his mentor had used to describe the many gods that ruled over their empire and how a man's conduct was under constant celestial scrutiny. Demetrius had also taken special care to explain the intricacies of citizenship and loyalty to one's country. Manliness, hygiene, the marriage vows, and even the mysteries of the marriage bed were all subjects of the young man's education.

Waves of memories washed gently upon Marcus's mind and then slowly receded. For a brief moment a touch of sadness invaded the boy's heart. This was the last day of his childhood. *No longer will I wear the necklace of a boy,* thought Marcus. *No longer will I dress in the garments of my childhood. From now on, I will wear the clothing of a man. My whole life is about to change.*

At tomorrow's ceremony, when his father placed a special toga over Marcus's shoulders and slipped a ring on Marcus's finger, everything would change. Marcus was amazed that in less than twenty-four hours his words would be measured by the same standard as his father's words.

Without warning the trickle of sadness in his soul flashed into a flood of self-doubt. "What if I fail?" Marcus blurted out. "What if I cannot remember all that I am to do as a man? What if…?"

"Marcus," called the soothing voice of Demetrius, "it is time."

Those three words were enough to reduce the storm in the boy's mind to a mere breeze. He realized he would not have to make the journey through manhood alone. After all, the gods watched over the conduct of men, and he had learned his lessons well. Marcus would do his best, and that would be enough. "Yes," Marcus said quietly, "it is time."

THE JEWS: OBSERVING A SACRED TRADITION

Traditions, pondered David. *I feel sorry for people who have no traditions. Traditions make life worth living. Father says they are like mile markers on our passage through time. Yes, traditions are very good things.*

This young Jewish boy had learned the lesson well, despite the many distractions of living in Eastern Europe after World War I. Life in the late 1920s was still very unsettled for all who had survived the horrors of the war. There were homes to rebuild, businesses to reopen, and the dead to mourn. Through it all, David's family held closely to each other, to their God, and to their traditions. He knew that by this time tomorrow he would have experienced the greatest tradition of them all for a young Jewish boy.

Tomorrow I will celebrate becoming a man, David thought with a smile. *Tomorrow I will become a* bar mitzvah—*a son of the commandment. However, I have no time to think about it now, for I must go help Father.*

Young David left the small house he shared with his father, mother, two sisters, and the three cousins who had been orphaned by the war. As his feet flew down the street toward his father's clock shop, he recalled countless happy days spent there watching his father work. Often the two of them labored in silence, simply enjoying the closeness of their fellowship. At times they would joke with each other. At least once a month his father told him that God trusted all watchmakers because the Almighty allowed them to "hold time in their hands." David and his father would both laugh, even though they had shared the same story many times.

From time to time his father used a simple lesson learned at the shop to help prepare David for success later in life. David noticed that certain themes were shared repeatedly. Quality of work, honesty, and the value of work itself were often the subject of impromptu teaching. His father often said that a man must learn to work and work to learn—in equal portions. In doing so, a man would be ready for whatever God called him to do in this life.

David soon found himself at the door of his father's shop. As he turned the ornate latch, he was pleased to think that his father's door was always open to him. With a twist of his wrist, he entered a world of clocks, watches, and wonder. The tiny bell above the shop door announced his arrival as he walked inside. David was proud that his father was a watchmaker. His mother often boasted that her husband was the finest watchmaker in all Europe.

As he had so many times before, David greeted his father with a hug and announced that he had finished his studies for the day. Then he sat on the tall stool next to his father's workbench and began to disassemble a broken watch. His fingers were not as skilled as his father's, but he was learning more with each new day, just by watching his mentor at work.

As he carefully looked for the source of the watch's problem, the boy's thoughts drifted back to one of his earliest memories of his father. It was David's first day of school. His father had lovingly wrapped him in a traditional prayer shawl and literally carried him to his classroom. *I was so proud that my father carried me in,* thought David. *He is not a big man, but his arms and hands are so strong. I knew he would never drop me.*

David chuckled to himself as he recalled how his teacher would write on the blackboard with honey instead of chalk. *When I would say a letter, my teacher took my finger and traced it. Then I got to lick the honey. It made me want to learn even more. I liked that tradition!*

With all the clocks and watches marking time around him, it was difficult for David not to think about tomorrow. He felt a mixture of excitement and anxiety at the thought of his special day—his day of *bar mitzvah*—and he put down his tools without realizing it.

Suddenly his father's voice invaded the stillness of his thoughts. "David, that watch won't be fixed by itself. Are you just daydreaming, or are you thinking about tomorrow?"

"Tomorrow, Father," David acknowledged. "I was thinking about tomorrow."

His father's stern face broke into a broad smile, and he chuckled. "Don't worry, my son. During this past year you have studied hard to prepare for your ceremony, and you will do fine. Think of the many times we have gone to the synagogue together. You know the service and understand how to read our Hebrew language. Remember, David, you will repair more than watches during your lifetime. This whole world is in great need of repair, and God has much for you to do. He will be with you."

His father's encouragement gave the boy confidence. David knew that tomorrow he would become an adult and would be responsible for his own conduct. *As an adult I must become a* mensch—*a generous, honorable, and compassionate person,* he thought to himself. He realized that this was a big task but knew it was well worth the price. David knew that the sacred writings of the Talmud promised that each son of the commandment receives an extra soul as he becomes more closely connected with God. David was cautiously confident that this spiritual connection would help him overcome the habits of boyhood.

In his mind, David rehearsed what he had to do in the morning. *First, when I wake up, I will dress in my new suit and eat a light breakfast with my family. Then, according to tradition, my family and I will walk together to the synagogue, where we will be seated in the front row of chairs. At that point I will put on my* tallith, *my prayer shawl, and try to relax.*

Suddenly the daydream became real and was as if David were actually there.

Innocent eyes rise to the platform and see the rabbi—looking directly at him! For a moment David is anxious, but the rabbi's friendly nod helps calm his fluttering stomach.

He then glances to his right and sees his father sitting straight and proud. Perhaps he is reflecting on his own special day, the one that happened here nearly thirty years ago.

David's mother gently whispers to him, "My son, you cannot fail! God and your family have prepared you well. Go and do your best." Her hand brushes his cheek, and the look on her face speaks of countless days and nights when she proudly held him in her arms. Without another word, her smile tells David that any sacrifice she made for him over the past thirteen years was well worth it. She would not trade her young son of the commandment for anything in the world.

Soon the ceremony filled with rich sounds and traditions begins. A cantor opens the main part of the service with a melodious prayer called the borchu. *Then the ark is opened and the precious Torah—the Word of God—is brought forth. Next, David's father and other men take turns speaking forth blessings and reading from the sacred writings.*

Soon it is time for David to ascend to the platform. As his trembling hands grasp the pointer he will use as he reads from the scroll open before him, his eyes scan the crowd assembled in the synagogue. They have come to celebrate with him on his special day of transition. It is tradition. A good tradition.

David pronounces the blessing and then reads from the ancient documents. His voice is strong, and after a few short moments, his hand has become steadier. When he has completed his reading, he gives the Dvar Torah—*his very first sermon, based on the passage of Scripture that he has just read. His words, a mix of boyish innocence and manly conviction, are deeply considered by those in attendance. After what seems like hours, David is finished and he descends the platform to rejoin his family.*

As he passes by, he sees a single stately tear wind its way down his father's cheek and then disappear into his thick black beard. His mother casts a sideways glance that says, "I knew he could do it," at the relatives and friends in the rows behind her. Then, David...

"David?" His father's call startled the boy back into the present. "My son, that watch is just as broken as it was ten minutes ago." Tapping his temple with his index finger, his father asked, "Have you returned to the synagogue?"

"Yes, Father," David answered. This time he was a bit embarrassed to admit that he was once again captured by the thoughts of tomorrow.

Then his father laughed that special laugh—the one that came from deep in his belly. "Come then, David. The sun is about to go down on today, and we must close up the shop. Here at work we will have many days like today, but there will be only one special day for you like tomorrow. Moreover, there is much to be done to prepare. Even now your mother is cooking for your party that will follow the ceremony."

Bubbling with excitement, his father continued. "Everyone will be there, and you will receive many presents, and we will eat, and we will sing, and we will dance, and... Well, my son, all I can say is that it will be a day you will never forget! Come, let us go home."

As they stepped outside the shop, David stood beside his father and waited for him to lock the door, just as he had so many times before. However, today his father did something different. He reached for his son's hand and dropped something into his palm. That something was a new key on a silver chain. David looked into his father's eyes and waited for an explanation.

"Today, David," his father said quietly, "today you lock the door. After all, God willing, this will be your shop someday."

David gripped the key tightly, and with his father at his side, he placed the key in the lock and turned it to secure their shop. Then the two of them began the walk home together, as they had done so many times before.

For them it was a tradition.

A good tradition.

THE MODERN WAY: STUMBLING TOWARD...WHAT?

Sunday morning. Nine-thirty.

Jason sat on the corner of the bed and tried to shake the sleep from his head. He still felt strange waking up at his father's house, despite the fact that he had spent every other weekend there since the divorce. Outside a frigid north wind pounded the window as if looking for a way in.

It's so cold here now, thought Jason. *It's so darned cold in here.*

For an instant Jason's thoughts flash back to the mornings when his parents were still together and he was little. He remembered sneaking into their bedroom and crawling in to snuggle with them as they slept. Memories of the feelings, sounds, and even pleasant smells of his dad's aftershave lotion and his mom's perfume flooded his senses. A small smile graced his face as, for one fleeting moment, he was warm, happy, and secure once again. With his mom on one side and his dad on the other, he had known that nothing could ever go wrong. Not even the dreadful, unseen monsters that lurked in the shadows of his room could invade that sanctuary.

Dad would play that game where he would snore so loud, and I would pinch his nose, recalled Jason. *Then Mom would tickle me until I begged her to stop...although I really hoped she wouldn't. Man, that was really...*

The sound of a truck roaring past the house brought Jason back to the present. His smile disappeared, and he felt foolish to have thought about things from so long ago. *Aw, what difference does it make anyway?* he rationalized. *Live for today, right? That's what Dad says.*

Rising from the bed, Jason quietly shuffled to the bathroom. Today the fair-weather friend of a mirror was on Jason's side. It showed that the biceps he was working so hard to build were starting to bulge a bit. Even better, the shadow on his upper lip was beginning to darken, and mercifully, the pimple on his chin had begun to retreat. It seemed as if he was making progress in his quest to grow up.

As he made his way downstairs, Jason walked past the door to his father's room. As always, it was shut. A few more steps and Jason entered the family room. He was shocked at what he saw and nearly staggered at the stench of the old cigarettes and stale cigars that lay in crowded ashtrays. Dirty cups and glasses were everywhere. Leftover food was scattered throughout the room, some on plates and some on the floor. Jason had never seen his father's house in such a mess.

Oh yeah, thought Jason. *How could I forget? Dad's big party…*

The house seemed strangely quiet after last night's wild get-together. Just hours before, the house had been filled with loud men who grew even louder as the night went on. Some of his dad's friends had come over to celebrate his new promotion. Although his father had politely asked Jason to "keep a low profile" during the party, Jason could not help but overhear what took place. From the darkness of the spare bedroom, he had heard the men offer many toasts to his dad. Jason remembered that one man with a deep, raspy voice kept repeating, "You finally made it, man! You finally made it!"

Jason quickly left the family room and went into the kitchen to find some something to eat. Near the refrigerator door, he saw his dad's calendar and scanned the month's events. Barely visible among the hastily written notes about business meetings, appointments, and garbage pickup days were some smudged pencil marks, *JBD*, on today's date.

JBD? the boy wondered. Then he got it. *Jason's Birth-Day.*

Jason had nearly forgotten that today was his birthday. It had not always been like that. In fact, he once would have felt some real excitement about his "special" day. Back then birthdays meant family, presents, and singing… However, as the years went by, birthdays had come to mean only one thing—disappointment. After the pain of the past few birthdays, Jason would not allow himself to become too optimistic.

JBD…what a joke, he thought as he turned away from the calendar in disgust. He knew the "special day" pattern all too well. For the past five years, at least one of his parents had had a schedule conflict with his actual birthday. His mom and dad were always so busy with work, social events, and lately, weekends away to "find themselves" that they rarely had time to come to his soccer games, school plays, or anything else important to him. Often they would reschedule his birthday celebration rather than reschedule their meetings. For a while Jason had not really minded. It seemed that the more events they missed during the year, the bigger the presents he received. In the past it had seemed like a fair trade-off. However, today he realized deep inside that something had changed. Jason no longer cared if he got any presents this year. He just wished that his family could eat and talk together—just be together. *What would really make today special is if Dad would just sit and talk with me without always looking at his watch. That would be worth a hundred presents—a thousand presents.*

Then Jason felt that familiar I-can't-deal-with-this ache rising in his chest, so he quickly slammed the door of his heart and began to reason away his feelings. Anything to stop the pain. *It's just a stupid birthday, anyway. So what if I'm going to be a teenager? What's the big deal? Besides, the guys in the neighborhood said they would throw me a real party tomorrow night. Those older guys sure act crazy sometimes...*

Jason got dressed and went back into the family room, thinking about how strange it was to call this room a "family" room, since there was never any family there. He considered cleaning up his father's mess, but he was unsure where to begin. Instead he retrieved the backpack containing his schoolbooks and seated himself at the kitchen table to work on an overdue assignment.

Most of my teachers are great, Jason thought as he worked. *They really care about us. But, man, some of them are hard to follow.*

School had become so confusing. Some subjects were in conflict with others, or at least that's how it seemed. One instructor taught that mankind was bad and that we should reduce the human population to avoid polluting "Mother Earth" any further. She made a point of calling creationism an ancient fairy tale and said she would not waste class time discussing it. According to her, God did not exist. Instead, she said, life began billions of years ago when some molecules came together and formed living beings. Over time these single-celled beings evolved into higher states of life. Man was now the highest form of animal and would continue to become bigger, better, and brighter. Yet Jason had seen enough television news reports to doubt the notion that human beings, on their own, were becoming better or brighter in any way. It was all sort of bewildering.

Then there was that special speaker who was invited to talk to the students about self-esteem midway through the second semester. Jason figured that school officials had scheduled the speaker because of all the problems the kids were having. So many kids had become violent and were talking back to the teachers. Also, he knew that several girls had become pregnant, and sadly, three of his classmates had committed suicide that year. The speaker had spent two hours trying to convince the students that they were "special" and that they were all really going to be "somebody" someday.

It does not make sense, Jason puzzled. *One teacher says humans are bad and that we sprang up from some mud a few zillion years ago. But then that other guy said I am special and someday I will be somebody. How does that fit together? Who's right and who's wrong? And if God doesn't exist, why does my football coach pray before each game? What's the point in that?*

Jason was too frustrated to get far on his homework. He reasoned that since it was late anyway, a few more days would make little difference. Mercifully, he heard his father open his bedroom door and shuffle out to meet him.

Despite the gray streaks in his dad's hair and his expanding waistline, Jason still thought his father was a wonderful sight to behold. He treasured what little time they had together.

"Hi, Dad!" Jason said with a smile. "Man, I'm sure glad you're finally up. I've been thinking a lot lately and wanted to run some things past..."

"You know, son," his dad interrupted in his most upbeat voice. "I've got some serious shopping to do before tomorrow. My new promotion came with a bonus, and I want to buy you something you will really like. So how about it? What do you want?"

Jason's heart began to crumble. "Um, dad, I really like what you buy me. But what I really want is just to hang out together. I'm growing up—I mean, I think I am—and I want to ask you about..."

"Oh, is that it?" his dad said nervously. "I know what you mean about time with your dad. My dad worked all the time, but I got used to it. Hey, we just spent the weekend together, didn't we? As far as the manhood thing, don't worry about it. Just look at the size of you! Manhood just...just...you know, just happens by itself. My dad never made a big deal out of it, and look how I turned out. You know, as I see it—"

Glancing at his watch, Jason's father interrupted himself. "Wow. Look at the time! We need to get going. Uh, glad we had this talk. We can talk more on the way. Grab your stuff and let's get going."

Minutes later Jason sat silently in the car, waiting to be driven back to his mother's house.

Soon his dad appeared and slid into the driver's seat. Backing the car out of the driveway, his father proudly asked, "What do you think of my yard? Isn't it beautiful? Of course, it doesn't just happen by itself. Takes hours each week, but it's worth it. Hey, a man isn't much of a man if he doesn't keep his yard looking great. Do you know what I mean, son?"

Jason nearly missed his dad's question. A single tear had slipped past his defenses, and he quickly turned away from his father. They did talk more on the way home, but it was all about his dad's yard, his dad's car, his dad's bills, and other aspects of his dad's life. They never once got back to Jason's questions.

Soon the car pulled up in front of his mother's house and came to a halt on top of the piles of leaves Jason had raked into the street. The young man composed himself, slowly got out, and poked his head through the passenger-side window to say good-bye.

"Well, so long, Dad," he said quietly. "I *will* see you tonight, right?"

"You bet, son. I wouldn't miss your special day for the world. It will be great! I'll be here at six, and I can stay until at least eight-thirty. Remember, it's your special day." Glancing at his watch, his dad exclaimed, "Wow, I really need to get going!" With that he tromped on the gas pedal and sped away.

Although his father wasn't aware of it, the car's rapid departure created a powerful vacuum behind it, causing the leaves that Jason had so carefully raked into piles to be scattered into a chaotic mess. With one foot on the curb, Jason watched his father get farther and farther away, until he could see him no longer. Then Jason went inside and locked the door.

2

BOYS
TO
MEN

MY HEART ACHES FOR JASON and the millions like him who must try to find the door to manhood and then travel the pathway to maturity by themselves. Unlike Sidimo, White Fox, Marcus, and David, many boys in contemporary society are lost in the shuffle of everyday life. Not only are wonderful opportunities to shape their characters and destinies missed during the most formative years of their young lives but their transition away from boyhood practically goes unnoticed. Today's boys rarely, if ever, learn from the adults closest to them what it means to become a man—or learn when they have become one. Instead they are left to search for answers in movies, song lyrics, the often ill-informed perspectives of their peers, and the mixed, even contradictory, messages coming from other "grown-ups" around them. Consequently we have too many Jasons limping through life. They are confused, hurting, and feeling terribly incomplete.

In many other cultures and eras, the message of manhood is and was straightforward. Older men and women from one generation pour themselves into the boys of the following generation. They teach, mentor, counsel, correct, love, listen to, and, in short, nurture boys to prepare them for the responsibilities of manhood. In return, the youth are expected to grow into increasing responsibility, accountability, and concern for others.

As the boys' levels of maturity grow, the adults in their lives empower them with increased freedom to make choices for themselves and their future families. By parental and communal design, each young man is provided excellent opportunities to become a productive member of his family and society. As they themselves are lovingly prepared for manhood, young males are taught that manhood is much more than having the physical ability to make children. It is having the maturity to love, lead, teach, and nurture children. Further, the younger learn from their elders that mature men do not dominate or harm their wives; rather, they learn to love, protect, and nurture them. In due time the cycle repeats itself, and these now-mature men help others follow in their footsteps, thus retaining and building on the foundations of their culture.

PURSUING A HEALTHY CYCLE OF MATURITY

This ongoing, cyclical pattern for building successful families and societies was noted by secular anthropologist Margaret Mead more than fifty years ago. In her book *Male and Female: A Study of the Sexes in a Changing World,* she wrote:

> The human family depends on social inventions that will make each generation of males want to nurture women and children. Moreover, every known human society rests firmly on the learned nurturing behavior of men. In all societies each new generation of young males needs to learn appropriate nurturing behavior.[1]

This truth has been well understood by many cultures throughout history. In stark and troubling contrast, our society has lost sight of what it takes to prepare young people to enter into responsible adulthood. Our abandonment of this sacred, time-tested cycle of maturity has led to countless problems for our culture, our families, and individual teens such as Jason.

Adults have become too preoccupied with the tyranny of the urgent and nonessential to effectively mentor, teach, and empower our sons and daughters as they grow. As long as our personal comfort zone isn't invaded by some powerful youth tragedy, we tend to ignore the real needs of the young people in our homes, communities, schools, and churches. In today's world it's just too easy for us to rush ahead with life, oblivious to the teenage time bombs that will someday explode across the headlines of our newspapers.

I confess that before 1997 I rarely thought about the state of our teenagers and the long-term implications of neglecting their transitions into adulthood. A news report about a teen who had gone over the edge might capture my attention momentarily, but the effect it had on me rarely lingered for long. To me, the statistics accompanying such reports were cold and devoid of any real meaning for my own life. High rates of suicide, teen pregnancy, crime, runaways, school dropouts, and drug and alcohol abuse among our youth were points of brief concern but hardly cause for serious reflection. Often I viewed these accounts much as I did the weather report or national unemployment rate. They were simply pieces of information rather than testimonies of ruined lives and wasted potential.

On those rare occasions when I did consider the plight of our youth, my thoughts generated questions without answers. I wondered why "good" kids threw away their precious lives doing such stupid things. Why would any young man want to join a gang and risk bodily harm, imprisonment, or death? Why would such bright children take drugs to numb their fertile minds? What was wrong with *them?*

Over time the increasing, often tragic, signs of our troubled youth caused me to wonder whether the problem wasn't more with *us* than with *them.* I also began to question why so many people—myself included—were too busy to deal with these issues. Were we like Jason's father, too preoccupied with our own lives to hear the questions our young people were asking? I eventually came to a painful and unavoidable conclusion: what was wrong with *them* was rooted in what was wrong with *us.*

From this new perspective, I could see that my wife, Kathleen, and I were neglecting some key ingredients in our children's development. I just wasn't sure what they were.

MAKING IT A PERSONAL QUEST

In early 1997 the need to discover how we could help our children transition into adulthood became my personal quest. I felt a true sense of urgency as our oldest son, Christopher, was going to turn thirteen later that year. Kathleen and I wanted to do something significant to help make his birthday a turning point in his life. By God's grace the answer came as I was returning from a trip to Pretoria, South Africa.

My close friend and longtime business associate James Glenn and I had been invited to South Africa to participate in an international Christian business conference. James is also pastor of a church in Saginaw, Michigan, and I was thrilled to have his company on this trip. Upon our arrival we had discovered that a kaleidoscope of fascinating people from all over the world were in attendance. James and I met with the president of Benin, a nation on the southern coast of West Africa, and we worked with him to develop a plan to improve the quality of life for the five and a half million citizens of his fine nation. On our final day in Africa, I was honored to have the opportunity to address the conference's general assembly.

Despite our full schedule, I was preoccupied with thoughts of Christopher's upcoming birthday, which then was approximately three weeks away. When the conference ended, James and I said good-bye to that beautiful land, boarded a plane, and collapsed into our seats. Before long my friend drifted into a peaceful sleep, while I pondered the significance of our trip.

Africa's wonderful, wild blur of colors and sounds provides an absolute feast for the senses. The cycles of life are evident everywhere. Newborn nations, like newborn antelope, learn to survive swiftly or die premature deaths. Change is continuous. Today's national hero is tomorrow's scapegoat. Men's legacies are established or destroyed by a risky decision, a bold action, or a few words spoken at exactly the right or wrong time.

My visit there provoked many new questions about my own life's purpose. Thoughts about my family, my personal legacy, and my oldest son's transition into manhood swirled within me. Even a brief reflection on my own mortality crept into the mix. Christopher wasn't the only one in our family who would have a birthday at the end of the month. I would reach the ripe age of forty-five on July 29. That fact alone led me to ponder some deep things about the future.

As our giant plane soared higher into the clouds, I began considering the whole issue of a person's legacy. I truly wanted to leave things here on earth better than I had found them, but I was unsure about how to accomplish that task. After numerous mental side trips around the subject, my thoughts centered on my children. I realized that each person's legacy comprises two essential parts. The first is *what we do with our own lives* while here on earth. Such things as the nature of our character, our contributions to society, our vocation, and our acts of service to others make up a large portion of our legacy. Of course, our mistakes, our failures, and any significant harm we do to others are part of our legacy as well. The second aspect of a person's legacy is based on *what our children do and what they become* during their lives.

This issue of legacy and its connection with our children really challenged me, especially when I considered how many young people were in trouble these days. Why didn't we parents do something more about it? If our love and concern for our children were not motivation enough, why didn't we act to protect our own reputations or legacies, which were so tied to our children's actions? It seemed that few parents had actual plans in place to bring about the desired outcome for their children's lives, and as a result, those children were growing up by default, not by design.

Going deeper, I wondered whether there were things that we parents were failing to do—things that actually *caused* our young people to stumble on their path to adulthood.

Eventually I adopted a more positive perspective and tried to figure out some basic strategies that parents could use to help our young people have the best possible opportunity for success. I used every moment that remained of my thirty-hour trip to sort through these issues until I finally arrived at a few solid conclusions. Here is what I discovered.

Conclusion #1: My Priorities Have to Change

As a typical "grown-up" male, I spent much more time on my vocation, ministry, personal achievements, recreation, and activities with non-family members than I needed to. As far as legacy goes, I owned my own business, had achieved some degree of financial stability, was a published writer, and so far, had not been a major embarrassment to my family. In short, I was doing a fair job building the personal side of my legacy ledger. However, I was saddened to realize that I was falling short in both the quantity and quality of time needed to mentor my children into adulthood. Sadly, I discovered that I had a better plan for my own retirement than I did for my four children's development. That needed to change.

Conclusion #2: My Children Need More Than Just Time in Order to Mature

Although I was a reasonably good provider for my family and spent a fair amount of time with my children, I'd never clearly identified what they needed in order to make the transition into productive adulthood. Unintentionally I had placed a higher priority on giving them brand-name basketball shoes than on giving them foundations upon which to build their lives. I finally saw that my lack of attention to guiding them into maturity could cause real harm to them later in their lives. I also realized that countless other parents were likely making the same mistakes with their own children.

Conclusion #3: I Had to Be Organized and Intentional in My Approach to Changing the Situation

To start with, I made a list of ways we could help our young people make the transition into successful adulthood. My initial list contained a wide variety of items, including spiritual instruction, education, and proper diet. Eventually I found that all of the items on my list could be distilled into three foundational elements: lifelong mentoring, intentional blessing, and the most dramatic, a rite of passage. It became clear that each child needed at least one adult to support and teach him or her about life's many pitfalls and opportunities. Next I realized that too many children grow up without the biblical blessing of words and touch. Instead they hear themselves described by peers and, in some cases, by their own parents as stupid, ugly, or incompetent, or in any of many other negative ways. Their hearts, minds, and self-images become scarred by the barrage of curses, and without an equal and opposing blessing, many of them walk through life with horrible misperceptions of who they really are. Finally I realized that even when children received some solid instruction and some level of positive reinforcement from those around them during their formative years, there was still something missing—a rite of passage.

ACKNOWLEDGING THE MISSING INGREDIENT

The rite of passage—our modern society's elusive, missing ingredient. It was something I hadn't thought much about before, and yet it now seemed so profound. The more I pondered the importance of a rite of passage and the corresponding mentoring, the more convinced I became that this was a key, not only to Christopher's future but also to the healthy maturing of other children in our world. Here is why.

In large part, adults are aware that many young people are troubled. However, I believe we have misdiagnosed the root cause of their troubling behavior. One of the most prominent words used to describe the baby boomers and following generations is *selfish.* While this term aptly describes many behaviors and attitudes, it does not go deep enough, and therefore it fails to uncover the genesis of their—no, *our*—predicament.

As a business consultant, I've learned that the way we define a problem determines how the problem will be solved. The more accurate the definition, the better the opportunity to find effective solutions. The *selfish* label is too vague and usually too simplistic to account for our society's endless problems that include divorce, child abuse and abandonment, something-for-nothing lawsuits, and the incredible lack of respect for others that permeates our world. Add to that the personal aimlessness, emotional distress, and general lack of peace running rampant in our culture, and it becomes clear that something more than selfishness is causing all this distress.

While self-centeredness may partially explain the increase in some of the problems listed above, it does not suffice as an all-embracing explanation. More important, it does not get at the root cause of these problems.

As I have listened to the accounts of so many troubled boomers, busters, Xers, and generation Next-ers, I've concluded that a more accurate description of their (sorry, *our*) condition can be summed up in a different word: *childishness.*

Too many individuals today have failed to make the transition from child to adult and yet struggle to discover what prevents them from doing so. It is well documented that many of our young people haven't had the benefit of supportive family relationships, mentoring, and other foundations for maturity. I have no doubt that this has contributed to some of the negative behavior in our teens and young adults today.

If that were the cause, however, then we would see problems only with children from bad homes, right? In reality, even in "good" homes where these positive things exist, children often increase in age without experiencing a corresponding increase in maturity. While they may avoid some of life's most obvious pitfalls, they often lack purpose, direction, and a clear picture of their own identities. These young people often retain many childish fears, attitudes, and negative patterns of behavior well into adulthood. Many are haunted by a sense that *something* is still missing in their lives. That something is a rite of passage from childhood into adulthood. I need to underscore this point. The foundational reason childishness persists well into adulthood in our society is our failure to create and implement transitional rites of passage for our youth. A rite of passage breaks the bonds of childhood and releases young people into their future as responsible adults. It works like this.

When a young male reaches his teen years, he instinctively looks for ways to affirm his manhood. In societies where rites of passage are part of the norm, each young male participates in a formal ceremony during which his manhood is publicly and undeniably affirmed. From that day forward, he is treated differently by those around him and receives more freedom, rights, and privileges. In response the young man begins to think and act more as an adult than as a child. For the rest of his life he pursues maturity rather than manhood.

In contrast, a young male living in a society with no formal rites of passage must find his own path to adulthood. Without formal affirmation of his transformation, he vainly tries to find manhood on his own through a variety of means. Sadly, his pursuit of manhood rather than maturity will lead him down many side roads that are fruitless at best, destructive at worst.

While the two concepts, manhood and maturity, seem very similar, they are as different as night and day. *Manhood* is bestowed upon a young male by the trusted elders (fathers, grandfathers, uncles, pastors, coaches, teachers) of his society during a rite of passage. *Maturity* is gained as a man grows in knowledge, wisdom, and character. Manhood is a gift that we adults give to our sons. Maturity is the gift that they give back to us.

On the long flight from Africa, it became clear to me that without a rite of passage and some very deliberate mentoring along the way, each of us remains trapped within a false image of who we are. As I looked more deeply into the matter of "growing up," I made a list of negative childish actions. Selfishness was definitely high on the list, followed by complaining, quitting when faced with a difficult situation, throwing temper tantrums, spewing threats of self-destruction, struggling with short attention spans, and demanding one's own way without regard for the needs of others.

Sadly, while these actions are often seen in young children, the list also describes far too many "grown" men in our culture. For example, consider the life of a fifty-year-old production manager I worked with several years ago. I will call him Joe to protect the guilty. During his twenty-year reign of terror in the workplace, Joe continually bullied, belittled, and intimidated everyone under his supervision. Like young children cornered in a school hallway, his employees cowered whenever Joe approached them. The reason? He would shout at, curse, and even threaten to physically harm any subordinate who dared to challenge his authority. Joe's childish behavior continued until someone with greater power came along and stopped him. After patiently attempting to change Joe's behavior, his boss fired him. Joe was a child in a man's body. He never made the transition to mature manhood.

We also see this childish pattern played out in scenarios that are even more destructive. Too many recent headlines have told the stories of men who became frustrated with some aspect of their lives and lashed out in uncontrolled violence. Unable to deal with life's inevitable disappointments in a mature manner, these disgruntled men have stormed into the offices of their supervisors, attorneys, or stockbrokers and begun shooting everyone in sight. Like little boys who hit their playmates when they don't get their way, these men—adult in body but still children in so many other ways—used deadly force to impose their wills on the uncooperative.

Yet another manifestation of this childish mind-set exhibits itself when adult men abandon their commitments, especially to their families. When we were children, we always wanted new things. Toys, sports gear, even cars were all "better" if they were new. We not only enjoyed them but also wanted to show them off to our friends. When they lost their luster, broke, or became a bit outdated, we whined, we cried, and we begged for another. Suddenly we were dissatisfied with what had previously brought us so much pride and happiness. Predictably, we then wanted to throw our "old" toys away and get new ones, believing that they would make us happy—which the new toys did, but just for a little while.

Compare this childish practice with many men's approach to marriage and family. When a spouse gains a few pounds, doesn't agree with the other's opinions as readily as before, or begins to wane in outward beauty, many men manifest the same type of childish behavior they did years ago. They whine, complain, lose interest, and start desiring a "newer" model. Sadly, such men have never grown up. No one ever lovingly challenged them, as Sidimo and Marcus were challenged, to put down their childish things and pick up the mantle of manhood.

Of course, there are countless men of varying ages who manage the stresses of life without running away from home or making armed assaults on former coworkers or fellow students. Since these men show no outward signs of significant problems or deviant behavior, then all is well, right? Not exactly. Here is why. Any man who grows up without intentional affirmation, mentoring, and a transitional rite of passage is, to some degree, wounded and uncertain about his own identity. In this condition, the man struggles to discover and release some portion of his potential. Conversely, a man raised by intentional design is much better equipped to understand his origin, purpose, responsibilities, and the potential for his life. With this insight he will be much freer to release the marvelous gifts and talents that God has placed within him. As we begin to raise our sons by design, they will be empowered to boldly express themselves in their work, play, relationships, emotions, and spirituality, as well as in a host of other wonderful ways.

DEVELOPING A NEW MIND-SET

It is clear that the lack of an intentional transition into adulthood creates a variety of problems for men of all ages. In an attempt to compensate for the lack of a transitional event, some teenage males unknowingly create their own rites of passage by resorting to violence, alcohol, other drugs, and sexual conquest. In the corporate world some men in leadership positions use the authority of their job titles to prove they have arrived, threatening others into submission. Like bullies who stalk junior-high schoolyards, these "grown" men live to verbally wrestle and pin their weaker opponents during staff meetings.

Often men in their late thirties, forties, and fifties stumble into what is commonly called a midlife crisis. During this time men become consumed with a desire to search for meaning and identity in their lives. This sounds strangely similar to the vision quest that White Fox undertook at age fourteen.

In today's society men seem to have a difficult time settling into life. Many struggle with a "Peter Pan syndrome." They do not want to grow up, and yet they realize they were created for a higher purpose than endless play in never-never land. How sad it is to see men at the end of their lives, estranged from their families, still unsure about spiritual realities, still questioning the reason for their own existence, and still wondering if they have succeeded in growing into manhood. Just as sad to see are the countless families whose sons fall into the predictable traps along the road of life because they don't know what a man is, much less how to become one.

If we are going to solve these problems, we will need to develop a new mind-set. We must no longer accept the unacceptable as inevitable. Teen rebellion, midlife crisis, and marital meltdown no longer need to be the normal pattern. In one generation our society can reverse this destructive trend and send our children down a positive path to success. I am convinced that lifelong mentoring, intentional blessing, and rites of passage for our young people are the foundations for the needed change of direction.

In the following chapters we will explore how to implement all of these concepts into one powerful plan for the children in our lives. While mentoring, blessings, and affirmations are ongoing aspects of the plan, the rite of passage is a singular, life-changing event that must be included in the developmental strategy for each child. The rite of passage celebration establishes the exact and undeniable day when a boy becomes a man. The importance of having a distinct time of passage into adulthood becomes clear when we understand the foundational differences between *manhood* and *maturity*.

Manhood is not something that a young male achieves by drinking, joining the military, sexual conquest, graduation from high school, or any other act or activity. Instead, manhood is something that is granted and affirmed by the elders of a young male's society, community, religious group, or family. As we saw in chapter 1, Sidimo, White Fox, Marcus, and David each became a *man* when the older males in their lives confirmed their coming of age, thereby settling the manhood question once and for all. As soon as the transition took place, each of these new *men* began to live life from a completely new perspective. Up until the rite of passage, each of them acted as boys, engaged in boyish activities, and under the guidance of parents and other mentors, spent considerable time preparing to become a man. However, as soon as the issue of manhood was settled at their rites of passage, their focus shifted and, as men, they began to pursue lives of maturity. Of course, no rite of passage made any of the young men instantly mature—they were not designed to. Maturity is a process and only comes with time, teaching, and ongoing life experiences. However, the rites of passage instantly and permanently transformed the identity of each young celebrant. The imaginary bridge from childhood was forever burned in the thinking of the young men and those around them.

Once having crossed over into this new territory of adulthood, no young man would consider a permanent return to childish games and a life of immaturity. Instead he gladly pushes forward on his journey to maturity and as a result receives heightened levels of respect, admiration, and responsibilities from those around him. In our own modern-day society, our embrace of planned maturity and rites of passage will eliminate a great deal of identity crisis for our sons and then make their pursuit of maturity more of a joy than a struggle.

As I thought about these things on the long journey home from Pretoria, I had no idea what fruit my quest would bear. By the time our plane landed in Michigan, I was completely worn out but elated at the results of our trip to Africa. James and I could see our families waving to us from inside the airport as we descended the ramp. Soon we walked into a wonderful welcome of hugs, kisses, and questions from spouses and children.

Later that evening I shared my thoughts on mentoring, blessings, rites of passage, and manhood with Kathleen. While we realized that there was no time to implement a solid plan of mentoring in the next few weeks, we did decide that Christopher would have much more than a standard birthday party to mark his transition into manhood. In less than twenty-one days, he would have a rite of passage.

---

1. Margaret Mead, *Male and Female: A Study of the Sexes in a Changing World* (New York: Morrow, 1949).

3

PLANNING
A MEANINGFUL
RITE OF PASSAGE

THE DAYS FOLLOWING MY RETURN from Africa were filled with a flurry of activity. I was two weeks behind in my work and, more important, in time spent with Kathleen, Christopher, Steven, Jenifer, and Daniel. There were letters to write, clients to contact, stories about Africa to tell—and a rite of passage to create!

Each evening after the children were in bed, Kathy and I would talk about Christopher's upcoming event. Our discussions and resulting conclusions were filled with rich emotion and sometimes painful reflection, especially for me. I often feel that time has become my enemy as I watch my son grow. With each passing day, he becomes more of a man and seems to change before my eyes. I am truly torn by this reality.

As a father I know I must one day release my son into his own future. Nevertheless, part of me wants to keep him as a little boy forever. I see that his once skinny arms and legs have developed into muscular limbs filled with energy and purpose. The little helper who used to stick by my side during work projects now has other things to do when my tools appear. At times I long to hear his squeaky voice calling, "Daddy," once again. I selfishly wish life could be composed of endless summers spent fishing or playing together. However, I also know that if I do not help Christopher continue to grow into a mature man, I run the very real risk of losing him to a lifestyle of childishness that would ultimately destroy him and our relationship. Therefore, for this reason as well as many others, I kept planning for his special day of transition.

One of the most interesting decisions Kathleen and I had to make was what to call our son's event. To call it a *party* made it sound too trite. The term *ceremony* made it sound as if the attendees would need to dress in flowing saffron robes and chant just to get in the door. We finally settled on the term *celebration* as the most appropriate.

Next we worked on the foundations for the celebration. We eventually concluded that two key ingredients were needed: a sharing of wisdom from special mentors and a time of spiritual blessing. Things were beginning to take shape.

GATHERING THE MENTORS

As we worked on the design of Christopher's celebration, I was reminded of the people who had invested in my own young life. This was a time of pleasant memories and reflection. I remembered family, friends, and unofficial mentors who had encouraged my own growth into manhood...

- My *mother* was always loving and kind, even when my older brother, younger sister, and I were less than deserving of her gentleness. Her love taught me to care for others.
- My *dad* showed me how to work and taught me never to complain about the hardships of life. I always felt so special when he let me help with one of his "grown-up" projects. He also instilled in me that the Golden Rule would never let me down, and that if I could not say something nice, I should not say anything at all.
- My beloved *Grandpa Henry* taught me about the outdoors and let me walk beside him, which was a great honor.
- *Grandma Alice* was the one who spent hours playing on the floor beside me, cultivating a vivid imagination within me.

- My stern but loving *Great-Aunt Virginia* instilled in me a desire to excel in my schoolwork and never accept less than my own best efforts.
- A pep talk from Roger Little, my *junior-high basketball coach*, gave me the confidence to push my physical skills as far as possible. As a result I became captain and most valuable player of my Class A high-school team and went on to play basketball in college.
- A *high-school biology teacher*, Fred Case, taught me to search out the wonders of this world through books. He made it fun to learn.

These fine men and women shaped my character during the first decade and a half of my life. Each provided crucial foundations for my own transition into manhood. Each gave time, love, mentoring, correction, and words of encouragement to a boy searching for the proper way to go in life. Although none of my mentors instituted a rite of passage for me, I knew I could rely on aspects of the love and support they had given me to help design the celebration for Christopher.

Christopher himself also had some great people who served him as mentors and coaches during the first thirteen years of his life.

- Three young men from our church, Tony Adamson, Mike Haak, and Brian Pruitt, spent considerable time with Chris engaged in sports activities, short impromptu Bible lessons, and generally having fun. Their acceptance of Chris helped his self-esteem and provided role models of healthy, active, Christian males.
- Two pastors, James Glenn and Ron Ives, took time with Chris to simply check on his progress as a young man in the making. A youth pastor, Dan Schoonover, took Chris under his wing and prayed for him during crucial junctures of his development.
- Both sets of grandparents showed genuine concern for Chris (and the other grandchildren) throughout his early years and affirmed his efforts at education, athletics, and spiritual growth.

While Kathleen and I did not have a specific plan for Chris's development, as we have since had for our younger children, it became evident that God had strategically placed key people in Christopher's life to provide mentoring, blessing, and affirmation. Now, as I planned his celebration, I was thankful for these key people in his life, several of whom would participate in his special night.

DEVELOPING THE TIME OF BLESSING

Without question, Kathleen and I wanted the celebration to have a strong spiritual foundation. Early in the planning stage I looked for and found two biblical accounts of blessing and celebration that really touched me. They gave me a good idea of what to include during our time of blessing.

A Patriarch's Love: Confirming a Son's Identity

The first story revolves around the Hebrew patriarch Jacob (see Genesis 47–49). When Jacob, old and bent, realizes that his time on earth is nearly over, he calls for his sons so that he can see them one last time and bless them before he passes on. A third generation becomes involved in the blessing when Joseph, one of Jacob's sons, arrives with his two young sons, Ephraim and Manasseh.

Old Jacob's eyesight is very poor, so he only vaguely sees the two grandsons and asks Joseph, "Who are these?"

Joseph's response speaks volumes to both his father and his two sons: "These are the sons that God has given me."

Abundant meaning resides in his simple statement! There would never be any confusion in the boys' minds about their origins. Nor would they ever wonder if their existence was the result of some random, cosmic mistake. Joseph's words clearly and proudly confirm that the boys belong to him. "These are the sons that *God* has given *me.*"

Grandfather Jacob's reaction is just as powerful. He immediately tells Joseph to bring the boys close to him so that he can bless them. As they come near, the old man rises slowly, painfully, to greet them. Countless days in the desert have taken their toll on his body. His beard and hair are no doubt as white as the frost on the high mountains. His cheeks must feel like aged leather, wrinkled and yet soft to the touch. I imagine hands of iron gripping the boys' arms and pulling them close. The boys are in awe of these hands. They surely remembered the stories their father had told them: Grandfather's hands had wrestled with God! However, today they will be hands of blessing—gentle and kind. Jacob pulls his grandsons to his chest, where he embraces and kisses them.

I wonder what Ephraim and Manasseh thought as they quietly accepted such a special blessing. Here they are in the presence of their father and grandfather, the two most beloved men in their lives. They realize their grandfather is about to die and yet, with an infinite number of other things he could have done with his final moments on earth, *he has chosen to bless them.*

As Ephraim and Manasseh look deep within Jacob's failing eyes, they see the reflection of thirty thousand sunsets. For an instant, the boys feel awkward. Uncertain. *What will he say about us, this man who speaks with God?*

The boys do not have to wait long for the answer. It is time for their rite of passage and for a blessing that will impart destiny into their young lives. In the presence of their father, Jacob places his hands on the boys' heads and says (in Genesis 48:15–16):

> May the God before whom my fathers
>   Abraham and Isaac walked,
> the God who has been my shepherd
>   all my life to this day,
> the Angel who has delivered me from all harm
>   —may he bless these boys.
> May they be called by my name
>   and the names of my fathers Abraham and Isaac,
> and may they increase greatly
>   upon the earth.

The boys are enveloped in a cloud of wonder. A surge of excitement courses through their bodies as they realize that their grandfather's sad passing means a new beginning for them. They will never be the same. With a glance at their father, they slowly move away from Jacob's side and sit quietly by the foot of his bed.

They can likely hear the footsteps of their uncles outside, who have come to their father's side for one last time as well. Reuben, Judah, and the rest have gathered to see their father before he experiences his own rite of passage into a timeless eternity. At Jacob's call, the uncles enter and receive his counsel, correction, and blessing. Jacob's words are spoken from the heart, and each son hears what his father has just for him.

Then, and only then, Jacob gives instructions concerning his burial, and as soon as he finishes, the patriarch draws his feet up on his bed and breathes his last.

How powerful that time must have been for everyone involved, especially for the young boys! During their grandfather Jacob's final moments, they received a sense of purpose that would sustain them on their journeys toward mature manhood.

Although I was not yet sure how to accomplish it, I wanted my own son to experience something similar, something just as memorable and powerful.

A Son Beloved: Pronouncing a Father's Pleasure

The second biblical account of blessing that impressed me is found in Matthew 3:16–17. It records the events that took place when Jesus was baptized in the River Jordan and the Holy Spirit descended on him. As Jesus rose out of the water, his heavenly Father declared from heaven, "This is my Son, whom I love; with him I am well pleased." It is also recorded that later, on the Mount of Transfiguration, the heavenly Father once again said, "This is my Son, whom I love; with him I am well pleased" (Matthew 17:5).

How significant that the Father said, *"This* is my Son." If Jesus in his humanity doubted his divine heritage for even a moment, these few words confirming his Sonship would have put those doubts to rest. However, if this were his Father's only purpose, he would have said, *"You* are my beloved Son," addressing Jesus alone. By saying *"This* is my Son," the heavenly Father served notice to all creation that the promised divine Savior had arrived. He let every being in the universe know who this man was and how his Father felt about him.

Ironically, or perhaps predictably, just a short time after the first wonderful blessing was spoken, this beloved Son was assaulted by the varied schemes of Satan. In Matthew 4:1–11, we see the devil tempt Jesus to turn stones into bread, to test the Father's love by casting himself down from a high tower, and to worship the deceiver in exchange for all the world's riches. Jesus, however, rejects all three temptations, realizing they are but smoke screens for Satan's real objective: to separate Jesus from the blessing, purpose, and identity that his Father had recently bestowed on him. This is why Satan begins two of his seductive statements to Jesus with the words, *"If* you are the Son of God..."

If Satan had somehow managed to confuse Jesus about his true identity or convince him that he was not the Son of God, then the course of human history would have been dramatically altered. Instead, Jesus believed his Father, received his identity, and dutifully carried out his heaven-sent mission on earth.

After studying these Bible passages, I was convinced that our celebration needed to include a spoken blessing, confirmation of Christopher's identity, and a declaration of just how pleased I was with him as my son.

PRESSING AHEAD

At this point, a vague picture of what the event would look like began to emerge. However, I was beginning to feel pressed for time. I quietly questioned whether we could create a proper rite of passage within a few short weeks.

In fact, as the preparations continued, a war began to rage within me. Often my mind made weak attempts to minimize the importance of the celebration, only to be overridden by a still small voice in my soul that whispered, *This celebration will change more than one life in some very profound ways.* In less than twenty-one days, I would understand what those words meant.

In the meantime, Kathleen and I pressed ahead in faith with preparations. We decided that since we had so little time to prepare, we would surprise Christopher with the celebration.

If we had it to do over, we would choose to prepare Christopher for the coming event as well as we could in the short time we had. While I will address this in greater detail later in the book, it is important to understand that families who have sufficient time to prepare for a child's celebration should definitely let him or her know well in advance that it is coming. The celebration itself then becomes the capstone on a lifetime of mentoring, blessing, and instruction for the child. This is the way that we approached the subsequent celebrations for our three other children. In Christopher's case, thankfully, keeping it a secret didn't take anything away from the evening's impact and was part of the fun for us. However, we quickly learned how difficult it is to keep something secret from an inquisitive, nearly thirteen-year-old boy!

During the early planning stages, we had some practical arrangements to make. First, we located a medium-sized conference room in a nearby hotel. We considered having the celebration at home or at our church, but for us the hotel seemed like the best choice. Of course, a wide variety of settings would work for a rite-of-passage event, including a wilderness cabin, a campground, a private home, a church building, or any other type of meeting hall. Many of the men who attended Christopher's celebration have since held rites of passage for their own children in different kinds of settings with equal effectiveness.

Next came the arrangements for food and beverages. We wanted the focus to be on the ceremony itself rather than on a dinner, so we chose to have cake, coffee, and soft drinks. This was easy to arrange, and it created a casual atmosphere of fellowship at the beginning of Christopher's special night.

Kathleen agreed to take care of these matters, allowing me to concentrate on developing the agenda for the celebration. Since I had no specific pattern to go by, I struggled with where to begin. However, slowly and prayerfully, an outline for the evening began developing in my mind.

A COMMUNICATION OF VALUE — FROM MEN

I knew that one very significant part of the celebration would occur when godly men communicated to Christopher something of value from their lives. Therefore I sent the following letter to a select group of men whose lives had demonstrated the qualities I hoped to see developed in my son.

Dear _____,

Greetings in the name of the Lord!

After prayerful consideration, I am writing to ask you and several other men to help with an event that is most dear to me. My son Christopher Brian Molitor is turning thirteen this month, and I believe that we need to celebrate his coming into the first stages of manhood in a special way. I am organizing a gathering of godly men who will pray and speak words of encouragement over my son at a "graduation" ceremony to be held on July 28th. I am requesting that you help in this celebration in some or all of the following ways:

Write a letter to Christopher that addresses growing into mature manhood and includes a selected passage of Scripture, a life lesson that you have personally learned, and a word of blessing. This is the most important aspect of the ceremony, as Chris will treasure these letters as he grows.

Commit to pray for Christopher during this time, asking that God will reveal his perfect plan for him.

Provide a small gift that is symbolic or has particular meaning for a young man growing up. This may be a book, something made by hand, an old fishing lure, a plaque or picture, etc. Please understand that the emphasis here is on the symbolic meaning, not on the gift itself.

Attend the ceremony if you are able. It will be held on Monday, the 28th, at the——— hotel in Midland from 7 to 10 P.M. Cake, soft drinks, and coffee will be served at the gathering.

Other options: God may give you another idea of how to bless this fine young man. Please feel free to be creative.

I realize that the 28th is drawing close and I am giving you short notice. Please forgive me for this. If you cannot attend, you may send your letters and/or packages to me at my home. This celebration gathering will be a surprise for my son, so please send your correspondence addressed to me, personally. If your schedule will not permit a mailing, then perhaps you can e-mail your letter and I will print it out for Christopher.

I am indebted to you for your kindness. If I can return the favor for a special young person in your life, just say the word and I will respond. I want to thank you in advance for helping me to send this fine young man into God's plan for his life! Any questions, please call me.

Brian D. Molitor

Despite the fact that these busy men had less than three weeks to prepare, their response to my letter was overwhelming! Businessmen, ministers, and friends from near and far wrote back with their support.

That was when the real fun began. It became increasingly difficult to keep the celebration a secret from Christopher. As the letters and packages arrived, Chris was usually right there, checking out the mail. On one occasion a dear friend of mine forgot to put my name on the envelope and instead addressed his letter to Christopher. Naturally, when it arrived, Chris picked up the letter and started walking toward his room with it. My poor son thought I had lost my mind as I dove across the room to snatch the envelope out of his hands just before he opened it.

As the letters arrived, I continued to work on the actual agenda for the celebration. I sensed that another part of the evening should be some dramatized skits that conveyed foundational life messages. However, I found it difficult to decide which lessons should be the focus of the evening, much less how to present them. After several days of fruitless planning, I did what we often do when we have exhausted our own supply of bad ideas: I prayed and asked God what to do. When I woke the following day, I had plans for three skits complete with props, such as pop bottles, one hundred pounds of shelled corn, bags of junk food, and tools. These skits would later prove to be a highlight of the celebration.

During this time, Kathleen and I made an important decision: we determined that she should not be present at Christopher's rite of passage. I will discuss our decision more later in the book but want to explain here that Kathy and I did this for two reasons. First, separating the genders during the relatively short duration of a rite of passage is consistent with the practices of many societies, past and present. I am convinced that this short separation helps solidify a fact that has been under assault in our modern society of late—that is, men are different from women. Men are not better, men are not worse; however, men are different. This leads to our second rationale for Kathy's not attending any of our sons' celebrations. The issues that men deal with, struggle with, and often fail to overcome are different. We wanted the men who attended to be completely free to share with Christopher about their struggles and victories over potentially sensitive issues. Had any women been present, this simply would not have happened as effectively.

So, along with taking care of details like talking with the hotel personnel to make sure the room was set up properly, we bought a new tape for the video camera (Kathleen had jokingly said that if I did not videotape the celebration, the hotel would become my new home). In addition to packing the video equipment, I packed my small camera and plenty of film. The plan was to take photographs to fill a scrapbook for Christopher after the celebration was over. Once all the key decisions were made and the final preparations were completed, we just had to wait for the special day...

4

LESSONS
FOR LIFE

MONDAY, JULY 28—the night of the celebration finally arrived. Christopher's grandfather, Jim Hayes, offered to take Chris and me out for a birthday dinner, even though Chris's actual birthday was still two days away.

Jim is a wonderful father-in-law. He is a bear of a man with a grip like a vise, despite the fact that he had recently reached his eightieth birthday. His easy smile and knowledge of home repairs helped me survive my early years as a homeowner. Grandpa Hayes was never more than a phone call away when I sheepishly finished a repair project with more pieces than when I began. Our dinner together was the perfect opener for Christopher's special night.

According to plan, Christopher and I met Jim at a local restaurant at five o'clock. As we talked about the day's earlier activities, I thought about how special it was to have three generations of men gathered together. Grandpa Hayes spoke of the relief he felt when he was finally able to sell some property that had been on the market for the past two years. Christopher offered to take him golfing later that summer, and I spent most of the time watching these two enjoy each other's company. At one point Grandpa Hayes asked Christopher if he had any plans for his birthday. Christopher's quiet response was that "nothing special" was planned. I just sat and smiled as I watched his grandfather's eyes twinkle.

SURPRISE, CHRISTOPHER!

We soon finished our dinner and said good-bye to Grandpa Hayes, who got into his car and drove away. As we left the restaurant, I asked Christopher with a straight face, "Where should we go now, pal?"

"How about the movies, Dad? There are some cool shows on tonight," he said excitedly. "They start at seven-thirty."

"Okay. But how about if we stop at the hotel first? There's a prayer meeting tonight, and I told the men that I would stop by."

"But, Dad, we only have a little time." Christopher looked disappointed. "When you guys get together, it's hard to get you apart. We'll miss the start of the movie!"

"Don't worry, son. We'll just stop in to say hello, and we'll leave whenever *you* say you want to, okay?"

My son reluctantly agreed, and we drove to the hotel. As we pulled into the parking lot, Christopher noticed several cars that belonged to the men from our church.

"Hey, Dad, there's Tony's car, and there's Pastor Ron's car, and..."

I just nodded and silently hoped I had given everyone enough time to get into the room before we arrived.

Chris and I entered the hotel and made our way down the hallway to the room. As we walked through the door, I was thrilled to see so many men had gathered to celebrate my son's special night. There were nearly thirty in all!

From all outward appearances, these men seemed very different from one another. Some were young and others old. Some had black skin, some brown, and others white. Some were wealthy, and others had very few material possessions. However, their genuine smiles spoke volumes about the glue that held them together: these men all shared a common love for their Maker, for their families, and for their friends.

I liked these men. They were not handwringers who huddled together to complain about the troubles of their lives. Rather, these were gentle warriors from all walks of life who had chosen to stand for what is eternally good. They were men who gathered to share the common load of life and to bear each other's burdens. Men who did their best to live out their commitment to God's truth. Their presence at my son's special night filled me with a renewed appreciation for the gift of friendship.

My only regret is that I failed to get a photograph of Christopher's face when he first saw all those wonderful men in the room. It took a while for him to realize that this gathering was being held in his honor.

I hustled around the room, making last-second changes in the seating arrangements, setting up the video camera, and putting the props in position for the skits. The room was ideal for our needs. We had a large area of comfortable chairs where the men sat and talked, and a formal seating area with tables, chairs, and a podium was arranged so that everyone would have a good view of the presentations and skits.

Seated in the far corner of the room was a grinning Grandpa Hayes, who had driven from the restaurant in record time and had arrived just before we walked in. Three of the men had brought their teenage sons—Caleb, Nick, and Patrick—to participate in the celebration as well.

It was obvious that my precious wife had been in the room earlier in the day. Colorful decorations brightened the walls. Kathy had also brought a large sheet cake that was displayed on a table by the entryway. At her instructions, the bakery had written a Scripture verse on the white frosting: *When I was a child, I talked like a child, I thought like a child, I reasoned like a child. When I became a man, I put childish ways behind me* (1 Corinthians 13:11). How appropriate those words! They brought tears to my eyes. Truly, this was going to be a rite of passage for my son. I silently thanked God for his grace.

After an opening prayer, we cut the cake and enjoyed refreshments and fellowship for the next half hour or so. I marveled at the fact that so many men were willing to give up several hours of their day in order to bless my son for a lifetime. Their laughter was genuine, their sharing heartfelt. A subtle fragrance and a sense of peace filled the room that night.

It was easy for me to picture Jesus' first disciples meeting like this. I could almost hear the soft steps of the Master as he moved among us.

His words rose up in my memory: "For where two or three are gathered together in My name, I am there in the midst of them" (Matthew 18:20, NKJV). Later that evening, he made his presence known to us in ways we could never have anticipated.

LESSONS FOR LIFE

After we finished our refreshments, the group gathered around the large tables to start the formal ceremony. Christopher and his young friends sat toward the front of the room, where they would have a clear view of the proceedings.

I opened by thanking the men for coming. As I looked into their faces, my mind was flooded with fond memories. I saw my friend Charlie and thought of the time we had hunted elk together in the mountains of Colorado. My eyes fell on my dear Christian brother and coworker James Glenn. The two of us had enjoyed an even deeper bond of friendship since our trip to South Africa. My great friend Pastor Ron Ives sat in the back of the room, his eyes already moist from the powerful sense of purpose we all felt just by being there.

I then moved ahead with the program, explaining to Christopher that some of the men had volunteered to help with several skits. This announcement brought laughter from the "volunteers." They vocalized mock protests and complained that they didn't recall freely signing up for theatrical assignments.

How Should a Man Deal with His Emotions?

Our first "volunteer," James, walked to the podium and began speaking about the role that emotions play in a man's life. He spoke from experience. James had grown up on the mean streets of Detroit, Michigan, and had become the man of his house at age eleven when his father abandoned him and his mother and siblings. James then turned to Christopher and solemnly shared that there were right and wrong ways for men to deal with their emotions.

Then, on cue, another friend, Tony, stormed to the front of the room. In his hand was a large, unopened bottle of soda water. Taped to the bottle was a sign that read MY LIFE. Tony began complaining loudly about some of life's problems. Christopher's young eyes grew wide as Tony's tirade became louder and angrier.

"Man, my wife sure makes me mad!" He seethed. "She's always making me jealous! She does it on purpose, too!"

Tony's anger seemed intensely real. With each harsh statement, he slammed the soda-water bottle into the palm of his powerful hand.

"My boss is such a jerk! Who does she think she is? I work like a dog, and she promotes somebody else!" His face reddened. "I should have gotten that job. It's not fair!" *Bang!* went the bottle as it crashed onto the tabletop in front of Christopher's face. His young eyes were riveted on Tony as the tantrum escalated.

"How am I ever going to get through this?" Tony said in a now fearful tone. "I could lose *everything* if it doesn't get better." He seemed genuinely scared as he complained about his frustrations and gave voice to his fears. By design, he continued to shake, slam, and even drop the pressurized bottle throughout the performance.

Then Tony's demeanor changed. His voice calmed, and he began reflecting on his faith in God and on his call to bless others.

"Despite all my troubles, I am a Christian, and I want to pour out my life for others. That is what God expects."

With that, Tony made his way to the front table where three empty glasses waited. He told us that the glasses represented the lives of other people. As he began to twist the top off the bottle, we could all see the words MY LIFE inscribed on its side.

As you could imagine, trouble was about to occur. Predictably, when the top of the bottle was removed, all of the intense pressure that had built up during the angry tirade was released in an explosion of liquid. Those in the front of the room dove for cover. Tony was instantly drenched from his head to his waist. Without a word, he vainly tried to pour what was left of the bottle's contents into the three empty glasses. Sadly, there was only enough left to cover the bottom of each glass. Even the paper sign on the bottle spoke volumes. It hung in soggy tatters, the ink running down the side of the bottle. Tony's "life" was truly a mess because his emotions were out of control.

The room remained silent as our soggy friend made his way out into the hall. Then James returned to the podium and solemnly asked us to ponder our own lives. He asked each of us to honestly evaluate how we, as men, handle our emotions. He challenged us to determine how much of our life was left to pour into others after we have given in to excess anger, rage, or other forms of futile flailing. The hardest question to face was this: did our out-of-control emotions rob our wives and children of a blessing?

Suddenly Tony reentered the room wearing a new dry shirt. In his hands was another bottle of soda water with another MY LIFE label on the front. He had the same angry look on his face as he began to repeat the complaints about his wife we had heard minutes earlier. He hissed through clenched teeth about the jealousy that tormented his soul.

As he finished venting this time, he again raised the bottle to slam it down into his fist. However, at the last second he did what no one expected him to do. This time, he gently placed the bottle on the table and fell to his knees. From this position of surrender, Tony poured his heart out to God. "Dear Lord, please help me deal with this jealousy." The passion in his voice was real. "It's eating me alive, and I cannot overcome it on my own. God, please help me."

Tony then rose to his feet, picked up the bottle, and put his "life" back in his own hands. His countenance changed again as another tirade of angry words gushed out. "Man, my boss is so unfair!" he raged. "Why didn't she pick me for the promotion? It just isn't right!" Again, the bottle was raised above his head and seemed destined for a violent crash. Would he slam it down again? No. Instead he gently placed it back on the table and walked slowly over to James.

"James, I'm really hurting. Will you pray for me?"

The two of them took each other's hands and prayed together. Tony looked relieved as they finished praying. One last time, Tony picked up the bottle representing his life and spoke. "There's too much happening today. I don't know how I'm going to make it."

The men in the room could easily relate to those feelings.

"It's just too much to take sometimes!" One final time the bottle seemed headed for a blow that would cause it to erupt when opened. However, Tony surprised us again. This time he gently set the bottle down and walked humbly towards Pastor Ron. His words were simple and quiet. "Brother, I need some help."

Many of us in the room were moved to tears as Pastor Ron simply hugged Tony. No words needed to be spoken. The moment was filled with power as God used one man to strengthen another. Then Tony returned to pick up the bottle and made his way to the three glasses sitting silently, waiting to be filled.

"I know that God wants me to pour my life into others," Tony said quietly as he twisted the cap on the bottle. Instinctively those nearest the bottle started to pull back. Would it explode as the first one had? When the top was removed, there was barely a sound. Not a drop was spilled. We then watched in wonder as one man symbolically poured his life into the lives of three others. Amazingly, each glass was filled exactly to the top as the final drop fell from Tony's bottle.

The men there had witnessed a critical life lesson: when we deal with our emotions properly, not only do our own lives flow much better, but also we have plenty to pour into our families and the other people God places in our path.

Tony carefully set his now-empty bottle down on the table. This time the sign on the side of the bottle spoke an entirely different message. The ink was dry. The sign was intact. One life had been emptied so that three others could be filled.

Christopher sat stunned, his young face filled with awe at the power of the message. In fifteen minutes he had learned more about how men should deal with their emotions than many men learn in a lifetime. And the night was just getting started.

Does a Real Man Have to Go It Alone?

Doug, a big man with salt-and-pepper hair, walked deliberately toward the front of the room. A devoted husband and father, Doug serves as an elder in a local church. His burly frame projects physical strength, while his kind and gentle manner reflects the love of the Father.

"Christopher," he called out in his soothing baritone voice, "please come up here."

After the exploding bottle in the last skit, my son looked a little hesitant to comply. Cautiously he left his seat and stood next to Doug.

"Chris, I have a job for you to do."

"Okay. What is it?"

"Just carry a couple of things to the back of the room."

"Sure, what are they?"

Doug stepped aside to reveal two fifty-pound bags of shelled corn that I had purchased from a feed store earlier in the week. Christopher's young muscles strained as he labored to pick up the first bag. He is a strong young man, but the bag of corn was like many situations in a man's life: it was hard to get a handle on! When Chris picked up one end of the bag, all of the weight shifted into the other end, and he nearly toppled over. He finally got the first bag balanced and started lugging it toward the back of the room.

After he had walked several yards, Doug asked him to stop. "Chris, how are you coming with that burden you're carrying? Is the job easy or difficult?"

Christopher responded with a typical male answer: "Well, it isn't easy, but I know I can do it." Doug's comeback captured both sides of a man's approach to handling the burdens in his life.

"Chris, it's great that you tried," Doug said kindly. "I can see that you're not afraid to work, nor are you a complainer. However, since you have another bag to move, how about if we just take a moment to pray. Let's ask God to show you someone in the room who might come and help you."

Chris seemed relieved by the suggestion. He immediately set the bag down, bowed his head, and earnestly prayed. "Dear Jesus, please show me who should come help me with this task. Thank you, Lord. Amen."

As his eyes opened, he immediately said three names: "Caleb, Nick, and Tony." The three quickly jumped out of their seats and moved toward the bags. Chris and Caleb took the first one, and the other two grabbed the second bag. In short order, the task was completed, and everyone returned to his seat.

While the lesson was intended for Christopher, everyone in the room could easily see the natural tendency in men to want to go it alone. We seem to think we can handle life by ourselves, no matter what comes along.

Doug then began a short teaching on the need to have friends we can count on to share our burdens and lend the support we need. He explained that men often become like solitary bull elephants. These majestic creatures are clearly in charge of their domain, but they manage it from the edges. They protect their herd and interact with others in their families and communities only when absolutely necessary. No one dares challenge these silent leaders—and no one tries to help them either. The loners' dominance lasts until they face enemies or obstacles they cannot overcome alone, and then, sadly, they perish.

The nodding heads around the room showed that Doug's points were well made and accepted. We all need others to help us through life's challenges. Truly, as it says in Ecclesiastes 4:12, a cord of three strands is not easily broken.

Doug then added an interesting twist to the skit. He questioned the three helpers about how they felt when Chris asked them to help move the bags of corn. One by one they responded.

"Honored."

"Chosen."

"I felt needed."

"Did anyone feel put out or upset when you had to leave the comfort of your chairs in order to help Chris?" Doug asked.

After a few seconds Caleb spoke up. "Jesus is our role model. He came to serve, not to be served. Sometimes we forget that. There's no way I could just sit here and watch my friend struggle with the load. Man, I wanted to help!"

Next, Doug explained how men often get into tough situations and, instead of asking God to show them the way out, try working harder on their own. Many heads dropped. We could all relate. God said his ways are higher than our ways and his thoughts higher than our thoughts (Isaiah 55:8–9), so why are we so stubborn sometimes? God always provides a way out for us, no matter what form of temptation, test, or trial comes our way (see 1 Corinthians 10:13). But to find God's way out, we need to ask him for the solution and then be willing to let others help us.

It was now becoming obvious that the truths shared during the celebration were intended for more than just a thirteen-year-old. The Lord had prepared a delicious meal filled with some of life's greatest lessons, and he was inviting each of us to dine.

As I looked at the smiles on the men's faces and reflected on what had happened already, it was hard to imagine that there was more to come. But as Pastor Ron walked to the podium, I soon learned that when the Lord prepares the meal, it truly is a feast!

What Kinds of Choices Will You Make, Young Man?

"A man must make many choices in his life," Pastor Ron said. "Right choices make for a good life; wrong choices make for a bad life. It is just that simple."

Clearly, Pastor Ron knew what he was talking about. He is a successful father, husband, and pastor, loved deeply by his family and his congregation. He had made some great choices along life's way. But one thing I like about this man is his willingness to share with others about a few of the wrong choices he made early in life. The lines at the corners of his eyes gave silent testimony to a period of hard living and bad choices.

"Christopher, I want you to go shopping," Ron encouraged. "Please come up to the front."

On a long table at the front of the room were several items "for sale." And what an assortment! They were arranged in two opposing piles. On the left side of the table were a bottle of whiskey, a fake pornographic magazine, some junk food, and a few children's toys. On the right side were a bottle of pure spring water, a Bible, a loaf of fresh-baked whole wheat bread, and a new hammer.

Christopher's face reflected a blend of joy and apprehension. As he started forward, so did two other men. Each "salesman" moved behind one set of items and waited for his turn to try to convince Christopher that he should shop there.

The first one to speak was Chuck, a wildly animated guy who began his sales pitch for the worldly items. "Hey kid!" he hollered as he reached out to grab Christopher's shirt. "Come here. I've got everything you need for success in this life. Check out this magazine, man. Look at these women. These are the real thing! This kind of stuff will make you a man!"

When Chris showed little interest in the magazine, Chuck's tactics changed, and he grabbed the bottle of whiskey. "Look kid, you're too uptight tonight. You need to loosen up a bit," he said. "Let's get rip-roaring drunk, and then things will look better. Eat, drink, and be merry—that's what the Bible says, right?"

"Ah, no, thanks— " Christopher said quietly.

"Okay, no problem," interrupted Chuck. "Uhhh…I can see you're a growing boy, so how about some chow? I got some great stuff here. Lots of fat and sugar. Plenty of special dyes to give these goodies a nice orange color." Chuck literally shoved the bag of junk food into Chris's face. "Let's eat!"

"I don't think so," Chris said as he pulled away from the salesman's impassioned pleas.

Chuck began to sound desperate as he noticed Christopher's attention shifting to the quiet man standing behind the other group of items for sale. "Listen kid, I know what you're thinking. It's time to grow up, right? Take it from me, there is always time for that—later. Here, grab some of these toys. You sure don't want to learn about work, do you? It's time to play, so let's play! The Bible says you're supposed to *play* like a little child, right? Hey, come on. Where are you going?"

"I'm going to look over here," Chris answered as he turned toward the other salesman, who stood quietly with his hands folded in front of him.

Chuck simply wasn't going to take no for an answer. "Wait a minute! Don't be stupid!" he screamed as his smile turned into a snarl. Picking up the porn magazine, he began his hard sell. "Blondes, brunettes, redheads! All *real* men love this stuff! Hey, what's the hurry? Come on, just stay with me for a little while. Couple of drinks can't hurt, can they? What's the hurry? Hey, no money down. I'll collect from you later."

Many of us in the room laughed at Chuck's antics as he tried in vain to hook the young man into staying. Yet behind our laughter, we remembered the many times we'd succumbed to the seductive call of bad choices and temporary pleasures. We were reminded that the Scriptures are to be prayerfully studied, not swallowed in simple sound bites—nor twisted, as Chuck was doing. We each carried the physical and emotional scars to prove the destructive impact of stopping and shopping at the wrong places.

Choices. What did Pastor Ron say? "Right choices make for a good life; wrong choices make for a bad life. It is just that simple."

The next salesman was another man from the area. His gentle demeanor and strong faith made him an excellent representative for his products from "Kingdom of God Enterprises."

"Son," he began softly. "Those things at the other end of the table may look or sound good, and they might be pretty exciting at first. But there is one major problem with them: they don't satisfy."

Those last three words hit the rest of us hard. *They don't satisfy.* So many of us had learned that the hard way. The heavenly salesman continued. "The problem is that you have to keep going back for more and more of that junk. I'll bet that other guy didn't tell you *that*, did he?"

Chris thought for a moment and acknowledged that Chuck had not.

Holding up the Bible, the salesman boldly spoke. "The words in *this* book will never disappoint you, son. You will never have to hide it or be ashamed of it. If you want to learn about women, this is the book for you. It will teach you how to love and respect them. Women are much more than just body parts. They are created in God's image. But this wonderful book isn't limited to just one subject. This is a handbook for your life!"

His words rolled like gentle thunder across the room. We knew that God was giving us all a reminder to stay with the words of life. We were convicted that there were too many times we ourselves had bypassed the Bible on the way to the television set or our favorite hobby.

"As for *his* brand of food and drink" —the salesman smiled and nodded his head toward Chuck— "they will definitely fill you *out,* but in the end they will leave you empty. It's easy to forget that we are the temples of the Holy Spirit, not toxic waste dumps. God wants us to put only good things into our bodies. Son, try this bread and spring water. They not only are good for you but also will remind you that Jesus is *the* Bread of Life and his Word washes us like pure water.

"Christopher, you have enjoyed a fine childhood. Your parents have cared for your needs, and you have lacked little as you have grown. You've played for hours with toys like those on the table over there. And yes, Jesus did say that we were to *enter* the kingdom as little children. But he didn't say that we were to spend the rest of our lives there just playing, remaining immature and unproductive. His Word tells us that 'if a man will not work, he shall not eat'" (2 Thessalonians 3:10).

That got my son's attention!

Young Man, Are You Ready to Fulfill Your Purpose?

"As a servant of God and as a man," the salesman added, "you will experience many times of enjoyment, fun, and laughter. But these are the results of being in relationship with your heavenly Father and obeying his Word and his ways. You will learn that there is nothing more enjoyable than being used by the Master to further his kingdom. Also, there are few things in life more satisfying than for a man to build something for and with his family. Christopher, it is time to set aside the toys of childhood, pick up the tools of a man, and pursue *your* purpose."

With that, my son picked up the hammer and stared thoughtfully at it. I confess that I briefly imagined him using it to build his dream house sometime in the future. In my mind's eye, I saw *his* sons—my grandsons—clinging to his legs as he tried to build. *Daddy, Daddy,* they called out. *Can we help?*

Then I remembered projects in the past when Christopher and I had worked together. Those first few were especially memorable as I spent more time undoing his messes than building. However, I now realized that in those God-ordained times, we were doing so much more than building doghouses or go-carts. Those projects were used to teach my son to work like a man and to press forward even when obstacles temporarily blocked the way. More important, God also used those times to bond our hearts together.

In that moment, it became so clear to me that the plan of God is to have one generation of men serve as the teachers, mentors, counselors, and friends to the next generation. What a wonderful plan! But how many boys and young men have never had an older man serve them in this way? How many men in the room with me were still hurting, still needing someone to affirm their manhood?

Pastor Ron's voice broke my train of thought.

"Christopher, it's time to make your purchases. You have heard both salesmen. What will you buy?"

I held my breath for a second as my son glanced at the first set of goods. Then he literally turned his back on Chuck and opened his shopping bag for the other salesman to fill. In went the Bible, bread, water, and tool. As my son made his way back to his seat, the men clapped and cheered.

None of us were naive enough to believe that a short skit would prevent Chris from ever listening to the voices of worldly salesmen when he was out on his own. However, we felt sure of one important thing: when he did hear those voices with their seductive promises, Chris would remember, *I don't have to shop here; I can make good choices. It is just that simple.*

The skit left us feeling full and yet still hungry for more. We were thrilled to think that this fine young man might never have to experience the pain so many of us had suffered from our shopping trips to the wrong places.

My mind was racing as I moved to the podium to announce our next step in the celebration.

5

LEADERS SHARING WORDS AND GIFTS

"SON, I HAVE SOME LETTERS HERE FOR YOU," I said to Christopher. "Some are from people you know. Others were sent by men you have never met—friends of mine from other countries. These are all special letters. I asked these men to pray before they wrote anything down, and I am sure they did. Son, I want you to understand that these men are husbands, fathers, businessmen, clergy, and community leaders. They are very busy men who have no time to waste, yet each was willing to seek God for wisdom that they could share with you."

My soon-to-be teenager sat ramrod straight and carefully considered my words. As he looked at the letters in my hand, I could see expectancy in his green eyes. I stole a brief moment for myself as I thought about how my son had changed since the day he entered this world. It was amazing how many stages he had already passed through. Could this be the chubby-faced little boy who just a few years ago viewed cards and letters as major roadblocks to the fun of opening packages at Christmas or birthdays?

It looked like him, but his face was now different. His cheeks were no longer chubby; instead, they were lean, and there was a hint of a mustache above his upper lip. When he was younger, a gathering like this would have intimidated him. He never would have been more than an arm's length away from me. At that age, an invisible cord tied us together. I would always lead, and he would always follow. Yet now he sat in quiet confidence at the head of the table.

For a moment I felt very proud at his growth. But in the next instant I was chilled by the unthinkable. *Does his growing independence mean that the invisible cord between us is being cut? Am I about to lose my precious son?* Mercifully, the answer came: *No, the cord that binds my son and me will never be severed. Instead, in God's perfect plan, it will lengthen. Just enough for him to experience the joys and sorrows of manhood, but never so much that we lose the special love we have for each other.* I could barely contain my emotions.

"This first letter is from a friend of mine in South Africa," I said to Chris. "He is a businessman, husband, father, and former soldier in Rhodesia. Most important, he is a man who honors God with his life, family, and work. After his letter, I'll read several others from people who could not be with us tonight. Then the men who are here have some letters and gifts for you."

I did a fair job of reading the first letter or two. The more I read, however, the harder it was to keep from weeping. The toughest letter to read came from my own father, who couldn't attend because he was recovering from a near-fatal heart attack. As I read my dad's letter, I remembered some of the places, times, and events he and I had shared over the years.

RECALLING A PRECIOUS RELATIONSHIP

In my mind's eye, I could see my dad coming home from his job as a superintendent at a General Motors plant in Michigan. My brother, sister, and I would excitedly watch for his car to turn into the driveway at the end of each day.

As I held Dad's letter, I remembered times spent trout fishing with him on the Pine River in northern Michigan. The opening day of trout season was a very special event in the Molitor family. There was gear to pack, fly lines to be oiled so they'd float just right on the surface of the water, trout flies to tie, waders to patch, and food to prepare.

I recalled that at age five I was certain I was old enough to go with my dad and his father, my beloved Grandpa Henry, when they made the annual pilgrimage to the river. But despite my pleadings and tears, I wasn't allowed to go with them. Not yet. The river was beautiful, but it was also dangerously unforgiving for a small boy who might fall into its swift current.

It seemed as if I would never get to go with my heroes! Upon hearing the bad news, I ran and hurled myself onto my bed for a time of very real sorrow. I hid under my covers, but I was careful to leave one hand exposed—just in case my dad couldn't find me concealed there. Soon I heard Dad's footsteps coming down the hall, and I felt my bed sag under his weight as he sat next to me. Over the years I have forgotten the exact words he spoke to me, yet I remember how he stroked my hair with his strong hand. There was comfort and even a sort of healing in my father's hands. Just that simple touch chased away my pain and reaffirmed his love for me. I realized then that his motive for keeping me home was protection, not rejection. That touch sealed his promise that someday I would go with him and catch my first trout.

Two years later my dream came true. Dad was pretty sneaky when it came to surprises. He called me into our living room about one week before that year's opening day. Just by the tone of his voice, I knew he was up to something. When I entered the room, I saw a complete set of fishing gear made just the right size for me. My eyes immediately fell on the most beautiful fly rod I'd ever seen. Its shiny blue finish and intricate gold-thread windings spoke volumes to me. I knew that it signified something incredibly important: I had made a transition in my father's eyes.

Several days later we made the long trip to our cabin for my first trout opener. I don't remember if I caught any fish that day, but it really didn't matter. I was with my two heroes—my father and grandpa—and that was enough for a seven-year-old fisherman with a new fly rod.

With these wonderful memories replaying in my mind, I started reading aloud the letter from my dad while Christopher watched and listened.

Dear Chris,

This is your grandfather writing. The one whom you used to call "Grandpa *Muttitor*" when you were only two or three years old.

Well, you are about to become a teenager! You are certainly ahead of your father and me at the same age regarding your beliefs and knowledge of our Lord. What we had was a general concept of sin, a locker room education regarding girls and sex (never did completely understand girls), and frequent admonitions to "be good." We were just lukewarm Christians well into adulthood. Fortunately we got there in time.

No one can really prepare you for the teen years. If we told you, you wouldn't believe us regarding all the physical, mental, and emotional changes that will take place. Keep the faith and conscience the Lord has given to you; the Golden Rule rarely lets you down.

Just so there is an equal opportunity flavor to these thoughts, your grandmother and I share them, and we are very proud of a boy named Chris.

Love,
Grandpa Molitor

As I finished reading the letter, I couldn't help thinking about the events that had nearly claimed Dad's life earlier that year and prevented his attendance on this special night. The ordeal began when Kathy and I received a chilling phone call from my mother at 2 A.M. Dad had suffered a severe heart attack, she told us, and was being rushed by ambulance to the hospital. As I drove the twenty miles into town, I was filled with fear. Dad and I had so much more to say to each other! Was this the end? At that point, only God knew.

The hospital was a blur of foreign sounds and smells. Soon family and friends had assembled there to wait for some word of Dad's condition. I spent much of that time in the hospital chapel with my faithful friend James Glenn. Together we petitioned our heavenly Father for an outpouring of his grace and mercy.

As the day wore on, a series of bad reports filtered back to us. Tests revealed severe blockages in Dad's heart, leading doctors to rush him to open-heart surgery. Hours passed. Next we were told he was in the recovery room. Then more complications occurred, and Dad was returned to the operating room for a second open-heart surgery. It was more than twelve hours before all the procedures were completed. Finally Dad was taken to the cardiac intensive care unit of the hospital. For nearly two weeks he lay unconscious, with only the steady, slow beeping of a heart monitor indicating he was still alive.

Twice each day my family and I were allowed to see him. He looked so helpless, like a little child. We would gather around his body, praying for God to heal him. One day as I sat on his bed, I realized I had been stroking his hair as he had stroked mine so many years earlier. Thankfully, two weeks later our prayers were answered, and he was released from the hospital to finish his recuperation at home.

On Christopher's special day, Dad was still recovering, and my precious mom was serving as his nurse. I knew Dad was praying for Christopher, and it was fun to think that someday the two of them might fish for trout together. I soon finished reading his letter and returned to my chair.

HEARING FROM MEN'S HEARTS

Next it was time to have the men in the room come forward to read their letters to Christopher. Each letter was unique. Each brought a slightly different perspective on manhood and the journey to maturity. When combined, the letters served as modern-day commentaries on key scriptures and a handbook for any man's life and conduct.

One by one, my friends came to the front of the room to share words written on paper, revealing the wisdom hidden in their hearts. Pastor Ron was the first to read his letter:

Chris,

What an honor it is for me to be a part of this graduation! I have enjoyed watching you mature into a young man. Challenges undoubtedly await you, but the deposit of God within you is more than able to face all of them.

Chris, a portion of Scripture that I have memorized and would consider a "life verse" for me in regards to goals and motivation would be Philippians 3:7–11:

"But whatever was to my profit I now consider loss for the sake of Christ. What is more, I consider everything a loss compared to the surpassing greatness of knowing Christ Jesus my Lord, for whose sake I have lost all things. I consider them rubbish, that I may gain Christ and be found in him, not having a righteousness of my own that comes from the law, but that which is through faith in Christ—the righteousness that comes from God and is by faith. I want to know Christ and the power of his resurrection and the fellowship of sharing in his sufferings, becoming like him in his death, and so, somehow, to attain to the resurrection from the dead."

A closing word of encouragement from me would be to develop friendships with your brothers in Christ. Chris, words cannot express the impact these types of relationships have had on my life. There have been times that just seeing another brother has imparted courage into me to press on.

Chris, I bless you in the name of the Lord Jesus Christ. May God's Word dwell in you richly and release life. May communion with the Holy Spirit encourage and comfort you. May the Father's love cause you to walk in courage and strength.

I am proud of you as a young man. I am very blessed to have you as a friend and as a friend of my son.

Pastor Ron

When he finished reading, Ron carefully handed the letter to Christopher and returned to his seat.

John Paige then made his way to the podium. John is a high-level corporate executive for a multinational company. Through men like him, Christopher saw examples of how God works both inside and outside of a church building.

Dear Chris,

I thought I would share with you what I have learned about being a "strong" man of God. The godly picture of strength is seen in how Jesus lived when He was on earth.... The picture of Jesus is one of a Man who is physically strong, possessing wisdom, and gentle with those weaker or less fortunate. Jesus was filled with God's wisdom and gentle strength.

Jesus is the perfect role model for a young man like yourself. Also understand that God doesn't expect you to become perfect on your thirteenth birthday either. What God desires from you and each of us is steady growth. Turn to God for direction in everything you do in life, and He will guide you.

John Paige
2 Timothy 2:22–26

Next it was Grandpa Hayes's turn to share his letter, which he asked me to read to Christopher. How special to hear the words of a man in his eighties! As I read, others in the room were studying the older man and the boy's reaction to his counsel. The men seemed to understand that each wrinkle in Grandpa's skin represented more than just age. Wisdom, experience, pain, victories, and suffering—all were found in the lines on his face and in the lines of his letter. Many of us shed tears as we heard what he had to say.

Dear Christopher,

I feel real honored to attend this very special occasion this evening in your honor. There have never been two grandparents who could be more proud and could love their grandchildren more than your grandmother and me. The Lord has really blessed us by sparing us for these many years to enjoy our little family. And we are hoping and praying that He may give us a few more good years.

The Lord has really blessed us with such a wonderful family. To begin with, you have been blessed with two wonderful parents and siblings, and you're being raised in a good Christian home. There are so many children today who aren't that fortunate.

There are so many more opportunities out there today than when we were growing up. I gave four years of my life in the navy to fight for my country and to make it a better world, and other than that it was just a lot of hard work to make a good living for my family. So my advice to you, Chris, is to get a good education, which I'm sure you will...

I have a little sentimental token here, Chris—a Christmas tree ornament—which was given to us by your mom and dad during the Christmas holidays in 1983. It was their way of letting us know they were expecting their first child. So your mom and grandmother shed a few tears together. We were all so happy. I am passing it on to you so that maybe someday, when you have a family of your own, you may use it on your own Christmas tree. May it always remind you of your grandma and me.

Chris, you have been such a joy to us over the past thirteen years. You are a very special grandson. If you ever need advice for anything, feel free to come to me at any time. But I'm sure your mom and dad will do a good job. I know you'll grow up to be a fine young man.

We love you dearly.

> With all my love,
> Grandpa Hayes—age 80

After Grandpa Hayes's letter was read, the other men came forward to share their thoughts with Christopher. Each letter was powerful and touching. Here are some excerpts:

First, I want to encourage you to begin to understand the special heritage you have in your family. God provided for a special dynamic to be possible within the family that cannot be found in any other social structure. Always remember, no matter where you are or what you are going through, whether good or bad, you must never hesitate to receive the love and comfort available to you through your family.

Next, understand that God has given you a dad who is special. I have the opportunity to meet hundreds of people as I travel around the world regularly. Please believe me when I tell you that there are very few men of his caliber in the world today. Having stated this, you must discover and take advantage of what God has in mind for you, in providing such a special man to be your father. You can always count on godly wisdom when you seek advice from your dad because he will always have your best interest in his heart. Nothing or no one should ever become more important in your life than your relationship with God.

The teenage years are some of the hardest years to serve God. One of the reasons is that there is a lot of temptation. It is very easy to stray away from God; however, I have no doubt that you will make it. One important thing is to stay faithful in having quiet times for prayer and Bible reading. I have struggled in this, and I have noticed that when I struggled with my quiet times, I also struggled in my walk with God. So stay strong in God and you will have no problem with fending off peer pressure.

My simple word of advice, of encouragement is to be strong, be courageous, and be of good cheer because the Lord will always be near.

Throughout the course of your life, I'm sure that you will encounter times that your faith in Jesus will be tested, times that you will stand in the face of mighty mountains and some not so mighty but still mountains. Those are the times that I want you to think of that tiny little mustard seed that Jesus spoke of. As small as the mustard seed is, Jesus said, if we have even that much faith, "nothing will be impossible for you."

Chris, if most men could live their lives over, they would want to begin where you are today. We know it's at the entry-way of manhood that one's vision of the future begins to take shape.

Childhood is great, but maturity is even better. As a child you have received great blessing from those around you. Certainly you have had opportunities to give and bless others also. As you mature, you will have increasing opportunities to give of your life, time, talents, spiritual gifts, money, etc....I strongly encourage you to give with the express purpose of encouragement and evangelism. "Live to give" always in the light of eternity.

"He is no fool who gives that which he can't keep in order to gain that which he can't lose." (Missionary Jim Elliot)

A man of God once gave me this phrase to consider: "Plant a thought and you will reap an action; plant an action and you will reap a habit; plant a habit and you will reap a lifestyle; plant a lifestyle and you will reap a destiny." I smiled and nodded my acceptance of the ideas he had expressed—but didn't take them too seriously. But later, as I pondered what his words meant, the Lord began to show me how thoughts are the building blocks that will shape our destinies. Our thoughts are the powerful "first steps" which deserve serious and prayerful discrimination.

I see you as a fine young man with a heart for God who, if given the right guidance, has a potential of becoming a great leader in the body of Christ. I am excited to be a small part in facilitating your growth as a man of God.

Now at the coming of age, this first stage of manhood, my advice and plea to you is *listen* to your parents. By listening and being obedient, you will avoid a lot of difficulties in life. One of the Ten Commandments, #5, says (Exodus 20:12, KJV), "Honor thy father and thy mother: that thy days may be long upon the land which the LORD thy God giveth thee." This commandment ends with a promise (see Ephesians 6:2). I had no one to tell me these things, but now I am relating them to you. Learn this now at your beginning of manhood, and you will be on the right path.

In the short time I have known you, Christopher, I have appreciated your love for the Lord and your quiet, respectful demeanor. At a time when many young men become mouthy and unrestrained, you have been a tremendous example for my son. Thank you.

There is only one sure way to be smart and flexible, to know when to hang loose and when to bite the bullet. There is only one way to be tough and kind, there is only one way to be focused and yet have peripheral vision. It is the way I am still learning, an art I have yet to master. It is always, in everything, in every decision, in every word to be led by the Holy Ghost. I pray God's strength and patience for you as you learn this art of walking in the Spirit.

During this time, while so much attention is coming your way, my strongest encouragement to you is to always put others first, especially those closest to you. Whether you like it or not, you are a leader, especially to your brothers and sister, even though you may feel as if they don't respect you at times. You have, and always will have, great influence on them.

Chris, I want you to know that I have tremendous respect for you as a godly young man. I know that this transition into manhood will bring with it even more respect as well as wisdom and maturity. Your future looks very bright, and there is only one thing that can dim it, and that's you! Remember, the best leaders always lead by making right decisions so they can lead by their successes, not failures. God has fully equipped you for success!

As I watched the last man leave the podium, it struck me that these men were the living epistles that Scripture speaks about. Imperfect men in an imperfect world being led by a perfect God. Each of their letters was a minisermon on life for any man. The letters told of lessons learned in the fires and floods of life. Some, with neither complaint nor excuse, told of the pain felt when a man loses his way. And yet, unlike many of the world's writers, who lament life's problems and leave readers in despair, these men pointed the way to the answers. Each man offered hope and a future to a much younger man whose life was filled with so much promise.

RECEIVING SOME POWERFUL GIFTS

Many of the men, along with their letters, offered Chris other expressions of their care and concern for him. Grandpa Molitor had sent along something quite special. It was a long-blade knife he had used as a Boy Scout in 1937. I remember watching my dad fillet rainbow trout with that knife when I was Christopher's age. The knife's blade was no longer shiny, and its sheath was weathered, but it was a treasure nonetheless. Later I told Christopher about the good memories that knife brought whenever I saw it.

One man gave Chris a beautiful woodsman's compass, and another gave him a road map. Each of these men spoke in parables about God's direction for a young man.

Others gave plaques, candles, music tapes, and CDs. A unique gift from a mountain climber in the group was a metal link used to safely traverse mountain slopes. On it was the inscription *"Jesus is your link to life."* Another man took the time to make a videotape of his "letter" so Chris could replay it at home. It included a song about manhood from a popular Christian music group.

James Glenn gave Christopher a beautiful silver nugget ring with a dove etched into the metal. It had been one of his prized possessions for over fifteen years, yet he gladly gave it to Christopher on this special night.

The list goes on. A Bible, a concordance, several books about manhood, a 1984 coin set, posters of Chris's favorite sports figures, and a *"Fishers of Men"* tie tack. Chris appreciated every gift. He knew that each came from the heart of a man who loved him.

I found it fitting that the gifts ranged from a new basketball to Oswald Chamber's classic book *My Utmost for His Highest*. A beautiful balance between the natural and the spiritual.

This part of the celebration went way beyond my greatest expectations. Yet there was still more to come, something I had not anticipated, a gift as moving and profound as any that had already been offered.

Joseph, one of the men there, asked if he could sing a song. I agreed and was surprised to learn that he had written the song just for Christopher only a week before. It is one of the most beautiful ballads about a father and son that I have ever heard. Let me excerpt a piece of the first verse and refrain for you here:

> Deep in the stillness
> > when the family would sleep,
> the Father would call him,
> > the Father would speak.

> O my beloved, O my sweet,
> > tender young boy whom the angels keep.
> How I love to hold you here in the dark,
> > holding the love of a boy in my heart.

The complete song describes the intimate relationship between God the Father and Christ the Son. The lyrics tell of how God can have that same kind of relationship with Christopher—with each of us—because of Christ's love and sacrifice. And we in turn can build our relationships with our sons on the self-sacrificing love of God. The words further urged Christopher and all of us to "listen to the Father, know your Father's plan," because that is where we find true life and maturity.

As the last sounds of Joseph's guitar faded, each man was momentarily lost in his own thoughts. Images of our own fathers and sons flooded our minds. Memories of our past. Visions of our future. All made possible by the Son who died for us all on a hill centuries ago. We were filled with gratitude. Slowly we began to look around at each other. A smile seemed to grace the face of each man in the room. Christopher and the other young men sat in the sweet stillness. They each had that Christmas-morning-and-lots-of-presents-under-the-tree look. Yet they knew that on this night they were receiving gifts that would never break or wear out. They knew that these offerings of knowledge and wisdom would be lost only if they chose to let them go.

And I knew it was now time to seal all that had happened. It was time to pray a blessing over my beloved son.

6

BLESSINGS ABUNDANT

JAMES GLENN ROSE FROM HIS SEAT and walked to the front of the room. He placed a chair in the center of the room and invited Christopher to come and sit in it. James then spoke of the importance of blessing a young man as he grows into manhood. He said that as light that dispels the darkness, the blessing of a father or other trusted mentor can safeguard a young man against much of the world's destructive influence.

James then reminded us about the war between cursing and blessing that rages for every young man's soul. He shared that our heavenly Father's blessing was greater than any worldly curse. He explained:

> In secret, a curse whispers in the young boy's ears, "You will never amount to anything." In response, the Father's blessing loudly proclaims, "Your God has plans for you. Plans of hope and a future."

> In secret, a curse whispers in the young boy's ears, "You are rejected and will always be alone." In response, the Father's

blessing loudly proclaims, "I will never leave you nor forsake you, and I will provide for you a friend that sticks closer than a brother."

In secret, a curse whispers in the young boy's ears, "You are weak and a failure. You will never succeed in this life." In response, the Father's blessing loudly proclaims, "You can do *all* things through Christ who gives you strength."

BRING BACK THE BLESSING!

When I glanced at Christopher, I thought of all the potential pitfalls that awaited him. All the traps I had blindly fallen into. My heart ached to think of the troubles he would suffer if he chose unwisely. It was almost overwhelming, and I was again struck by the awesome responsibility of fatherhood.

Then I remembered a special time of prayer for my son that had occurred more than a decade earlier in a unique place and in a unique way. When Christopher was just a baby, I was involved in a statewide prison ministry in Michigan. I would go with a team of men into maximum-security prisons, where we would stay for four days at a time. Typically, we would sleep inside the prison, walk in the prison yard, and eat in the prison cafeteria. It was not a glamorous ministry, but it provided some of the most meaningful spiritual experiences of my life. The ministry consisted of music, fellowship, small group discussion, personal testimonies, and a series of teachings on the spiritual dimension of life.

Our ministry always had a makeshift chapel in the prison. It was nothing fancy, but we knew that God would honor our efforts to do his will, regardless of where we were. Our speakers would always go into the chapel for prayer before their presentations and return there immediately afterward to thank God for using their words to heal hurting inmates. There were always several men praying in the chapel during the entire four-day ministry, so the presenters had plenty of prayer support.

On one occasion I was asked to share my personal testimony of what my life had been like without Christ and how it changed once I committed my life to him. It was painful to honestly recount my mistakes and to share about the many times that sin had been stronger than my desire to do right. I knew, though, that I needed to be vulnerable before these men confined by concrete walls and rolls of razor wire. They needed to see that Jesus Christ truly changes lives.

I told the inmates of my life's troubled times and spoke of being near death on several occasions. As I shared about my failures and past sins, I could feel a weight of guilt and shame lifting from my shoulders. The healing continued as I spoke about the goodness of God, how he had given me a wonderful wife and then one (at that time) fine son, whom we had named Christopher. Also, I told of how God had placed me in my own business and had made it possible for my family to have a home of our own.

As I finished my presentation and returned to the chapel, an incredible sense of peace filled my heart. I was thrilled to think that I had really made it out of the snares of my youth.

Suddenly, as I was about to enter the chapel, my joy turned to terror. I was gripped with an unshakable fear. In my mind I heard the words, "You might have made it, but your son won't." I stumbled into the chapel and sat down. My mind raced. *My son. My precious Christopher. What will happen to him? What lies in store for him? Car wrecks? Gun shots? The cruel blade of a knife? Will he reject the God who has become so real to me?* I could hardly bear these thoughts.

So I did the only thing that made sense to me. I pitched myself forward onto the floor and began to weep. The cold concrete pressed into my face as I called on God's mercy for my son. From the depths of my soul, I cried out to my heavenly Father. I once again begged him to forgive me for all my sins. I begged him to erase any divine judgments that were recorded against me. I implored him to start something new in my family and with my generation. I cried out for him to touch my son and the children who would come after him so that the Evil One could not harm them. My faithful brothers came around me to pray and to cry with a brother over his unspoken sorrow. Their gentle hands on my back brought comfort as I wept bitter tears and shook with fear. Slowly the torment and grief began to subside.

Then another thought entered my mind, quieter than the first, but infinitely more powerful: *I will watch over your son.* I recognized the voice as that of my heavenly Father. With those few words, the peace of God descended on me and turned my grief into rejoicing. I have carried that assurance with me since that amazing day.

I will watch over your son. These soothing words came back to me as I watched James approach Christopher on his special night.

"I want several of you men to come forward and pray for Christopher," James calmly directed. "But before we pray, I have a question for you, Chris." Turning to Christopher he asked, "What do you want us to agree with you about when we pray?"

Christopher thought for a moment and then responded, "I want to do what God wants me to do, and I hope he will give me some friends I can walk with along the way."

The rest of us in the room were astounded at his request. Several men moved near my son and began to pray. At first I could only watch. Here were men, firm in their faith, blessing my son. They were pastors, computer experts, heavy equipment operators, and businessmen. All speaking blessings over this young man who meant so much to me.

After a few minutes, I took my place in front of Christopher, placed my hands on his head, and prayed. I affirmed him as a man of God. I blessed him in the name of the Lord. I made a public commitment to be there for him whenever he needed me. Finally, I proclaimed the words that every child must hear from his father.

"Christopher, you are my beloved son, in whom I am well pleased!"

Faces glowed. Tears flowed. Hearts were knit together in marvelous ways. Christopher knew that God had already answered part of his prayer. The men who surrounded him were his friends. After the time of prayer ended, my son rose to his feet and the men in the room hugged him. As we began drifting back to our seats, James spoke again. "We are not quite done here," he said, pointing to the empty chair. "I think the Lord has one more thing in mind."

THE BLESSING OVERFLOWS

"We came together tonight to bless Christopher," James said with a smile, "but it's obvious that God wants to do more than that. I was raised in a home in the inner city of Detroit, a home without a dad. I'm not complaining, but tonight I realize what I've missed. Can any of you relate?"

Heads nodded all over the room. Our friend had summed up what many were silently feeling.

"Is there anyone here who would like to come up and receive prayer?"

At first no one moved. But then one man slowly walked to the front. He sat in the chair and motioned for the others to pray for him. He sat stiff as a board, tensed against the healing touch of the Lord. His eyes were shut tight. As a boy he had been abused and later abandoned by his father. A lifetime of confusion, hatred, and bitterness welled up inside him. Some of the men around him seemed to know just how to pray.

"Father, I ask that you would show your love to your son."

"Lord, bless this man whom you died for. Heal his hurts."

Other men spoke affirming words over his life.

"We love you. We appreciate the blessing that you are to us."

"You are a great friend. I am glad that God brought you into my life." With such heartfelt words, ordinary men carried out God's work in this man's life. Restoration. Reconciliation. Hope. Healing.

After several minutes, our friend started to relax. A smile came over his face as he squinted at the men huddled around him. Cleansing tears trickled down his cheeks, carrying with them the toxic pain that had been stored inside. Like a river overflowing its banks, the celebration washed over everyone there.

Before we finished, six more men came forward for prayer. Each had a personal reason for coming. Most felt a deep sense of loss due to their earthly father's inability to love and bless them when they were boys.

The last man who asked for prayer had a different need. He said that the celebration revealed his *inability* to properly love and bless his own young son. Through all of the letters, gifts, and skits, he was convinced of his need to show the heavenly Father's love to his twelve-year-old before it was too late. He then told of his horrific childhood and of a father's words that cursed him every day that they were together. Our friend was constantly told by his father that he wished the boy had never been born. As the ultimate insult, the father told his son that he had tried to have the boy aborted all throughout the pregnancy. Our friend had carried that hidden pain for over thirty-five years, but the celebration had opened a door to healing that he thought was permanently closed. This precious man was not disappointed that night. God did a deep, lasting work in his heart.

To close out our evening, I asked Joseph if he would sing his new song, "O, My Beloved," one last time. After he had sung the beautiful melody, it was time to leave. Amazingly, it was nearly eleven-thirty.

THE RIDE HOME

Christopher and I said good-bye to our friends, carefully packed up the mementoes, and walked out into the star-studded evening. We were tired and drained. Completely empty and completely full at the same time. As we drove away, Chris put his head against the car's headrest and closed his eyes.

"What do you think about tonight, son?" I asked.

"It was awesome, Dad," Christopher said sleepily. "I can't believe all those men came. You and Mom are something else. I never dreamed I would have a celebration like that."

Then he fell asleep.

I took the long way home that night. I wanted to savor the evening as long as possible, not wanting it to end. My thoughts went to my other precious children: Steven, Jenifer, and Daniel. Their special nights would soon arrive as well.

Then I thought of their future children and grandchildren. As I pulled into my driveway, I smiled at the beauty of God's plan of blessing. As long as there are sons and daughters, there must be celebrations. It doesn't have to end.

I gently woke my son and helped him upstairs to bed.

"Good night, son," I whispered. "I sure do love you."

"Thanks, Dad. I love you, too," he said with a yawn. "Man, that was awesome."

KEEP GROWING HIM, LORD!

The day following the celebration was a typical summer day at our home. At about seven-thirty, my youngest son, Daniel Elijah, made sure I knew it was morning. Prying open my eyelids, he whispered, "Come on, Dad, get up! Dad, let's play!" Soon the rest of the family shifted into high gear. The lawn mower roared, basketballs bounced, children squabbled and played.

Christopher was the last one to get up that day. The excitement and lack of sleep the night before had taken their toll. When he finally came downstairs, his brothers and sister surrounded him with questions about what had happened the night before. It was great to see Chris hug his mother and excitedly share with her and his siblings about his celebration.

Kathleen began reading the letters the men had written. She made it only halfway through the first letter before her tears began to flow. Steven, Jenifer, and Daniel listened intently to stories of exploding soda bottles, bags of shelled corn, and a special song. They knew that they, too, would have a celebration one day.

Christopher carefully made a list of each man who attended, jotted what they had shared with him, and planned to send each one a personal thank-you note.

Watching the wonderful mayhem, I was filled with awe and thanksgiving. I paid special attention to Christopher and wondered, *How will the celebration touch his life? Was it really a turning point or just a nice party?*

It has been over seven years since Christopher's celebration, so I have had some time to observe his behavior. While I realize that he still has a long way to go on his journey to maturity, there have been some interesting developments.

For the first few days after the celebration, Christopher seemed to be his usual self. However, as several weeks went by, I began seeing a definite change in some key areas of his life. His approach to household chores, for instance. He had always tried to be obedient when it came to work around the house, but he had a hard time remembering to do his assignments without being asked. Also, when he was younger, he'd typically do a halfhearted job whenever he had work to do. Those were the days when, if we asked him to clean his room, he'd reluctantly agree—and then simply stuff his closet full of everything from tennis shoes to damp towels. This is one of the areas that changed following the celebration. His work ethic improved. Chris started completing his chores without being asked. Not only did he do them, but also he did them with more attention to detail than before.

Chris also seemed more eager to take on new challenges. For example, a few days after the celebration, I discovered that a tire on my truck had gone flat. Typically my children would stand by and watch me work on this type of project, but not that morning. Christopher volunteered to change the tire. I confess I had my doubts about his ability to handle the task. The spare was located under the car, and the jack was one of the new ones that baffles even the best mechanics. Nonetheless my son was adamant about changing the tire, so I agreed to let him do it. This time, I was the one who watched. I gave him some brief counsel about safety before letting him begin, and to my pleasant surprise, he followed the proper procedures from start to finish. He was rightfully proud when the job was completed. So was I.

Another area that continues to change since his celebration is his relationship with his younger brothers and sister. Prior to his rite of passage, Chris seemed to tolerate them but certainly didn't treat them as well as he treated his friends. Following the celebration, he become progressively more attentive and friendly toward each of them. It has been especially gratifying to see him interact with his younger sister, Jenifer. She is sometimes left out of the fun when the young men of the family get rough with each other. At times Jeni has rightfully lamented that she had no one to play with. Christopher's kindness to her has brought about a change in her attitude. She is happier now that she knows he cares for her.

Still another area of change that Kathy and I have noticed is Chris's approach to worship and other aspects of his relationship with God. Our Sunday church services often begin with a time of praise and worship. More often than not, the adults in the service sing and praise the Lord while many of the young people passively sit in their seats. We have been thrilled to see Christopher join in the worship and really enjoy it.

One of the most satisfying aspects of the new Christopher comes in the area of identity and self-confidence. He has always been a great son. However, sometimes he was too timid and compliant for his own good. Kathy and I now notice that he shares his views more easily on a variety of issues. He speaks with a new boldness and assurance, believing he has something of value to share. In his earlier years Chris was rather shy in school and unsure of his own abilities. He makes friends more easily now and yet still holds on to very high standards of conduct. At a time when many of his peers were experimenting with sex, alcohol, and other drugs, Chris remained committed to making good choices. Predictably this brought some persecution from others. Just as predictably, others are drawn to Chris to learn why he has the courage to resist.

Along with Christopher's newfound confidence has come an increased ability to laugh and enjoy life. It is important for parents and young men alike to understand that maturity doesn't mean "no fun." Too many adults seem to lose their sense of humor as they grow older. God intends for joy to accompany us on our journey to mature manhood. Joy and laughter are not childish; rather they are wonderful signs that a man's faith, hope, and life are all pointing in the proper direction. In the years since his celebration, I notice that Christopher laughs more often and more deeply than before.

I want to be very clear about these changes. Christopher has not completely mastered the art of mature manhood now that he has left his teen years! Like the rest of us, he still occasionally does a poor job with a work project, is less than kind to his siblings, and has doubts about his future. The big difference now is that he recognizes these problems as matters of maturity rather than manhood. In other words, he knows that as a man, he should continue to strive for excellence in these areas. When his performance is not what it should be, he doesn't mentally slide all the way back into boyhood again, nor does he question his manhood. Instead he simply accepts that he has to improve in some specific areas of his life. This allows him to prayerfully pursue the achievable goal of increased maturity rather than struggle to attain something that he already has—his manhood.

Please understand that not all of Christopher's positive qualities came as a result of his celebration. His mother and I have done our best to teach him right from wrong for many years. Although we did not have a concrete plan to do so, we provided a great deal of mentoring for him from very early on. To the best of our ability, we taught Christopher about family relationships, work, worship, and many other aspects of maturity over the years, beginning when he was very little. I am sure that some of the lessons are just now beginning to sink in. In addition we always instinctively knew how important it was to affirm his efforts and good qualities. Our words of intentional blessing helped Chris grow in confidence and reach for new heights.

The point here is this: celebrations will not instantly create a perfect man. They are not designed to. The rite of passage is one part of a comprehensive plan for each child's development. However, I am convinced that something wonderful happened deep inside this young man during the ceremony. Was it an imparting of godly gifts when the older men prayed for Christopher, or did the celebration release qualities he always had within him? Was it the letters or gifts or skits that changed my son's approach to life? Perhaps it was a combination of all these things. While only God knows the exact answer, it is obvious that something significant changed in my son. The Lord did a deep work, and by his grace, Christopher continues to grow and mature. He has become a better man. A celebration will do the same for the young men in your life as well, especially when it is part of your overall plan for their success. In the next chapter, we'll see why rites of passage are so powerful.

7

BOYHOOD
TO MANHOOD:
WHY CELEBRATIONS WORK

IN THE YEARS FOLLOWING Christopher's rite of passage, I spent a great deal of time thinking about the celebration concept, its applications, and its impact. Initially I questioned whether a rite of passage would actually help young males make the transition into mature manhood. After a few years of participating in numerous celebrations and seeing their impact on both those being celebrated and those in attendance, my question changed from "will it work" to "why does it work?"

Today, after over seven years of studying this powerful concept, I understand at least some of the reasons why rites of passage are so effective in men's lives.

WHEN AM I A MAN?

Foundationally, rites of passage work because they answer the one question that nearly all young males need answered: when do I become a man?

The Pain of No Answer

A friend of mine, Charles, recently shared a profound incident that happened to him just after he entered into his teen years. One weekend Charles was riding in a car with his father, headed to northern Michigan for a weekend away. Since it was just the two of them, my friend thought it was a great time to ask his dad about something that had been troubling him for months. After traveling a few miles on I-75, Charles mustered up sufficient courage to pop the question.

"Dad, uhh…when do I become a man?" he asked expectantly.

Charles hoped his dad would respond with something out of a 1950s Hollywood script. He anticipated that his dad would look lovingly into his young eyes, pat his shoulder with a strong right hand, and then explain exactly when and how a boy becomes a man. Sadly, that never happened. Instead my friend's father did something that, decades later, still amazes him.

According to Charles, his dad chuckled and, without so much as a sideways glance at his son, changed the subject. That was it.

Charles explained to me that even though the incident took only moments to tell, it took years to overcome. He sadly told me of the painful struggles with his own identity as a man and how the uncertainties had guided his choices in life. He went on to share that he had wasted much of his life experimenting with sex, drugs, and violent sports, looking for something to signify that he had arrived at "manhood."

My friend's story didn't surprise me. In fact, it confirmed the desperate need young men have for a solid answer to the "manhood" question. Charles's scenario is all too common in today's society. It is replayed over and over again. Predictably, a boy in his early teens asks a logical question about his impending manhood, and the man in his life—if one exists—doesn't have a clear-cut response. This leaves the young male alone to figure it out by himself until he has children of his own. Inevitably they will ask the same question and, unless something changes, will get the same response. This trend doesn't have to continue, but we men need to have a serious change of heart if we are ever going to stop it.

The Confusion of Changing "Mile Markers"

Not long ago, I shared the celebration concept with another man and was amazed at his response. He adamantly told me, "Everyone knows there's no way a thirteen-year-old boy is a man!" This gentleman then offered several rambling explanations to support his belief. He used the legal drinking age, the age for military service, and the age for young people to legally drive as the true milestones to manhood. I found it fascinating that each of these ages of "accountability" or "manhood" was different. Not only did these "ages of accountability" differ from state to state, but also they had been changed many times in recent years.

I tried to tell the man that when I was in my teens, the drinking age in Michigan was changed from twenty-one to eighteen. This may have been partly because we were drafting eighteen-year-old men—or were they boys?—and sending them to kill and die in Southeast Asia, yet they couldn't legally drink a beer when at home on leave. Also, during that time period, a sixteen-year-old could drive a car twenty-four hours a day. He simply got his license and that was it. Today both of these ages have changed again. The legal drinking age is now back to twenty-one, and while a sixteen-year-old can still get his driver's license, he can't legally drive after midnight.

None of this seemed to matter to this man. His words simply underscored the confusion our society has concerning entry into adulthood. Gordon Dalbey writes about this sad perplexity:

> What does my own culture offer as a validation of manhood? The driver's license at sixteen; the freedom at eighteen to join the army, attend pornographic movies, and to buy cigarettes and beer. The message is clear: becoming a man means operating a powerful machine, killing other men, masturbating, destroying your lungs, and getting drunk.
>
> We are lost males, all of us: cast adrift from the community of men, cut off from our masculine heritage—abandoned to machines, organizations, fantasies, and drugs.[1]

When the man finished his half-baked lecture, I asked him one simple question: "Then exactly when *does* a boy become a man?" Like my friend Charles's father, he had no answer. He finally sputtered that he really didn't know, but he was just sure that it wasn't at age thirteen!

THE POWERFUL SOLUTION: IT'S A DECLARATION!

In reality the answer to Charles's and every other young male's question is simple yet profound: a young male becomes a man *when the elders of his family and/or broader society declare him to be one.*

This was true for Sidimo, just as it was true for White Fox, Marcus, and David. In those cultures young males accepted their parents' and other elders' declarations about manhood as truth. As soon as they reached the appropriate age and participated in their rite-of-passage ceremonies, they were accepted as men and then began to live according to these new adult expectations.

I readily acknowledge that it's wise to withhold certain privileges and responsibilities from young men. I am not in any way advocating that we lower the legal age for certain activities, such as driving, drinking, voting, serving in the military, or getting married. Many young people are simply not ready to handle such things without a great deal of counsel, mentoring, and support from others. However, this is not because they aren't *men*; rather it is because they are not *mature*.

If we, as a society, continue to consciously or unconsciously connect manhood with any of these events, then we unintentionally encourage our young males to think—and act—like children during their teen years. We condition our young people to believe that legal drinking, driving, and having sex are somehow rites of passage into adulthood by themselves. In this frame of mind, is it any wonder that our young people act like immature kids far into their teens, twenties, and beyond? Also, isn't it obvious why our young men are so drawn to these "grown-up" activities? Could it be that they are trying to attain their manhood earlier than when their society tells them they can have it?

It makes infinitely more sense for us to condition our young males to accept their manhood at an early age and then help them grow into maturity. Then they will be ready to make good choices about such matters when they arrive at whatever age the privileges are granted.

We must realize that young males like my friend Charles need an adult to simply and confidently answer their questions about growing up and take them through the door to manhood. A celebration, hosted by a loving father or mentor, is the one event that will mark that special day of transition from boyhood into manhood. It is the day that will answer all the questions about "when." From that day on, the questions of our young males will focus on how to act like a mature man rather than on when or if they will become one.

THE CORNERSTONE OF MANHOOD

I am convinced that a celebration leads to mature manhood just as, in orthodox Christian teaching, salvation leads to sanctification. Here is why. A person becomes a Christian at the moment he or she accepts Christ by faith and is thereby born anew spiritually. This person's rightful position and identity is as a full-fledged member of God's family. The person can never be more of a Christian than he is at the moment of acceptance. He can become much more spiritually *mature* but not more of a Christian. Scripture does not teach that we earn our Christianity by degrees, levels, or ages. It teaches that acceptance of Christ is the door through which one enters into the faith and is fully accepted into the fold.

Naturally, the new convert must be taught what the works of a mature Christian are and how to do them. These works include a renewal of the mind and heart, which leads to changes in one's attitudes, behavior, communication, and worldview. Clearly each Christian goes through a process of maturity. However, the process cannot begin until one has become a child of God. Before any maturing takes place, new converts must accept that a miraculous transformation has occurred and they have transitioned from one state or condition into another totally different one.

In a like manner, a young male must first accept the fact that he *is* a man if he is ever to do the *works* of a mature man. Obviously, a teenage male is not fully developed physically, mentally, emotionally, or spiritually. However, at his rite of passage, he is formally and publicly welcomed into manhood. From loving elders he learns that he was created to be a man and that there are good works prepared in advance for him to do (see Ephesians 2:8–10). Once the parents and other elders formally declare that the boy has become a man, then the boy is positioned to experience a miraculous change. Once he accepts his manhood, his goal is now to grow into maturity as a man. The celebration acts as the door into manhood, just as salvation is the door to sanctification and maturity as a believer. After a boy walks through the door to manhood, the rest of the journey to clearer identity and maturity begins in earnest.

If, on the other hand, a young male never walks through the door to manhood, he is condemned to wander for years outside of his intended domain. The teen is then left to stumble into his future by default rather than boldly pursuing it by design with the help of mature men. Without a transitional event to mark a boy's passage into manhood, he is sentenced to spend many years trying to discover ways to affirm and confirm his own coming of age. Sadly, he will look for an *action* rather than for an *event* to mark his transition. Our young people today are vainly substituting their first cigarette, drink, sexual encounter, theft, gang fight, or even murder for a true transitional event. It is infinitely better for mature adults to lead our young males into defining rites of passage that usher them into the realm and ranks of manhood.

TURNING OUR HEARTS TOWARD OUR CHILDREN

In the years since Christopher's celebration, I have witnessed—and experienced—another significant reason for the effectiveness of celebrations: rites of passage not only change the hearts of our youth but also dramatically change the hearts of fathers and other elders. On that special night so long ago, Christopher was not the only person who changed. The celebration changed me as well, in some very profound ways. It certainly caused me to look inside myself and to look at my own past to discover why I think and act as I do. That special night also forged in me a steely commitment to raise my children with great purpose and to view each of them as a wonderful work in progress. Much of my own selfishness vanished as God broke my heart for my own family and gave me a new love for each unique child. I now try to take more time each day to intentionally mentor, bless, talk with, play with, listen to, and love Christopher, Steven, Jeni, and Daniel. Because of my first son's celebration, I have become a better father. The other men who attended the celebration have changed also. Most have held celebrations for their own children and have refocused their attention on what is of primary importance in life—their God and their families.

In the years since the first celebration, my love for my own children has overflowed. I now find myself consumed with the quest to discover ways that concerned adults can help our next generations grow, mature, and succeed. My pursuit has led me to conclude that there are three foundations upon which we can build our efforts: lifelong mentoring, intentional blessing, and rites of passage. These three concepts, when utilized as parts of an overall plan for our children, will produce incredibly positive results. Together these elements provide the essentials for a young person's success. The rite of passage is a central aspect of the plan, but for maximum positive influence, it must be preceded and followed by mentoring and intentional blessing. The following two chapters will explain how to make these concepts part of a powerful plan to build character and confidence in the next generation.

---

1. Gordon Dalbey, *Healing the Masculine Soul* (Dallas: Word, 1988), quoted in Gary Wilde, *Mentoring: An Example to Follow* (Colorado Springs: ChariotVictor, 1997), 13–14.

8

LIFELONG
MENTORING

AS IMPORTANT AS RITES OF PASSAGE ARE, it is crucial that we not view them as isolated events that magically produce mature young men in a few short hours. In today's fast-paced life, one could be tempted to see a celebration as an end in itself. Instead, the celebration marks the end of childhood and the *beginning* of manhood. For maximum influence on a young person's life, the celebration needs to be preceded by mentoring and intentional blessing by parents or other trusted elders. Additional mentoring, blessing, and support then follow the celebration and, ideally, continue in various forms throughout life.

In reality none of the young men from chapter one reached maturity solely based on his rite of passage, vision quest, or any other one-time event. Instead the various passage ceremonies solidified and affirmed what the boys' elders had been teaching them throughout their lives. Each boy's parents and other mentors spent countless hours observing, teaching, listening to, and correcting their young charges. These mentoring relationships began very early in the boys' lives and continued after they had transitioned into manhood. A stand-alone rite of passage devoid of any pre- and post-celebration instruction about maturity will always fall short of its intended goal. Conversely, continuous instruction about manhood, maturity, and increased responsibility without a corresponding rite of passage will leave a male longing for a sense of graduation from childhood. The celebration serves as the ultimate affirmation that a young person has passed into a new season of life. The bottom line is that both a rite of passage and lifelong mentoring are needed to maximize a young person's potential.

While I consider intentional blessing to be part of the mentoring process, some specifics should be explored in detail. Therefore we will examine the concept of intentional blessing in the next chapter to learn how it dovetails with the mentoring process and adds power to a celebration. First, though, let's look at mentoring.

MENTORING FOUNDATIONS

Mentoring is a much-discussed concept today; however, it certainly is not new. We've seen the mentoring relationship in cultures as diverse as those of Sidimo, White Fox, Marcus, and David, and we can see in the biblical record how Jesus mentored his disciples and his disciples mentored others. Most, if not all, parents teach, train, discipline, and mentor their children in a variety of areas and have done so for generations. Programs such as Big Brothers Big Sisters of America have been in existence for nearly a century, and in recent years many local and national programs promoting mentoring have been initiated. While each initiative has some distinct aspects, they all have one thing in common. They seek to place young people with trusted counselors, supporters, and instructors who will help with the transition from childhood into productive adulthood. In other words, they promote mentoring.

Entire books have been written on mentoring, so this chapter is not intended as an exhaustive study on the subject. However, I want to share specifically about the important role of mentoring in the context of rites of passage.

A Natural Necessity

Two foundational truths about mentoring need to be clearly understood right off. First, mentoring, teaching, and training by a trusted adult are vital for our young people's successful development. Each boy comes into this world ignorant of the dangers around him and unaware of his own abilities and options. Early experiences with pain and pleasure provide some framework for survival but do little to help the child reach his full potential. It is the quality and amount of instruction and support from others that largely determine the boy's eventual maturity and success.

Second, in the absence of positive adult role models, young males will find their own role models or mentors. A primary example of this occurs when boys join gangs despite knowing that their new mentors participate in illegal and dangerous activities. The desire to be under the care of someone who is stronger and wiser is very powerful. It should be. God put that desire into our very being as a means to draw us to our fathers, mothers, and other mentors. It is for this reason that the absence of positive role models creates a void quickly filled by someone less qualified.

Predictably, young boys lacking discernment are often attracted to external (and false) signs of maturity. Wild parties, drugs, violence, lawlessness with seeming impunity, sexual encounters, expensive cars, and rolls of cash all tempt boys to attach themselves to clueless leaders headed for destruction. These false mentors teach their young disciples a host of concepts about life, maturity, and manhood from their own twisted perspectives.

Not all mentors a boy might select are so obviously detrimental; in fact, some may be concerned teachers, coaches, or other leaders outside the home willing to serve as positive role models. However, why leave such a vital aspect of a young person's life to chance? The lack of intentionality on the part of parents and other elders subjects our sons to a flood of influence from role models who may not embody the worldview, character, philosophy of "success," or spiritual values we want for our sons.

Tragically, when we abdicate our roles as mentors and encouragers, we also hand our sons over to painful confusion about their value and identity. When this occurs, everyone in the equation suffers. Our sons experience the hurt of unfulfilled relationships with the most important people in their lives, and we parents miss a central element of our own God-ordained purpose: to serve as loving leaders for the next generation.

The good news is that it does not have to turn out that way; the very opposite can be true! I have seen mentoring bear abundant fruit in the lives of young men as the elders in their lives prayerfully and joyfully guide them on their journey to mature manhood. Our sons, families and nations will be healed when every boy and young man has the support of a father, mother, or other trusted adult willing to serve as coach, teacher, disciplinarian, loving confidant, and advocate. In short, as a mentor.

The Original "Mentor"

The term *mentoring* is actually based upon both the actions and the name of an ancient Greek named Mentor. In the classic Greek tale the *Odyssey*, Mentor is a friend of Odysseus, the king of Ithaca, a small island kingdom. More important, Mentor is the trusted tutor of Telemachus, the son of Odysseus. In the story, Odysseus reluctantly departs from his family to go and fight another man's war. Rather than leaving his son solely in the care of his mother, Odysseus chooses Mentor to be the boy's guide, teacher, and protector. Over the next twenty years, Mentor remains faithful to his task and even risks his own life for Telemachus during his father's long absence.

After many years away, Odysseus attempts to return home to his family with his ships filled with treasure from all of his exploits. Unfortunately things do not go as planned, and this absentee father is once again swept away. Odysseus eventually returns, having lost his worldly treasures, and finds his home in chaos. (Why am I not surprised?)

The Modern Mentor

This ancient tale contains amazing parallels to what is happening in the lives of our young people today. Too many modern families are thrown into chaos as parents depart, either physically or emotionally, to fight battles for significance, financial increase, and/or identity. That is the bad news. However, as in the *Odyssey*, there are many adults today with the courage and wisdom to stay and serve the new generation rather than going off to fight for a less vital cause.

Mentors for today's young males come in many shapes, sizes, and colors and are called by many different names. First and foremost, they are called *dads*. Despite some reports to the contrary, our world is still filled with fathers who are deeply dedicated to the development of their children. Other titles of mentors include youth pastor, coach, teacher, grandfather, uncle, older brother, stepdad, foster parent, and scout leader, and there are other possibilities.

In addition, since the function of a mentor is slightly different from the function of a role model, it is clear that mentors can also be called mom, grandmother, aunt, and foster mother. Across the world, mothers are investing themselves in the lives of their sons. Countless single moms are raising sons, and these sons can certainly turn out well if a plan of mentoring, intentional blessing, and rites of passage is successfully designed and carried out. Mothers also have important, unique roles in the lives of their sons in nuclear homes where both parents spend time mentoring, teaching, and disciplining their boys. For example, my wife does an outstanding job of teaching our children life lessons during trips to town, at bedtime, or at the dinner table. Without question, mothers can be excellent mentors and teachers for their sons.

However, I need to present the complete picture here and say that there is one thing that a mother can never be for her son: a male role model. Boys must grow up around some positive male role models so that they can observe what it means to be a *man*. In homes where a woman is raising a boy alone, it is crucial that she find a trusted man to serve her son as mentor and role model before, during, and after his celebration.

TAKING TIME TO TEACH

Whatever our family structure and whether we are dads, moms, grandparents, or teachers, it is important to understand that mentoring relationships can only develop when we spend time with the children. If that were not the case, then parents could simply provide their children with exhaustive lists of do's and don'ts and life would be error free. Probably about three pages of *Thou shalt not kill*, *Thou shalt not covet*, and *Thou shalt clean thy room* would do it, right? Hardly. If time is not intentionally set aside for interaction, recreation, and shared observation of life, then it is likely that the relationship between a young person and his or her mentor will remain quite shallow.

Successful mentoring occurs when a close relationship combines with well-conceived lesson plans. Having a deliberate plan for mentoring and a few key life lessons helps to ensure that our children mature by design, not by default. When we know what lessons, skills, and truths we want our children to learn, then we can intentionally look for opportunities to teach those things.

One of the basic life skills that I wanted each of my children to learn was how to enter a store, interact with clerks, and make their purchases. Simple stuff but essential to success as an adult. When they were younger, I had my children accompany me into stores to simply observe the process of buying goods. After we were on our way back home, I would explain why I smiled and called the clerk by name. In addition, I would explain why I chose one brand of product over another. I would briefly talk with them about product cost, volume, quality, and so on. Finally, I told them about the payment options of check, cash, or credit card. Once they understood these basics, it was time to move to the next step in the mentoring process.

Once my children got older, I had them go into the store with me, told them what I wanted to buy, and then had them analyze the products and prices to see which we should choose. Finally, I would give them enough money to cover the cost of the product and have them pay the clerk. In the beginning this was scary stuff for eight-year-olds who could barely see over the counter. However, after a few initial tongue-tied attempts, each of them developed confidence and learned vital lessons about treating others with respect, the value of money, the importance of comparative shopping, and many other life principles.

Like shopping in a store, some of the best teachable moments happen during times of informal sharing rather than during a more structured, classroom type of instruction. For example, my family and I grow a large garden each year. Kathy and I see this as a wonderful opportunity for teaching foundational life principles to our children. Our garden begins with a time of discussion, planning, and layout led by our children, not by us. Each one draws a diagram of the garden area and decides where various plants and seeds should go. We then discuss the diverse plans and agree on a final layout of the garden. Next comes the hard work of rototilling, raking, and removing any weeds that survived the previous winter's freeze. Soon plants and seeds are purchased and carefully placed into the soil. As summer progresses, we take turns inspecting the garden and sampling the various types of produce as they ripen. At times we have an overabundance of tomatoes or green beans and we talk about what to do with the excess. Some of these plants are sold to willing grandparents, and at other times they are given to needy people. When the growing season ends, we till the soil under and wait to repeat the process in the spring.

At each step Kathy and I watch for opportunities to impart wisdom about one or more of the life lessons that we have chosen for our children to learn. The garden layout discussion opens the door for teaching about planning and working with others. The manual labor of preparation fosters dialogue about industriousness, as well as the principle of sowing and reaping. Times of selling and/or donating produce to others generates discussion about money and the importance of blessing the less fortunate. At other times lessons about teamwork, dedication, handling disappointment, and resolving conflict are shared with our small band of "farmhands."

Whether over a garden or any other activity, you will find that time spent together inevitably puts a teacher and student in the most fertile learning laboratory of all—life. Even the most mundane activities have teaching potential. One of most memorable life lessons taught at the Molitor household can be summed up in one sentence: "It's amazing what you find...*when you clean*." After numerous repetitions of both the statement and the practical lessons learned when we actually do clean a closet or drawer, my children are finally catching on to my not-so-subtle message about clutter. The bright light of understanding comes on whenever we shovel out a closet and locate a long lost shoe, missing baseball glove, or crumpled ten-dollar bill. Now I only have to begin to say, "It's amazing what" —and one of my young ones will finish the sentence for me— "you find when you clean!" Of course, their eyes roll and they repeat the phrase with a less than sincere tone. However, I am thrilled to report that they have become progressively more adept at keeping order in their rooms, school backpacks, and yes, amazingly, even their closets.

Over the years, Kathy and I have tried to follow the pattern set forth by Jesus, who taught his disciples experientially rather than in a classroom setting. He brought forth profound life lessons from a wide variety of things, including rocks, trees, clouds, and his day-to-day interaction with people. The key to his successful mentoring was that he took time to walk with and talk with his disciples each day. We try to use this "capture the moment" method to impart foundational life lessons to the young disciples under our roof as often as we can. The same pattern is easily followed while discussing events that happen at school, during athletic competition, and in a host of other settings.

As we take advantage of teachable moments to impart life lessons to our children, inevitably each of us will fail at some point to live up to the very principles we hope to teach. Be encouraged that our young people need to learn from role models who are positive—but not perfect. This means that we can use our own failures as teaching points alongside those things that we happen to do well. Times when I have lost my temper and said things that were hurtful to either my wife or children have been turned into life lessons when I swallowed my pride, apologized to the offended party, and then explained to the children that what I did was wrong. The lessons that our children need to learn are all around us, even when we have a bad day. Do not be afraid to share your struggles and failings with the young people around you. They are aware of them already, and with your explanation of the situations' causes, consequences, and options for handing them better, your children will learn how to avoid making the same mistakes themselves.

FRONT LINE LESSONS

I cannot overemphasis the impact of life lessons on our children. Remember "the shopping trip of a lifetime" skit that we did at my son's celebration? The one in which the salesman tried to get Christopher to compromise his stand on substance abuse and immorality? Amazingly—or perhaps, predictably—that skit played out in real life during Chris's junior year in high school when he was invited to spend the weekend at a classmate's cabin. Chris went on the excursion, expecting to have a great couple of days swimming, boating, and hanging out with some friends. When he arrived, he discovered that the weekend get away was a coed affair and that the cabin came complete with an open bar. By nightfall many of the young men and women there were drunk and had paired up to sleep together. Chris told me that he had been approached many times by well-meaning peers trying to get him to join the crowd. The guys invited him to get drunk, and more than one girl invited him to share her bedroom. He declined all the offers and ended up spending a miserable night on a couch, by himself. My son dejectedly drove home the next morning feeling much like Elijah, who once felt as if he were all alone in his stand for righteousness.

Chris and I talked about the situation later, and it took a while for him to realize the significance of his actions in the face of such strong peer pressure and the old-fashioned, in-your-face temptation. He had been miles from home, in a situation where he could have compromised his standards and no one other than God would have known, and yet Christopher chose wisely.

Life lessons learned from trusted mentors stick with our young people. Life lessons—learned in time—change lives.

THE BOTTOM LINE ON MENTORING

Mentoring moments can happen at any time for the simple reason that life lessons are everywhere. The key to success is consistent communication and strong, healthy relationships between mentors and the young people under their care. Regardless of which life lesson we hope to teach, the process is always the same. The mentor simply watches for the appropriate teaching opportunities to arise, and then he or she shares in a manner that best communicates that lesson. Mentors should never nag or use the lessons to embarrass a child in front of others. To do so would decrease the level of trust and potentially shut the door on future lessons.

Clearly, the onus is on parents and other mentors to establish both the relationships and the plans for ongoing interaction with the young people in their lives. Don't worry about the young people's response to increased closeness and more time spent with a parent or other mentor. Given time, it will be overwhelmingly positive. Today's youth are full of questions about life, relationships, love, finance, nature, and a host of other subjects. They just need someone around them willing to explore the answers. Always give them the space and time they need for themselves, but watch for crucial openings and teachable moments. Mentors don't force; they lovingly guide.

Those of us who have raised young children remember their endless streams of "Why" questions that seemed to diminish as they grew. At one point I assumed that the rate of questioning slowed or even ceased because the young ones had gotten most of the answers they were looking for. I now realize sadly that the children stopped asking the questions for one simple reason: in our own busyness, we stopped answering.

WRITING YOUR OWN STORY

There are many of us who can relate to the story of Odysseus and Telemachus, the son he left behind. Too many have left home literally. Others of us have physically remained within the walls while our hearts drifted far away. Instead of raising and mentoring our children, we are off fighting battles of our own choosing. Like Odysseus, many of us depart to fight someone else's battles while allowing our own homes to fall into disrepair. One more business deal, a bigger paycheck, and that elusive promotion to the next rung of the corporate ladder all seem worth pursuing "just for a little while."

Sadly, those laboring in what we commonly call "full-time ministry" also hear this same seductive call. Pastors, evangelists, youth ministers, and missionaries often sacrifice their own children's well-being in order to pursue God's call to help a hurting world. To be sure, parents have to work in order to release God's gifting within them and to put food on the table. And, of course, ministers of all sorts must pursue God's divine callings upon their lives, or this world would continue its downward spiral into chaos. However, as parents, we must be certain that our work, ministry, and life are in balance at all times.

The voice of the world loudly screams at everyone to do more, get more, and go more, and that bigger is better. Its twisted reasoning says that ministers should abandon their children in order to preach to throngs of people and that the rest of us should work two jobs to earn more money—for the children. Countless thousands fall for this siren-like song each year only to learn too late that they have crashed their family's ship on the rocks of excess.

Fortunately, there is a clear point of balance that can be found by every parent and mentor willing to stop long enough to listen to the sure voice of God. Our Creator's laserlike logic cuts through all the noise and confusion with just one simple parable about a shepherd who would leave the flock of ninety-nine to search for just one sheep that is lost. Some ministers need to walk away from their flocks temporarily to find that lost sheep that only they can reach. Some businessmen need to radically change their approach to finances and redefine the term *prosperity*. Keeping up with the Joneses only makes sense if Mr. Jones has time for his children. If he doesn't, why try to keep up with him? He is headed the wrong way.

In today's world many women are in the world of business as well and have the same opportunity to get out of balance as their male counterparts. Single mothers are often torn between earning a living and spending time with their children. The challenges associated with this conflict are enormous but not insurmountable. Balance points exist. We simply must be willing to find them.

I strongly suggest that men and women of all professions take time to consider that the loving God they serve is able to balance both their callings to the world and the one sure ministry that they have been entrusted with—the one to their children. Those who choose to change their work schedules and even their vocations in order to support their children's development will never regret it. Those who do not will likely spend years wondering what might have been.

GOD'S VOICE

There is one parallel in the *Odyssey* that should inspire parents and mentors alike. At crucial times in Telemachus's life, one of the Greek gods would actually speak through the boy's protector, Mentor, in order to provide vital direction and answers to his heartfelt questions. As parents and mentors, we can allow the true God to speak through us and provide those answers to the young men under our care. What an honor and responsibility we have been given!

We have the opportunity and obligation to teach the foundations of life to this next generation. If we simply create a plan and set aside time for interaction, our words and insights will prepare our sons not only for their celebrations but also for the rest of their lives.

9

INTENTIONAL BLESSING

IN THE BOOK OF GENESIS, we are treated to the amazing account of Creation and catch our first glimpse of the Creator's love for humankind. For those who mistakenly believe that God is some sort of cosmic bully, they need only to read the first few pages of the Bible to understand his heartfelt devotion to his people. It was there, in the beginning, that our heavenly Father first showed us what it means to bless our own children.

THE POWER OF THE SPOKEN WORD

In the beginning God was confronted with a situation that to any of us would have seemed hopeless. Genesis 1:2 describes the earth as "a formless empty mass cloaked in darkness" (NLT). Not much to work with, but for an all-powerful God it was all in a day's—okay, six days'—work.

I find it fascinating that with an infinite number of options available, God chose to deal with the chaos in a very simple manner. Instead of releasing the energy of a thousand nuclear warheads to reshape the very molecular structure of the mess that we now call earth, he simply spoke the right words and watched the miracles happen.

As we read further, we learn that God continued to use carefully chosen words to bring our entire universe into existence. Planets, stars, oceans, plants, birds, and animals of all kinds materialized with just a few spoken words from the Creator. God obviously understood the power of words to bring about change.

The crown of God's masterpiece came on the sixth day, when he made "man"—male and female. The Scriptures tell us that humans are the one and only being that God made in *his* own image. In other words, rocks, trees, and butterflies were all created by God; however, none of them are made in his image and likeness. Nothing in all of creation is capable of making decisions to act like, be like, and love like the Creator—except for human beings. Once you let that fact sink in, life gets very interesting.

THE POWER OF INTENTIONAL BLESSING

Just imagine the scene on the amazing day. Surrounded by the beauty of the first garden, our heavenly Father has just finished creating the first man. Named Adam, he stirs on the warm grass and takes in his first breath. The rush of life-giving air fills his lungs and sets off an amazing chain of internal processes for the first time in all of eternity. Adam's heart begins to pump blood into each tiny capillary of his body. Muscles contract, stretch, and flex. Brain waves and miles of nerve fibers begin to register and catalog each marvelous new sensation. Air rushing into his nostrils carries the fragrance of flowers bursting forth from the fertile soil.

Then comes another new sensation for Adam that we now call *sound*. Invisible waves emanating from a thousand sources begin to wash over the tiny bones and membranes and nerves in Adam's ears. Wind in the trees, birds singing, a friendly splash of water nearby all are logged into Adam's mind. Finally this new man is ready for the final stage of his awakening. Slowly his incredible eyes begin to open, and the light of his first day gently passes his eyelids. As they quickly adjust, this first man's eyes take in the indescribable beauty of Eden, the place his Father, our Father, has made for him. The colors are breathtaking. Bright sun, blue sky, and green plants all fill Adam with the wonder of a child.

The marvelous carnival for Adam's senses continues unabated until he hears a new and different sound. This sound is quiet, yet irresistible. Adam turns his head to see what all men, deep within, continue to long for.

A Father on His Knees

In Genesis 1, verse 28, we discover that the very first act of our God toward his new son, Adam, was to *bless* him.[1] Once we understand what sort of blessing God gave, we get a deep appreciation for the love of our heavenly Father. The original Hebrew word that we now translate as *blessing* is *barak*, which is a root word meaning "to kneel." It refers to an act of adoration, in which one greatly praises and salutes another. Now, if your view of God is that of a cold, vengeful ogre, then this will be a very difficult passage for you to reconcile in your mind. However, if you are at least willing to consider another perspective, this passage will thrill you. In reality, God can be most accurately viewed as a heavenly Father who longs for fellowship with his sons and daughters. How do I know? Because what actually happened on Adam's first day was this. He turned his head and saw his Creator actually *kneeling* beside him. He looks full into the face of his heavenly Father. When their eyes meet, there is an instant bond of love between them. No walls. No shame. Just love.

According to the Scriptures, Adam's first view of his God and Father is summed up in one Hebrew word: *barak*. Kneeling, loving, and adoring. Just picture it. Here was God himself, kneeling at the side of his "newborn" son, simply adoring him. Isn't that a marvelous picture? Like a modern-day father, with face pressed against the hospital nursery's window to get a better look at the marvelous creation who bears his likeness, so God looked at Adam and came to a profound conclusion: it is good.

Reading further, we learn that the heavenly Father then proceeded to share with his son about all that he had created for him. God spoke with Adam about the wonderful opportunities he would have as they walked together throughout eternity. The heavenly Father blessed his son with his words, his countenance, and his very posture. What a great model for us to follow.

The Blessing in Modern Times

In times past people understood the power in the true meaning of *blessing* and used it, as Jacob did, to affirm and direct the lives of following generations. Sadly, our modern society has transformed this life-changing concept into a meaningless phrase devoid of any real significance.

This degradation of the term *blessing* is seen and heard in many segments of our culture today. Movie stars stand at well-lit podiums and proclaim how "blessed" they are to receive an award for their latest performance. Christians across the world use the term *blessing* to describe anything and everything good that happens to them on a daily basis. Those of us in the fold often describe an unexpected tax return or a job promotion as a "*blessing.*" In reality these situations are cause for thanksgiving but simply do not line up with the biblical use of the term.

We have already seen that the Old Testament Hebrew word for blessing encompasses the concept of kneeling and adoration. In the New Testament the term actually comes from the word *blood* and from the idea of consecrating an altar by sprinkling it with blood. The word was originally used to describe "the act of making or proclaiming something holy, or to set something apart for holy purposes." Several additional descriptors associated with blessing help capture the broader meaning of the term in the New Testament. According to Webster, "to bless" means to *make happy, to consecrate by prayer, to praise, to magnify, to keep, guard, preserve, endow, enrich, gladden, thank, and finally, to bring comfort and joy.*

In the deepest sense, we bless someone when we speak words of encouragement and affirmation to him or her. To consider that our words can actually be used to set our sons and daughters apart for holy purposes is truly awesome. A timely, well-chosen word from a parent can encourage, enlighten, strengthen, and safeguard a child against the assaults against him or her that inevitably come. It may be even more awesome and sobering to consider that a parent's words can also be used to discourage, weaken, and literally open the door to those who in the future would wound our children.

The Power of Death and Life Is in Our Words!

It is difficult for some to understand that a few simple words could really be that powerful. In the book of Proverbs, King Solomon tells us that death and life are in the power of the tongue. In other words, the things we say can either infuse life, hope, joy, and confidence to our children or be used to crush their fragile egos and damage their developing identities. The disciple James reminds us that both *blessing* and *cursing* can come from our mouths. For this reason it is imperative that parents and mentors learn about the power of their words and use that power to bless the young people in their lives.

A blessing is passed on when a respected elder such as a parent, grandparent, or mentor speaks words of encouragement and affirmation to any young person. Words of blessing must not be reserved for only the best and brightest young people or for those who are known for their outstanding performances, appearance, or potential. In fact, often those who seem to have the least amount of talent need to hear our words of blessing the most.

Once adults know the power of their words, an affirming blessing can be spoken over virtually every young person on the face of the earth. Far too many parents are quick to point out faults and slow to identify strengths of the young people around them. Their careless words often become curses that cripple the very identities of their sons and daughters. We must balance our criticisms and silence with words of encouragement and praise. Their world is full of comparisons and unattainable models of what a young person should look like and act like. It is also full of acid-tongued peers who, like barnyard chickens, look for any sign of weakness in others and quickly take advantage of it. Our children are constantly bombarded with messages, subtle and otherwise, that they just don't measure up. God will use a parent's words of blessing to neutralize these negative messages and impart hope to their children.

I once overheard a parent babble about the dangers of complimenting a child "too much." Intrigued, I inserted myself into the conversation to see what I could learn. From the lips of this well-meaning adult came some of the most absurd nonsense that I had ever heard. According to her, too many compliments and too much encouragement will *spoil* a child. Not one to let folly go unchallenged, I ask for clarification on what it meant to "spoil" a child. She explained that children become spoiled when adults "build them up too much." As I listened, I could feel my face getting hot from frustration.

Opting for reason rather than wrath, I took her argument to its absurd conclusion. I offered that if children were spoiled by too many compliments and too much encouragement, then logically the best way to preserve our kids would be to continually point out their weaknesses and to do our best to discourage them. Things got quiet.

I then went on to share my views on the importance of blessing our young people by pointing out their strengths and acknowledging their efforts. The woman thought for a moment and then responded that perhaps her position had been a little too extreme. For a brief instant, I thought that she was about to embrace the concept of blessing. She did not. In her next breath, she concluded that the best way to keep a child unspoiled was to simply say nothing about them one way or another. True story. Sad story.

Based on the term she used, *spoiled*, this woman evidently confused precious children with month-old cabbage. If I am not mistaken, things don't spoil or fall into disrepair when they receive too much care or attention. Instead they spoil when someone fails to take proper care of them.

Of course, there is a balance point here. Children need to be corrected when they err, and they need their parents to point out areas for improvement along life's road. Failure to discipline and correct our children when they are in the wrong or when they become too demanding will result in serious problems for them in the future. There is nothing noble or redeeming about ignoring a whining, rebellious child. Parents have to provide proper guidance, training, and when needed, correction for each child. This is an essential aspect of the lifelong mentoring that we explored in the previous chapter. However, the child who constantly hears about his shortcomings and never receives words of encouragement will soon withdraw into a protective shell or lash out in frustration. Likewise, a child whose presence and efforts are ignored will hear not silence but a loud message: "You aren't worthy of my attention." Our words literally shape the destinies of our own children and the other young people entrusted to our care. We must choose and use them wisely.

BLESSING AND CURSING IN ACTION

Quite a few years ago I was asked to serve as the coach of my son Christopher's eighth-grade basketball team at a small school in Midland,

Michigan. At that time I was not quite sure what I was getting into, but after having played the sport for many years, I wanted to give coaching a try. I agreed to serve as the coach and began to prepare plays and strategies for success. I confess that somewhere in the deep recesses of my mind I pictured a string of great victories, bonding with young men who were both skilled and dedicated to the sport, and of course, the school's trophy case brimming with shiny trophies with our team's name on them. I could hardly wait to get started!

That vision of grandeur lasted right up until the opening minutes of our initial practice session. It was then that I first met the members of my squad. Christopher was the only player with any previous experience. Four of the young guys had never before even played the game of basketball. To make matters even more challenging, two of them had emotional problems. One was under heavy medication and suffered from attention deficit disorder. Two came from broken homes. I quickly scrapped plans to put that Coach of the Year award on my mantel and tried to keep from panicking. It took about a week for the initial shock to wear off, but once it did, I realized that coaching was more than diagramming plays and layup drills.

Slowly I began to understand that I had been given a wonderful opportunity to work with young guys who needed something good to happen in their lives. With this in mind, I developed a plan to help the players with both basketball and life. Together we set some goals based on team unity, mutual respect, and learning the fundamentals of the game. Whenever any of my players made even an attempt at one of these goals, I acknowledged his effort. In those rare times when a shot was made or a good pass was completed, I would erupt with loud cheers. The smiles that spread across the faces of the players told me that we were all making progress. I did not overlook or ignore the mistakes made by the boys. Otherwise they would not have made any improvements. However, when mistakes were made, I would quietly explain what should have taken place and how to get it right the next time.

During those preseason practice sessions, I learned some fascinating things about relating to young people. It soon became obvious that the more I affirmed their efforts, the harder they tried.

Once in a while, I found myself shouting instructions in a voice that was more loud than loving, more drill instructor than coach. When this occurred, there was a visible change in the countenance of the player who bore the brunt of my tirade. Whenever this happened, I would stop the practice long enough to explain my tone and intent to all the players and to apologize to those I had upset. Sadly, I came to realize the reason that my amplified volume had such a negative impact. Some of the boys had never heard an adult male raise his voice with anything other than anger toward them.

When the big night of our first game finally arrived, I met with my team in our makeshift locker room for a pregame pep talk. It was the first time I had actually seen my guys in their raggedy game uniforms. They were a remarkable sight as skinny arms and legs protruded out of shirts and shorts several sizes too large. Their faces showed a combination of excitement and anxiety. My own son, Christopher, looked young—too young—to be leading this group into battle against our rivals from nearby Bay City. Our opponents had won the league championship for several years running, and everyone knew we were in trouble.

At the appropriate time, we left the sanctuary of our locker room and entered the gymnasium, which was filled with frantic fans, screaming cheerleaders, and anxious parents.

Our opponents were already engaged in their pregame layup drills. They were quite a contrast to my kids, as each player was decked out in a brand-new crimson uniform, complete with warmup pants and sweatshirt. And these kids were huge! Two of them had slight mustaches, and their starting center stood a full head taller than Christopher, our biggest player.

Just before the opening tipoff, our school's athletic director hushed the crowd and said a quick prayer into the microphone. I don't recall the exact words. I vaguely remember, however, that she asked God to bless all in attendance with love for each other, prayed for an outpouring of Christian sportsmanship on the court, and then finished with an admonition for everyone to act in a way that would please God. With those sentiments ringing in my ears, I began to think that we could at least have a pleasant evening engaged in friendly competition with like-minded people. That vain imagination lasted until the initial jump ball, which the opposing team got and immediately dribbled in for the first of many scores.

Incredibly, the coach for the opposing team barked at his players to guard our kids all over the court. This meant that my team could barely inbound the ball, let alone move it down the court to score. Each time our young point guard, Michael, tried to dribble or pass his way through their swarming defense, the ball was stolen and the other team scored. Early in the game an opponent smashed his elbow into Michael's nose, causing my player's eyes to fill with tears. I confess that I struggled to keep back my own tears that night. I have never felt so frustrated or betrayed in my life by the opposing coach, a man who only moments before had piously folded his hands and said amen to the prayer that spoke of sportsmanship and Christian charity. What a joke. I was amazed that he failed to comprehend what his tactics were doing to my young players.

We survived the first half of the game and retreated into our locker room trailing by a score of 35 to 0. At that point, I really don't know who was more shook up, my players or I. During those few quiet minutes, I did my best to encourage the boys and to affirm their efforts. I told them to ignore the score and instead work on little things that would eventually lead us to a victory later in the season.

The second half went much the same as the first, with the opposing coach doing his best to crush our team with the full-court press, double-teaming our guards, and goading his players to become even more aggressive than before.

During the fourth quarter of the game, I began to notice something unusual about the opposing players. Despite the fact that they were hugely successful on the scoreboard, they showed no signs of joy or satisfaction at the victory they knew would soon be theirs. But why? My answer soon came and stays with me to this day. *They* were the ones being crushed during the contest. Somewhere in the din of the crowd that jammed that small gymnasium, I could hear the opposing coach as he screamed at the young-men-in-the-making who were suffering under his "leadership."

"SMITH, GET HIM!"

"THAT WAS STUPID!"

"GET YOUR BUTT OVER HERE ON THIS BENCH!"

His face red with rage, this poor excuse for a coach, mentor, or man berated and belittled his players from the initial moments of the game until after the final horn had sounded. The young men in the crimson uniforms would not even look into the face of their coach as he yelled at them during time-outs. The coach stomped his feet, threw towels against the wall, and kicked chairs during his nonstop tirades. Each word that he spoke cracked like a whip on the backs of these boys, and while they played the game with skill, I could see the pain in their eyes.

When the game finally ended, I walked my players into our locker room and began to acknowledge their efforts with carefully chosen words. We had actually scored eight points by the game's conclusion, and our players had never quit. That alone gave me enough ammunition for several minutes of sincere praise for my young warriors. It was that night that I first coined a phrase that we kept as our official team motto for the rest of the year. I simply told them that when I looked at each of them that night, I did not see the score or any mistakes made during the game. Instead what I saw was *the heart of a champion* in each of them. While it is difficult to explain, I believe that when these young men heard themselves described in that way, something very special happened to them. Something on the inside.

As the season went on, my young guys continued to practice hard and learned to work as a team. Despite their best efforts, we continued to lose each week. Confidence was low as we began one of our final games of the season. While this game started like all the others, we somehow managed to tie the score by halftime. In the third and fourth quarters our boys played well and actually got to within one point of our opponents a couple of times. Amazingly, with less than thirty seconds to play, my young lions clawed their way into a position to win if we could somehow steal the ball and make a last-second shot. Of course, with our string of losses, very few people in attendance believed that our boys could do it. The opposing fans, unaccustomed to losing, raised their voices, stomped their feet, and clapped their hands to try to rattle my young players. During our final time-out the noise level was so great that our players literally couldn't hear any of my instructions. (With my record as a coach, perhaps that wasn't all bad...) Things looked bleak. With us down by one point and the other team having the ball, and with only seconds to go, the odds of our winning were slim. I began to mentally prepare another "nice try" speech to my kids as we took the floor for the final seconds of the game.

The entire sequence of events that followed is lost to me now. I can clearly remember their team taking the ball out of bounds. After that I can only see disjointed frames of those few last seconds in my mind's eye. I remember the blur of white and maroon jerseys flying across the hardwood floor. An errant pass. Our forward, Darrell, leaping, twisting, somehow deflecting the ball. Then the ball, the precious ball, bouncing, rolling, dancing toward the out-of-bounds line. More colors, faster this time. My son Christopher diving, fingers stretching, grabbing the ball and throwing a pass to his teammate Andrew. Then a mad scramble. All hands reaching, players tearing frantically at the ball. Fans standing. Screaming. Andrew, surrounded by opposing players, launching the ball toward the basket. The scoreboard's lighted numbers flickering, changing, counting down to another crushing loss. Young hearts beating fast, eyes wide, running. The ball. The ball arching up, then floating. Hanging. Falling. Brown leather passing smoothly though white nylon netting. Then, joy. Just joy. I remember the joy on the faces of my boys as it dawned on them that they had just done something that some of them had never done before. They had won! They laughed. I cried. We *won*. True story.

The annual winter sports ceremony came at season's end. This brief event was typically attended by the players, a few parents, the coaches, and some school officials. With our dismal win-loss record, our boys knew that there would be no team trophies to show off.

All they expected, therefore, was that each of them would come forward to the little makeshift podium and receive a paper certificate with their name on it. This would be followed by an unceremonious return to their seats to await the close of the ceremony. I had other plans, however.

Unbeknownst to them, I had gone to a local trophy shop and ordered a trophy for each boy. On it was the player's name, the date, and the inscription *The Heart of a Champion*. At the appropriate time I stepped to the podium, took the microphone, and called each boy forward, one at a time. As each one arrived, I reached out and put my arm around his shoulder. Then I took a few minutes to tell all in attendance about his strengths, efforts, and accomplishments. When I finished, the next boy would come forward and the process was repeated. Soon the parents and players alike understood that the season was about much more than points scored and games won. Tears flowed down my cheeks as I did my best to speak life, success, and blessing into each young player. For some of the boys, I am certain that it was the first time they had ever heard a grown man affirm all the good that God had placed within them.

The last one in line was my own son, who had worked so hard that season and had helped us win that memorable game. When his turn came, I pulled Christopher to my chest and told him that God had lots of games for him to win if he would just stick with it. I truly sensed that God was using the simple words of a father and coach to wash away a season's worth of frustration for this boy who one day hoped to play basketball in college.

After the ceremony I walked back into the tiny gym and sat in my coach's chair to replay the events of the previous five months. Funny, after all the difficulties of the long season, my thoughts went back to the time we walked onto the court for our first game. I wondered what happened to our opponents. The ones in the crimson uniforms who won the game that night but lost so much of themselves when cursed by the careless words of their coach. Perhaps I will never know what became of them, but I am certain that unless their parents or other concerned mentors have intentionally spoken words of blessing to them, these young men remain deeply wounded.

To this day I still keep track of most of the players from my own team. These young men went on to enroll in colleges across the country and are pursuing their God-ordained destinies. When I see them, they still call me coach. I like that. Christopher never gave up his dream of playing basketball and became the starting center on his high-school team. In that role he won many games, just as I knew he would. His teammates voted him captain in his senior year and selected him as their Most Valuable Defensive Player. He even set a school record by blocking ten shots in one game, and his name now stands on the school's permanent record board. Several months after his final game in high school, Chris graduated and was excited to see what God had planned for his future. While much of it is unclear, we soon learned that a few more basketball games were included in those plans. You see, that little guy in the raggedy uniform grew a bit. He is now over six feet seven inches tall and can shoot like a pro. Right after his high-school season ended, he was invited to try out for the team at Southeastern College in Lakeland, Florida. Chris made the trip and spent two days playing against college juniors and seniors. Did I mention that after his tryout, the basketball coach at that college offered Chris a spot on his team?

Once I got the news that Chris had made the team, I called his new coach, John Dunlap, to see how things had gone. It became very clear to me that Coach Dunlap was a wonderful man who deeply cared for his players. Coach told me that he had seen many things in my son during the tryout that he really liked. In addition to his skills on the court, the coach said he was impressed by Chris's attitude, his hustle, his ability to work with others on the team, and his determination. After we hung up, I had a thought. Maybe, just maybe, those qualities could be summed up in just a few simple words: *The Heart of a Champion*. It sure is fun to think so.

My experience with the ragtag basketball team helped me understand the power of words to shape the lives of young people. Somewhere along the way, I learned that God had provided another tool for building healthy children—healthy touch.

THE INTENTIONAL BLESSING OF TOUCH

Through God's marvelous design, we are able to bless our children in two foundational ways—with our words and with our appropriate physical touch. Included in the second category are hugs, putting an arm around a child's shoulder, tousling the child's hair, and giving high-fives.

It is a sad commentary on the state of our world today that I have to add the word "appropriate" to the concept of physical touch. It is no secret that too many adults have abused their roles of authority and actually harmed the children under their "care." What a twisted irony it is that the very hands God created to bring comfort and joy to children have been used against them. Because of this sad fact, I want to clarify that this section on the blessing of touch is intended primarily for loving fathers, mothers, grandparents, foster parents, and others who have been given official custody of children. I am in no way giving license for any other adult to touch children, no matter how pure their motives might be. With that disclaimer in place, let's look at what God had in mind when he gave parents and other trustworthy mentors the ability and desire to bless their children with loving touch.

A Father's Hands, a Mother's Touch

I marvel at God's wisdom and creativity when he made our hands and fingers. We use them countless times each day with scarcely a thought about their dexterity, flexibility, and sensitivity. They await our unspoken commands to lift, carry, twist, tap, pound, shake, type, and carry out thousands of other subconscious instructions. Obviously these silent servants make life much easier for us. However, God intended for our hands to meet not only our own needs but also the needs of others and to bestow upon them the blessing of touch.

Scientific research continues to show amazing connections between touch and development in both animals and humans. Years ago psychologist Harry Harlow did some experiments using infant monkeys and proved that the lack of physical touch was very harmful to them. Young monkeys who could see, hear, and smell their parents and others of their kind but not touch them developed severe emotional and behavioral problems. Those deprived of touch became extremely retarded in their behavior and fell into patterns of constant grooming, self-clasping, social withdrawal, and rocking.

Of course, we are not monkeys, so does this research have any bearing on the human race? I think so. One of the most striking examples of this was discovered in Romania, where long-time communist dictator Nicolae Ceausescu ruled with a very hard hand. His ruinous policies resulted in countless orphans being kept in near isolation for extremely long periods. These children were essentially warehoused and left by themselves except for obligatory feedings and changing. After Ceausescu was executed in the coup of 1989, the world got to see the impact of this deprivation on young bodies and souls. On average, the children were in the third to tenth percentile for physical growth and horribly delayed in motor-skill and mental development. They rocked and grasped themselves like the young monkeys in Harlow's experiments and grew up with abnormal social values and behavior. While they were deprived of many things during their sad childhoods, I am convinced that a key missing ingredient in their sad lives was that of loving touch.

In 1992 some people a bit closer to home had the same conviction and decided to try to prove that touch was a vital aspect of good health in humans. Researchers from Harvard, Duke, and other prestigious schools came together to create the Touch Research Institute at the University of Miami School of Medicine. Their task was to determine if the touch of human hands would contribute positively to treatment programs for a variety of patients. Here is what they found. *Touch* facilitates weight gain in preterm infants. *Touch* positively alters the immune system. *Touch* reduces pain, reduces stress hormones, and alleviates depressive symptoms in young patients. In addition, *touch* in the form of a short massage three times each day actually caused cocaine-exposed premature babies to gain 28 percent more weight than those not massaged. Amazingly, their studies on medical students proved that a single massage increased the number of disease-fighting T cells in the blood and caused the students to become more active. There is more. Women treated with simple *touch* therapy experienced markedly less pain during childbirth. Other adults found that simple *touch* resulted in less depression and reduced chronic pain. Preschoolers who received short periods of touch therapy before bed had more restful sleep. (Remember when Mom used to rub your back at bedtime?) The research continues to see how touch can helpfully augment treatment of long-lasting diseases, like most cancers and Alzheimer's.

Knowing that God placed enormous power in the touch of our hands, we now must begin to use this power to bless the young ones within our reach. Again, I am certainly not talking about the kind of touching that seeks its own pleasure or reward. Nor the type of touch that brings any harm or discomfort to those being touched. Instead we are called to release the kind of touching that conveys acceptance, kindness, reassurance, and unconditional love to the children placed in our care.

The Touch of Jesus

We see a wonderful example of this in Mark 10:13–16. In this biblical account, we read that many adults were bringing their children to Jesus so that he could touch or "bless" them. For reasons unknown, some of the disciples attempted to stop the children from getting close to Jesus. Naturally our gentle King corrected his disciples and reminded them that the very kingdom that they were seeking had more than enough room for children such as these. Once released to approach Jesus, the children came and experienced the wonderful love, gentle touch, and words of blessing from God in the flesh. According to the Scriptures,

Jesus took the children up onto his lap, put his hands on them, and blessed them. This same account is found in two other places in the gospels, and by some detailed word study, we can grasp the fullest meaning of what actually happened.

To begin with, the words used to describe the young ones who came to Jesus refer to infants, toddlers, *and* half-grown boys and girls. Clearly these were not just tiny babies that Jesus held momentarily, like a politician at a photo-op, and then hurriedly gave back to their parents. The phrase "laid his hands on them" is actually rooted in the Greek word *haptomai*. It means to "touch or handle something as to exert a modifying influence upon it." In other words, he touched them in order to bring about a positive change in the children themselves. Clearly there is power in the touch of loving hands.

The final component of this scene is the blessing itself. The Greek word that is translated "blessing" is *eulogeo,* meaning "to speak well of." By putting these concepts together, we see the beauty of what really happened when Jesus touched the children. What follows is my expanded version of what transpired that day.

Jesus was going about his Father's business when adults began to bring their children to him to be blessed. The disciples of Jesus rejected these young people and tried to send them away, supposedly so that Jesus could get on with more important matters—whatever those were. Once this was discovered, Jesus made clear that ministry to these young people did not represent a hindrance to the kingdom of God but in fact was precisely what God had in mind for his kingdom. The young ones then came to this trusted adult, Jesus, who brought them close to himself, some even sitting on his lap. Once there, each child was touched by anointed hands in a way that caused him or her to feel his power, love, and acceptance. The touch of this trusted adult brought healing to many and freedom from the fears that children have as they grow up in uncertain times. Before leaving his presence, each child heard Jesus speak positive words—just for him or her—that affirmed the good that was within the children and the good that awaited them in the future.

Imagine the impact on each child who was welcomed, accepted, and touched by Jesus. These young people were truly blessed to have the Prince of Peace touch them.

Following in His Footsteps

With Jesus no longer physically walking the earth, are our own children to be denied this sort of blessing? Not if we do our part. You see, Jesus was and is our example in all things. Our characters, our prayer lives, our views of right and wrong all spring from the teachings and life of Jesus Christ. However, if Christ is truly our role model, then let us not stop there. Let us welcome the children, first our own and then those who have no one else to hold and bless them. Let us get past our own fears of rejection and do as Jesus did with the children. Love them. Touch them. Bless them. Affirm and comfort them with words that will counteract the countless curses heard by every young boy or girl. Jesus did. We should too.

THE BLESSING OF PRAYER

One last simple yet powerful blessing must be mentioned here. That is the blessing of prayer. Despite our best efforts, our children can still suffer negative experiences that can only be touched by God's power. Broken hearts and shattered dreams happen in this life, and at times the emotional trauma runs too deep for even the best affirmation of a parent to heal. Thankfully, God has made a way for us to involve him in the lives of our precious young ones. It is called prayer.

Kathy and I have made a habit of praying for our children every day. We pray for God's protection and favor and for His will to be done in their lives. In addition, if they are struggling with any problems in school or with self-esteem, or with anything else for that matter, we cover them in prayer. Remember, God responds to prayer and not just need. The Scriptures are clear in saying that he knows what we need before we even ask. Our heavenly Father still requires, however, that we come to him in prayer. A simple prayer from a loving father or mother releases the resources of heaven to come into your child's life. What an honor to have the Creator of the universe respond to our requests and petitions. What a mistake to leave prayer out of the plan as we build the lives of our young men and women. Pray for the children. Jesus did. We should too.

---

1. Since there is some question as to when Adam was joined by Eve, I will simply use Adam to show the marvelous response of our heavenly Father to his newborn child.

10

THE POWER
OF A PLAN

WE HAVE REACHED THE POINT in this book where some summation may be helpful. Three individual concepts have been introduced: rites of passage, lifelong mentoring, and intentional blessing. Although separate and distinct, they work dynamically when combined into a strategic plan for any young person's development. Either parents and other mentors must intentionally choose to create such plans for the children under their care, or by default they leave these children's futures to chance. There is an old saying that has great implications for our children today: "If you don't care where you are going, any road will take you there." In other words, if you really don't have a destination in mind, it is never clear when you are going in the right—or wrong—direction.

IF YOU FAIL TO PLAN, YOU PLAN TO FAIL

Very few things in life work out the way we would like them to unless we have a plan in place. As an example, imagine what would happen if a family tried to go on a week's vacation without any planning. What if everyone just jumped into the car and started driving? The result of that sort of folly would certainly be a vacation that was far less than it could have been. Chances are, the family would have no place to stay and nothing to do and would never be sure they had arrived. Even if the family ended up at a nice place, a resort perhaps, they would be ill-equipped to enjoy it. The sunscreen, golf clubs, clothes, beach towels, etc., would have all been left behind. In like manner, when we fail to plan strategically for each child's growth and development, we put at risk something infinitely more valuable than a vacation—the child's destiny. We can do better than that.

For most people, planning is an extremely common activity. Getting dressed in the morning, taking a trip to the grocery store, and arranging work schedules all involve planning. People not only plan but also use a host of devices to keep them on track as they pursue their plans. Palm Pilots, day planners, calendars, and even hastily scrawled sticky notes all serve as reminders that there are tasks to perform and goals to accomplish.

Planning, in its most basic form, is very simple. Set a goal and then determine what steps are needed to accomplish that goal. Simple. Using this approach, people have accomplished incredible tasks. Impassable rivers have been spanned by complex suspension bridges; people have flown to, walked on, and returned from the moon; diseases have been cured by deliberate, painstaking research; and in perhaps the ultimate test of planning, entire families get to church on time—occasionally.

Few people would dispute that little or nothing of merit ever gets accomplished without a systematic, comprehensive plan. However, if that is true, then we must ask a very basic question: why not use this same deliberate approach in raising our children?

GETTING STARTED WITH THE PLAN
FOR YOUR CHILDREN

Webster defines the word *plan* in this way: *to design; to devise a diagram for doing, making or arranging. To have in mind as a project or purpose. An outline; a diagram; a schedule; a map.*

So, as a parent or mentor, you begin the planning process by simply thinking about those qualities that you hope to see in your children as they grow. I suggest that you literally write down a list of the attributes of successful young adults. Your list will include what you hope to see in your children physically, spiritually, emotionally, vocationally, and in other areas as well. Hygiene, social awareness, grooming, relational skills, manners, financial management, and compassion for the less fortunate should also be considered. In fact, you may well identify any number of other areas of development that you believe to be important.

Once all of these concepts are identified, you will have a fairly complete vision of the qualities and knowledge you hope to see develop in your children as they grow. You must then create a plan for imparting them to your children. The foundations for your plan will be lifelong mentoring, intentional blessing, and ultimately, a rite of passage.

As you begin, though, understand that each child is unique and is born with special gifts, talents, and tendencies. This is vital to understand, especially if you have more than one child under your care. One child may excel in schoolwork, and the next may struggle just to keep up with his peers. One child may be a gifted musician and the next unable to carry a tune in a bucket. One child may be a star athlete, while his younger sibling wants nothing to do with sports. As a parent or mentor, you must show your children that although they differ in skills, interests, and abilities, they all have equal value. If you clearly favor a particular child based on his or her performance, you will do a great disservice to the others. I strongly suggest that you never compare one child to another. Instead, identify and encourage the special gifts, abilities, and efforts of each child. No son or daughter needs to hear that he or she is not quite as good as, smart as, handsome as, or any other thing as, a brother, sister, neighbor, or some other young person. Comparisons by parents or mentors are always painful and will be perceived as curses, not blessings, by the very children we hope to motivate. With that in mind, let's look at how to put together a plan using mentoring, blessing, and a rite of passage.

How It Works

Ideally, even before our children are born, we determine that we will be intentional about raising them, leaving little to chance. However, many of us who are parents realized the need to do this well after our sons and daughters came into this world. When this is the case, we simply begin the process wherever our children are along their journey to adulthood.

Let's say that as a parent, you make your list of positive qualities that you want to see in your child, and on that list are *industriousness* and *perseverance*. Your vision then is to see your child grow up with a strong work ethic and a determination never to quit until a goal is accomplished. Now the mentoring begins.

As soon as your child is able to comprehend, begin to talk to him or her about the joy of hard work and the pride of accomplishment. Encourage the child to observe and participate in any home repair or chore that is safe for him or her such as washing dishes, fixing a bicycle, or patching a hole in the wall. When they are young, children can bring tools, hold a flashlight, put away the clean pans, and so on. Young children's tasks should not be too difficult, nor should they take too long. As your children grow, both the complexity and duration of their tasks can increase. Throughout the process, you simply talk with the child about what is being done and why it is being done. Other lessons will include the importance of finishing what you start, doing a quality job, and cleaning up afterward.

The lesson can be further strengthened by reading appropriate bedtime stories, such as *The Little Engine That Could.* For those of you who missed it during your own childhood years, this story tells of a heroic little train that saves the day by hard work and perseverance. His unfailing confession of "I think I can, I think I can, I think I can..." plants wonderful seeds in the fertile minds of young people that later grow into their own determination when faced with challenges.

Of course, you are not going to get too far with this bedtime story if your son or daughter is a teenager. So is the lesson lost? Not at all. You simply adjust your teaching/mentoring approach to his or her level. For older children you would forgo the book and simply share with them real-life examples of hard work and perseverance. Michael Jordan failed to make his high-school basketball team in his sophomore year and went on to become one of the greatest players of all time. His secret? Hard work and perseverance. The life stories of people like Thomas Edison, Abraham Lincoln, great missionaries and adventurers like Stanley and Livingstone, and a host of others will motivate young people with the same simple message of success—I think I can, I think I can, I think I can...

By sharing similar examples and demonstrating the qualities to your children on an ongoing basis, you are laying a foundation for their futures as adults. For example, while we don't expect our adolescent sons to work eight hours a day, and we know they won't see *all* tasks through successfully, we want to teach them that these are things that *men* do. It is expected that when they become men at their upcoming rite of passage, they will be increasingly diligent in doing and completing their schoolwork and chores. Ultimately, when they finish their schooling, it is expected that they will work hard, earn as good a living as possible, and provide for their own families.

Now we introduce the concept of intentional blessing into the mix. As the mentoring, teaching, and training continue, you look for any and every opportunity to affirm your child when he or she demonstrates hard work and perseverance. For example, I recall many times when one or more of my children helped with a home repair such as clearing a clogged drain under the kitchen sink. Once I realized that some work was needed to fix the pipe, I would invite my young ones to help. This meant that they walked with me into the garage to get a bucket, pliers, rags to wipe up the water that was sure to be all over the place before we finished, and any other tools needed to complete the project. Rather than just grab these things, I explained why they were needed and how they would be used. Then I had each child carry at least some of the tools back into the kitchen so that he or she would feel part of the process. Next we would all crowd around the sink and begin to unscrew the drain pipes to find the problem (which was usually something like a plastic toy or Popsicle stick). Once the problem was solved, we would clean up any mess and put away our tools. All during the process, I watched for any and every sign of positive involvement from the children. When I asked for a wrench and a child actually handed me the correct tool, I made a point of thanking him or her and telling the child how great it was that he or she was able to identify tools at such a young age. Remember, intentional blessing is all about affirmation of the good within our children. My sincere words of praise for the child's efforts served to affirm the value of work and the child's own competence.

As the children grew and matured, I began to give them increasing responsibility for projects around the house. After a while, I no longer had to fix clogged drains. Instead I would ask one of my young ones to fix them under my guidance. Predictably, the child would then go to the garage, find the proper tools, and fix the problem. The years of mentoring had taught the children how to make the repair, and the intentional blessing of affirming words along the way had given them confidence to not only try but also succeed.

Ideally, by the time his rite of passage arrives, a boy will have had years of mentoring and have heard thousands of words of blessing about his work ethic and perseverance. These fine attributes can be further affirmed at the rite of passage itself, either in the father's letter or in a positive skit. Following the rite of passage, these qualities can be affirmed on an ongoing basis as the young adult moves toward more independence and, eventually, out on his own. Remember, it is at this point that the parent begins to treat the former child as a young adult and helps him make good choices rather than making the choices for him. This mentoring relationship continues for a lifetime.

The Keys for Success of Your Plan: Commitment, Time, and Prayer

In the purest sense, there are three keys to the success of your strategic plan. They are your sincere commitment to the plan, spending sufficient time with each child to implement the plan, and prayer throughout the process. I am convinced that the first thirteen years or so of a young person's life are the most crucial in terms of his or her ultimate success in this world and that we must be there to guide the child using the simple tools discussed in this book. However, your commitment and gift of time and prayer to your children will prove life-changing regardless of their ages. Just remember that the best plan in the world will *not* change any child unless a parent or other mentor takes the time to implement it.

Set goals for yourself. As part of my plan to bless my own children, I make a very concerted effort to speak at least one positive word and to touch each of them at least once each day. This is often as simple as putting my arm around their shoulders, kissing them good night, affectionately rubbing their heads, and whenever possible, giving them a loving bear hug. It has been fun to see how much the height of the hugs has changed over the years. When my children were very young, I would get down on my knees and embrace them as they toddled over to me. Now my oldest sons are both over six feet tall, with Jeni and Daniel not far behind. What a joy it is for me to now reach *up* to hug them whenever I get the opportunity.

It is easier than you may think to take the time to follow through on your plan once you place yourself in your children's world and begin to feel what young people actually feel. For example, take time to consider what areas they may be overly sensitive about and where they may be struggling. Your words of intentional blessing will counteract the countless curses thrown at them by others in this world. If you think back on your own childhood, you will probably become aware that every child hears or thinks that he or she is plagued with at least one thing horribly wrong with his or her body: a nose that is too big, teeth that are less than perfect, a body that is too fat or too thin, complexion problems, and so on. Each day, our children are bombarded with media images of "perfect" people with perfect figures who are surrounded by perfect friends flashing their perfect smiles for the camera. Words of blessing and the healing touch of a parent or other respected mentor will cancel a child's perceived curse of imperfection and replace it with a wonderful sense of self-worth.

I encourage you to praise your children continually for a variety of qualities, efforts, and accomplishments. Let them hear you say that you see them as loving, caring, strong, courageous, wise, skillful, handsome or beautiful, nurturing, great thinkers, problem solvers, and so on. Regularly point out and confirm each of the skills, talents, gifts, and other attributes that God has given them. It is crucial to affirm both effort and success. This is a vital part of the overall plan designed to build spiritual awareness, self-confidence, and a healthy self-image.

For some parents this whole concept may seem a bit overwhelming. This is especially true if you were not raised in a setting where parents lovingly taught, spoke words of blessing, touched with kindness, and hugged as a means of showing affection. As a result of abuse or neglect that they suffered as children, some adults struggle with outward demonstrations of affection, even to their own children. I am sympathetic to these difficult situations; however, past pain doesn't have to result in withholding your words of blessing and healing touch from this next generation.

This is where prayer, the next key, comes in, not only for parents struggling to break free from the patterns of their own childhoods but also for all parents. In its simplest form, prayer is asking God to get involved in our situation. People of faith understand the wisdom of inviting the Creator of the universe to participate in their lives and in the lives of their children. One simple prayer puts things in motion that otherwise would never have happened. A life of prayer opens doors for our children that would have otherwise remained closed.

While this book is all about the role of parents and other mentors in the lives of children, it by no means minimizes the fact that the children themselves belong to their Creator. We are only stewards, wonderfully tasked with caring for God's own sons and daughters for the few years that we have with them. We would be wise to check with God about these marvelous members of his family each day to see if our vision and approach to mentoring lines up with his. Obviously, we pray for our children when there is some sort of problem or crisis such as illness or accident. However, we can and should develop lifestyles of praying for our children on a daily basis. Again, I realize that some parents may not be comfortable praying for and with their children; however, these are very important things to do. Saying grace before meals and nighttime prayers not only brings God's blessing but also provides our children with a model of spiritual awareness for them to follow. Even if you start slow and start small, you will still be glad that you started.

If you simply begin to try to implement your plan for your children, great things will begin to happen. Before long, you will find that mentoring, speaking words of blessing, appropriate touching, and daily prayer become natural expressions of your love for the children under your care.

When we train our sons and daughters as Mentor did with Telemachus, bless them as Jesus did with the children who came to him, and then prayerfully host rites of passage to confirm all that they have become, we can rest in the fact that we have done everything possible to help our children develop into mature adults. God will do the rest!

IT'S NEVER TOO LATE

I'd like to conclude this chapter by relating some things that have helped many men with their reactions to this mentoring, blessing, and rite-of-passage concept. I hope you are very excited about the celebration idea and about designing and implementing a positive plan for your child's development. Frankly, I have rarely spoken to anyone who wasn't overwhelmingly positive toward it. However, upon reflection, you may also feel some sadness—perhaps even some anger—that no one had this kind of plan or held this type of event for you when you were younger. Many men reflect on how their lives would have been different if parents or other mentors had helped with the transition into adulthood with a celebratory blessing. Others had parents who abandoned or abused them, leaving them to move into the adult years with deep scars rather than with affirmations of love and confirmations of growing maturity. These situations can stir up some very powerful emotions. If that is you, please keep reading. I have some very good news for you in chapter 16, "Healing a Father's Heart." For now just know that you are not alone and your situation is not beyond hope.

There is another scenario that can trouble some men as they read about rites of passage. It may be that your children have grown and moved away from home and you're feeling regret that you missed opportunities to bless and celebrate them when they were younger. In either case, I want to encourage you that it is never too late to be healed, and it is never too late to be a blessing to your own children, regardless of how old they are.

To you who are still hurt by the lack of care you received from your natural parents, please know that God has promised to be a father to the fatherless (Psalm 68:5). He is capable of healing your wounds and turning your sorrows into joy (Psalm 30:11). You can call on him to meet your every need, even those from many years ago. If this describes you, then I suggest that you begin to share how you feel with your wife, a good friend, pastor, priest, or counselor. As we discovered at Christopher's celebration, many men are bound with anger, bitterness, and a sense of sorrow over what did or did not happen to them in the past. Just talking about it helps. Talking and then praying about it will definitely open new doors of healing for you.

Also, if you regret never having helped your older children transition into adulthood, know it is *not* too late. Your words can still bless your children, no matter how old they are. Your sons and daughters still need to hear you say, "I love you," and feel your concern for them.

If you have older children or even grown children, how do you bless them? It's simple. Pick up the phone, jump in your car, or get on a plane. Do whatever it takes to reconnect with your precious offspring. You may feel a bit rusty, but the blessing you'll bring them will still have an incredibly powerful impact upon their lives—and upon yours as well.

For those who have younger children, I encourage you to begin immediately to create and implement your plan for their development. You will be amazed at how God will bless you, your children, and your children's children through a lifelong commitment to your precious children. A few kind words of blessing, some loving instruction, a little prayerful encouragement, and then soon—too soon—it will be time for that special night of celebration for your child.

Now, let's look deeper into how you can implement the powerful concept that ties the plan all together: the rite of passage.

11

FOUNDATIONS FOR YOUR OWN CELEBRATION

I HAVE HAD THE HONOR of attending and hosting many celebrations in the years since Christopher's. From these experiences, I have compiled the following foundational issues that should be considered when planning a celebration.

IT IS NOT OPTIONAL

First, I believe that a properly planned celebration is an essential part of every young person's life. To put this in the plainest terms possible, a rite of passage is not optional; it is necessary. There is no alternative to acknowledging a boy's transition into manhood if we truly want him to succeed. A big birthday party won't do it. A trip to Disney World won't do it. Parents, grandparents, or other concerned elders must accept the responsibility for planning and hosting a celebration for each child in their lives.

The questions below are the typical ones I'm asked when people first begin thinking about planning their own celebrations. I hope my answers will give you some practical guidance as you move ahead with your own rite-of-passage plans.

SHOULD I PREPARE MY CHILD FOR WHAT'S AHEAD?

The answer here is definitely *yes*! I had little time to do this for my first son, since I had only three weeks between the time that I decided to hold the celebration and the event itself. This meant there were no long discussions with Christopher about the meaning of the event, his changing role in the family, the steps to maturity, and so on. I simply built upon the lessons and discussions that we'd had prior to the event and then used the celebration as a foundation for our continued mentoring.

With so little time to prepare, I decided to surprise Christopher with the event. In retrospect, I would rather not have surprised him; instead I would have explained the scope and intent of the event to him as soon as possible. Even two weeks' notice would have been good. Thankfully, Chris's maturity level and our preexisting strong relationship made the surprise aspect of the event a nonissue.

Obviously, with my second son, Steven, I had a much longer time to reflect on and then talk with him about the full meaning of his rite of passage. I strongly recommend using this reflection, discussion, and preparation model for all celebrations. However, I realize that many parents will find themselves in the same situation I was in with my oldest son. They will not have years to prepare their boy for his transition and will simply have to start wherever they are in the process.

For those parents who have the time, it's best to hold extensive discussions with your son prior to the event. Your talks should focus on the rite of passage itself and what it means for the young man's future. Clearly, these discussions set up vital aspects of the event itself, even though they may take place months prior to the celebration. Fathers should be mentoring their sons all along but especially in the months prior to their rites of passage. It will be good to talk through new expectations, changing roles, and any new responsibilities that will be given to your son.

My long-term vision is for these celebrations to become part of our family culture for generations to come. Once we held Christopher's event, Kathy and I had three years to prepare for Steven's celebration, five years to prepare for Jenifer's, and seven years to prepare for Daniel's. We have used this time to have ongoing discussions (mentoring) about adulthood, maturity, and growing responsibility with each of our younger children. As a result, each of them eagerly anticipated their own special day of transition. I am thrilled to say that the rite-of-passage concept is now becoming ingrained into the very fabric of our immediate and extended family—so much so that I look forward to participating in the celebrations of my children's children.

The point here is that you should introduce the celebration concept to your children as soon as you possibly can. If you missed this opportunity with your first child, then don't miss it for your second child. If you missed it for all of your children, then don't miss it for your grandchildren.

WHAT IS THE BEST AGE?

No two sons are exactly alike, and no two sons mature at exactly the same age. Your first son may be ready to accept new levels of responsibility at age thirteen, while your second son may take longer to mature. Certainly the reverse could be true as well, so don't feel as if you need to host each child's celebration at exactly the same age.

In addition to maturity level, there are other factors that influence your timing. For example, if your family is going through a particularly hectic time near your son's birthday (such as a change in location or a serious illness of a loved one), then you should consider delaying his celebration for a month or two. If he has been anticipating his rite of passage on or near his birthday, then let him know what is happening and why it will be better to postpone it for a season.

I decided to hold my second son's celebration approximately six months after his thirteenth birthday. At that point his words and his actions assured me that he was ready. His maturity grew tremendously during those extra six months, and he was ready to receive the blessing of the celebration.

As a parent or mentor, you should prayerfully consider each boy's readiness for this life-changing event. It is clearly more art than science, so I cannot give you any exact guidelines to follow for scheduling a rite of passage. Some boys will be ready for the added responsibility and freedom much earlier than others. Others will take more time to reach the level of maturity and understanding required for the celebration to be truly meaningful. I will offer this one piece of advice, though: if in doubt about a young person's ability to comprehend the celebration's meaning, then wait a few months, do some additional teaching on the subject of manhood and maturity, and *then* schedule the event.

Having said all of that, I believe that there is something very special about affirming manhood and womanhood during the early teen years. Many cultures throughout history have identified the preteen and teen years as the time when their sons make the transition into manhood, and the situation is similar for girls. In our modern culture we clearly recognize that the teen years are unique, but regrettably we have not known what to do with them! Rather than fearing this period and viewing it as a time of impending rebellion, we can now begin to celebrate it as a time of orderly transition.

As I mentioned previously, when we seize the opportunity to help our youth move into adulthood, we prevent them from having to create their own rites of passage—rites usually marked with conflict and experimentation with so-called grown-up things, such as alcohol, other drugs, and sex. When we help them establish their God-ordained internal identities, we help them avoid creating false identities through externals such as wild hairstyles, body piercing, tattoos, and counter-culture clothing. When we communicate the understanding that there is a proper time and method for them to "grow up" and become self-supporting, we then help our young people avoid poorly planned schemes for independence, such as dropping out of school or running away from home.

There is no question that we parents will close the door on many of our teens' potential problems—struggles with low self-esteem, poor self-image, lack of purpose, despair, cynicism, and rebellion—by implementing plans for mentoring, intentional blessing, and finally, rites of passage into adulthood. Since the roots of these problems often grow during the early teen years, I am convinced that our modern-day sons and daughters will benefit from celebrations that occur between the ages of thirteen and seventeen.

But what about those parents who have older sons? Have these youth missed out on the opportunity to grow into mature adulthood? Not at all! This type of celebration will be extremely effective for a young man of eighteen, twenty-one, or even older. Indeed, this ceremony can be a life-changing event even for men who have reached their thirties, forties, and beyond. The old saying "better late than never" definitely applies here. The real key is that older, mature men are involved in the celebration to confirm, affirm, and bless the celebrant's manhood.

While this type of ceremony can be connected to a teen's birthday, it may also be linked with other special events occurring later in a young man's life, such as graduating from high school, voting for the first time, or entering college. In other words, you don't have to wait until a particular birthday rolls around to host the celebration. Use any opportunity you have, as soon as you can. You and your child will be glad you did. Our entire society will benefit as well.

WHAT IS MOM'S ROLE?

Another central issue concerns the role of a boy's mother in his celebration. Kathleen and I agree that whenever possible a mom should help plan the ceremony and spend some special time with her son prior to the gathering. She may do such things as take him to lunch or prepare his favorite meal before the evening's celebration. Also, she may want to write him a keepsake letter that he can open when he returns home. However, the bottom line is this. We have concluded that *it is better if the mother not host or attend her son's celebration.*

I realize this is a very emotional subject that takes some time to think through. Some moms initially bristle at the suggestion that they not attend. They reason that they have spent the past thirteen-plus years carrying, nursing, nurturing, comforting, feeding, teaching, and generally caring for this youngster and, therefore, deserve to be there on his special day. I acknowledge that in many homes, mom has been the most significant woman, and perhaps the most significant person, in her boy's life. Nothing will ever change that. Nevertheless, a celebration marking a boy's transition to manhood is an event best accomplished in the presence of other men.

Kathleen actually came to this conclusion first. She believes there must be a time when a mother releases her son into the care of the trusted men in her home, extended family, church, or broader community. From her perspective, releasing does not mean abandoning or ignoring the boy, nor does it mean that the boy will no longer need his mother. It simply means that there is a change in the mother-son relationship. I turned Kathleen's thoughts on this subject into the following note to a universal son. It might help both women and men understand the concept of "releasing" from a mother's perspective:

My son,

Since before you were born, I have nurtured you, cared for you, and protected you. But now it is time for you to take an important step. Today I am releasing you to become the man you were created to become. It is time for you to take more responsibility for your own actions. I will always love you as my son, but from this day forward, I will also respect you as a man. I will no longer try to control your actions, but I will work with you to think through your future. You have a special place in my heart. Now go for this short time to discover your special place among the men. When your celebration is over, come back and share with me what you have learned and who you have become.

Love,
Your Mother

I greatly appreciate Kathleen's perspective on this issue. She helped me sort through the emotions involved so that we could arrive at the best conclusion for everyone involved.

Now, here is the balance point. Husbands and fathers should be especially sensitive to the mother's feelings before, during, and after her son's rite of passage. Dads can help moms understand and enjoy all that takes place there by videotaping the proceedings and by taking some photos as well. It's an emotional time for everyone involved, so some extra concern, communication, and caring will help the rite of passage be a smooth and rewarding event for the whole family.

DOES IT HAVE TO BE A SPIRITUAL EVENT?

I want to emphasize the fact that rites of passage are profoundly spiritual events. I know of no culture, past or present, that held rites of passage for its youth and yet failed to embrace the deeply spiritual aspects of the ceremony. While these cultures would never agree on one approach to theology, they would clearly agree on one foundational truth: life is more than what is seen with the natural eyes. In sad contrast, our modern-day society, in all of its arrogance and ignorance about God's sustaining grace, tries to pull further and further away from its deeply rooted spirituality. What a sad mistake.

We must not allow our children's rites of passage to become fancy birthday parties, devoid of spirituality, God, or religious foundations. To do so would be a grave mistake. I am convinced that this is a time for parents to decide intentionally who they are and what they themselves believe. Remember, there is no such thing as an unbeliever. Everyone believes in something or someone as the ultimate authority in his or her life. This ultimate authority is the one counted on in times of trouble and the one who determines right and wrong, thereby guiding many of life's decisions.

For some people this ultimate authority is self, and for others it is some form of government. This paradigm seems to serve them well as long as life flows smoothly forward. However, when faced with the reality of a terminally ill child, a terrorist attack, or some other crisis, they realize that their "ultimate authority" is woefully inadequate.

For me and millions of others, there is a spiritual dimension to life, and someone else is in charge of this universe. This "someone else" left a clear account of what is right and what is wrong, showing us how to deal with life and death on the earth. The account is found in the Bible, and that someone, God, responds to prayer and any sincere attempt by his children (of any age) to reach him. Our heavenly Father offers life to a world that sees too much death. He ordains that each child is born with unique qualities, purpose, and value. And to each child he gives the promise of hope and a future. This is my worldview. These are rock-solid beliefs that carry me through all of life's joys and sorrows.

My worldview can't help anyone else unless he or she embraces it too. This is something that all mothers and fathers must settle in their own thinking before launching their children into such an uncertain world. The parents' view of spirituality will obviously affect their approach to mentoring, intentional blessing, and the rite of passage. Parents with no spiritual foundations struggle to construct meaningful messages for their children during this critical time of transition. Some may try to encourage their young charges to "dream big" or to "leave the world a better place than they found it." Others may attempt to instill a benevolent worldview by promoting the Golden Rule. Still others may exhort young people with sound bites such as "stick to your guns," "stay true to your values," or "to thine own self be true." Any and all of these concepts sound great; however, they become problematic if presented without explanation of the spiritual roots from which they grow. Each child so charged will eventually ask the simple question *Why?* "Why leave the world a better place if this is all there is? Why stay true to *values* if I live in a world that has no absolute truths? Why *do unto others* if there is no eternal scorecard, rewards, or consequences? Why not just live for today if there is no eternal life? What difference will *anything* I do really make…?"

In reality, our understanding and application of truth, morality, values, hope, and personal purpose spring forth from our spirituality. As a Christian, my spiritual foundations come from the Holy Bible. From its pages, I have learned how to have a personal relationship with God and about God's view of values, morality, purpose, relationships, and much more. Once I embraced these truths, I was able to teach my own children how to apply them to their own lives, present and future.

I would respectfully say that no man can give his children what he does not have himself. No one can affirm what he does not believe, so I strongly encourage parents and other mentors to sort out their own spiritual foundations before trying to help their children build theirs. I am convinced that this universe is decidedly spiritual, and therefore those who live in it must embrace spiritual realities or be condemned to flounder around until checkout time. We can do better than that.

I have heard many well-meaning parents say that they didn't want to push their children toward any particular religion or to influence their views of God. Instead they wanted to let their young people "find their own way." What utter nonsense! In my view, that is the most irresponsible position a parent could take with life's most important issue. Imagine the drastic impact on a child whose parents took this approach to some of life's lesser matters. A young boy with no instruction on hygiene would never brush his teeth or comb his hair. Too much bother. A teenager with no guidelines on diet would certainly live— and prematurely die—on junk food. Tastes better. A child with no parental support or insight about the value of education would certainly never enter school. Too much trouble. Few parents would think of abdicating their responsibility for instruction in these basic matters. So how much more should they direct their precious children into a relationship with a loving God?

The point here is simple. Parents must take sufficient time to determine their own position on spirituality before they attempt to host a celebration. Once their own spiritual foundations are laid, the parents can begin to share them with their children as part of their mentoring plan. A powerful culmination of this sharing can then take place during the celebration when their son is released to pursue God for himself, as a man. The living and active faith seen in parents makes the celebration and time of prayer at the end infinitely more powerful than if there is no faith at home.

As a final thought here, please understand that parents don't have to be spiritual superstars for this to be genuine. They simply need to have a real desire to know God and follow him to the best of their abilities. This sincerity, not perfect attendance at church or deacon board membership, will be seen, admired, and emulated by their sons.

HOW WILL PRAYER PLAY A PART?

If there is ever a season to set aside distractions and spend time in reflective prayer for your son, it is prior to the celebration. There is no substitute! The impact of prayer will be evident in many ways during the celebration. Parents should prayerfully consider whom to invite, where to have the gathering, and what to include on the agenda for their son's rite of passage. These are all-important aspects of the event, and nothing should be taken for granted. Prayer will help the men know what to write, say, and give to your young man. Prayer will seal the blessing for your son when the celebration ends. Prayer is the greatest assurance you can have that your celebration will accomplish its immediate and eternal goals.

IS BIGGER REALLY BETTER?

When it comes to goals, you may be wondering about the best size for the celebration. Our society continually preaches that bigger is better than small, fancy is better than plain, and enough money will make anything succeed. Don't get caught up in any of this nonsense when it comes to your son's celebration. A prayerfully focused celebration held in a cement-block basement and attended by just a few men will be infinitely more powerful than some godless grand production in a fancy conference center. Quality, not quantity, is key here. Keep praying about it, and the answers to when, where, and who will soon be evident.

MANAGING THE EVENT ITSELF

Now let's get down to the details of the celebration itself. What specific plans will you need to make in advance? What particular arrangements and activities will you need to consider? Naturally there are many options, and you should feel free to be creative. However, I do have some general suggestions that can help with the planning process.

Choose a Practical Location

Remember that the celebration is primarily designed to allow young men to receive blessings, affirmations, and encouragement from older men. Thus the event may be as simple or as elaborate as you choose. The impact will come from the depth of what is shared rather than from the setting itself. Therefore, many different locations can be appropriate, including a home, hotel, church, campsite, or rented meeting hall.

I recall a wonderful letter that I received from a missionary in Africa. This man had received a copy of an early manuscript of this book and wrote to tell me of his plans to celebrate his son's transition into manhood. He was going to host the event at his son's favorite spot beside a river and waterfalls in Nigeria. He and his son would journey there in a Land Rover, accompanied by a few of their male friends. The agenda for their special day was to spend time relaxing by the water, cooking his son's favorite meal over the open fire, and then sharing some letters and gifts from other men. Sounds great!

Just be sure to select a location that will comfortably hold the number of people you invite and allows sufficient room for all of your planned activities.

Timing

Just as there are many alternatives for *where* to hold a celebration, there are a lot of options for *when* one can be scheduled. You can plan yours for any day of the week, but you need to consider work schedules, school obligations, air travel for guests, and other potential conflicts.

Most that I have attended have been held on weekends. Be sure to allow sufficient time so that you are not rushed. This once-in-a-lifetime event must not be overshadowed by anything else.

Arrange for Refreshments

It's a nice touch when some refreshments are provided during the celebration. They may be eaten before or after the event. Refreshments may include a formal dinner, snacks, a cake, beverages, or any combination that is appropriate for your boy's special event. But please don't think that you must have a catered dinner to make the celebration a success. In fact, food and refreshments are add-ons to the celebration. They are not essentials.

Contact the Guests

The number of men attending the celebration may range from three to thirty. I would discourage a gathering larger than that, as it creates problems with space and overextends the length of the event. Here again, more is not necessarily better. Your boy will be blessed that just a few men cared enough to attend his special event. He will also know if some came simply out of obligation. You would not want any of your male guests sitting there preoccupied with other things, so choose wisely.

Invitations should be sent out at least two weeks before the event. However, four weeks' notice, or more, is preferable in order to allow time for the adjustment of busy schedules. You can use my letter as a model or write your own. Just be sure to include place, time, and all other details, including what you are requesting the men to contribute. Don't assume that the men will understand the rite of passage concept initially. Lovingly explain what you are doing, give the reasons for the event, and state specifically what you need from them. Have them contact you prior to the celebration if they have any questions so that they come prepared to properly serve your son.

Plan for Skits and Dramas

Skits and dramas can be powerful tools for teaching life lessons. They take the old adage of "a picture is worth a thousand words" to a new dimension—a *demonstration* is worth a thousand pictures! This means that whatever skits you choose must be designed to lovingly and powerfully teach lessons that your son will need for the future. Let me head off any potential skit problems with a few dos and don'ts:

DO be very creative in your skit design. There is no shortage of challenges that we face in life, so there are countless life lessons that can be powerfully portrayed in a skit or drama. Today's man must deal with emotions, friendship, work, education, choices, purity, faith, and a wide variety of other issues. Any and all of these are great foundations for skits. They don't have to be funny or elaborate to be effective. But your dramatized lessons can be very, very creative. Just make sure they are appropriate to your son's age, maturity level, and life experiences.

DO select your participants wisely. Make sure that each person involved in a skit is credible and able to handle the tasks assigned. By this I mean don't have an avowed atheist attempt to portray a message about the importance of a spiritual foundation for life! This will not be well received. Also, be sure you don't assign someone to be part of a skit if he tends to want to attract attention to himself. Putting a would-be comedian in front of a dozen other people is a recipe for disaster in the context of a celebration. The focus must be on the lesson, not on the people taking part in the skit. Select participants who are levelheaded, outgoing, and not prone to act silly. Then make sure they have time to prepare for their parts.

DON'T make the skit your ultimate "weapon." A skit is not the appropriate vehicle for "finally" getting a particular point across to your son. It is not to be used as a weapon to browbeat a young man. A frustrated parent may have been talking with his son for years about the need for better grooming, industriousness, spirituality, or any other subject. The night of his special celebration is not the time to ram the point home one more time. This would be a lecture in disguise. Please don't bother. It would cheapen the rest of the event and probably ensure another few years of noncompliance by your son. I encourage you to trust the celebration process and allow your son to grow toward maturity after it is over.

DON'T design a skit that would embarrass your son. Avoid humiliating your son by pointing out his weaknesses or his past failures. For example, if he has been in trouble with authority in school, a skit about respecting teachers would be a bad idea. Also, if he has struggled with or gotten caught with alcohol or other drugs, a skit about the dangers of substance abuse would be inappropriate. The young man would perceive this as an attempt to embarrass him in front of respected elders. Clearly, that's not your goal.

DON'T gloss over the details. Good skits take detailed planning. As the host, your role in the skit process is threefold. First, prayerfully design skits that will teach and minister to your son at his celebration. Second, prayerfully select the right people to be in the skits. Third, carefully write out the skits along with the primary lessons to be covered, detailing what props are needed, so that your volunteers will clearly understand your vision and their responsibilities.

And here is a final hint: When you design your skits, be sure that *all the props will be available when you need them.* You don't want to be making changes at the last second because a prop is unavailable, broken, or just overlooked.

Be Open to Including Alternative Activities

For various reasons, some people will not feel comfortable with skits and dramas at their son's celebration. Either they are unsure of their abilities to perform, or they determine that their son will not favorably respond to a skit. In such instances, there are many alternatives that can make the celebration interesting, powerful, and memorable for your son.

One alternative is to prepare a poster board or sheet of paper with your son's name at the top. Pass the board around to the attendees and have them write two words that describe your son. Words like *diligent, strong, brave, smart,* and *loving* will greatly encourage your son and help him see himself as others see him.

Another alternative is for the dad or grandfather to share positive stories and remembrances about the son from his childhood. These must be positive and not embarrassing for the young man. His first fish, first building project, or a particular act of kindness or bravery would all remind your son that he has had a positive impact on his family and his world since he first arrived.

Yet another alternative or addition to skits and dramas is to present your son with a scrapbook of his photos and accomplishments from the past. This type of presentation would make an excellent foundation for the young man's future.

The bottom line is this: the celebration should be designed in a way that creates powerful, positive memories for your son. He will remember the sights, sounds, messages, people, and emotions for a lifetime. Take time to design the celebration with this in mind.

As a final thought, remember that the underlying motive for the celebration is love. Thankfully, love covers a multitude of sins, errors, and mistakes, so you don't need to worry if something doesn't go quite as planned. Love will take care of it. As you plan your celebration, please just relax and follow your heart. It is going to be great!

12

CELEBRATION
FOR A SECOND SON

PARENTS WITH TWO OR MORE CHILDREN quickly learn that each one enters this world with a unique set of gifts, talents, abilities, and challenges. One child is compliant and shy; the next is much more independent and boisterous. One loves an orderly room and puts everything away in its proper place. The next child, more prone to sloppiness, is oblivious to the new strains of mold growing in the wet towels under his never-made bed. No two are exactly alike.

The plan for each child's development, therefore, must also be customized to meet a variety of unique needs, personalities, learning styles, and attention spans. Parents who are willing to invest the time can find creative ways to help each child grow, using the foundations of mentoring, intentional blessing, and the rite of passage. Over the past twenty years, Kathy and I found that God had some special plans for each of our four children. Our task was to discover the best ways to motivate, educate, and at times, refocus each one. Once we had completed the celebration for our first son, we began to focus our attention on the next three children. Special emphasis was placed on preparing son number two for his rite of passage.

Steven was born three years after Christopher entered this world. He came very close to not being born at all. When Kathleen was pregnant with him, she had some serious complications, including hard contractions at just over twelve weeks. As a result her physician put her on strict bed rest for the remaining six months of the pregnancy. No, that is not a misprint—six months. If she had been on her feet for even a short time, it would have put our unborn son's life in the gravest peril.

This was the most difficult time of our young married life. I had recently started my own human resource development company and had to travel extensively or risk losing our only client. This left Kathy to watch over three-year-old Christopher as she lay flat on her back for the entire day. When I was gone, friends and family came over to assist with chores, cook meals, pray, and entertain Christopher. The process challenged both our faith and our endurance. We learned to pray without ceasing, as numerous times we had to rush Kathy to the hospital to stop contractions. On one particular night, we had two frightful trips to the emergency room as new complications jeopardized the lives of both mother and baby.

I gained an incredible amount of respect for my lovely wife during this time. I cannot imagine spending six days in bed with little to occupy my time—let alone six months! However, my wife possesses a powerful combination of mother's love and warrior's heart. For her the pregnancy was neither convenient nor enjoyable. Instead it was painful, restricting, and frustrating. If she had wanted to end the pain, she could have simply left her bed and gone for a walk. The baby would have been lost, but she could have gotten on with her life. However, that is not how God created her. She sacrificed six months of her life to secure the life of our son, Steven David Molitor.

We warmly recall that during her time of bed rest, Kathy's physician wanted us to keep track of the baby's movements within the womb. This was the primary means of determining the impact of all the complications on his health. Using this method, "healthy" meant that Steven would give mom a kick at least ten times during the course of a day. Kathy usually recorded ten kicks within the first hour that she was awake. Steven, though still within the womb, let us know that he was alive and well. By God's grace he entered the world some six months later and has not stopped kicking up his heels ever since.

THE ANTICIPATION BUILDS

Steven was just over ten years old when we held Christopher's celebration. He was fascinated by the stories of the skits as well as the gifts that his older brother received. I was quick to tell him that his special day would arrive in due time and explained the basic concept to him as well.

During the following three years, Steven went through many of the typical changes for a boy his age. He grew taller and stronger. His voice changed from tenor to baritone. Girls caught his eye, and judging by all the phone calls that he received, he had caught theirs as well. Steven began to focus on the future instead of simply living in the present.

It was fascinating to watch Steven's view of his impending celebration change as well. Soon after his older brother's event, he began asking me when his own special day would arrive. At that point his motivation had more to do with a gathering and gifts than maturity and manhood. That's consistent with being a ten-year-old boy. However, as his own celebration neared, Steven began to grasp its true meaning. He no longer talked about what he would *get,* in terms of things; instead he began to consider who he was to *become* as a man.

It was during this three-year period that Kathy and I became very deliberate about our plan of mentoring and intentional blessing for Steven and his younger siblings. As the months went by, we continually watched for teachable moments and opportunities to affirm the identity of each child. Simply knowing that the time of transition was coming helped our family adjust to the changes that would follow each child's rite of passage. Clearly, this planned approach to childrearing had become a way of life for us all.

Steven was not the only one who had three years to think about his celebration. As his father, I spent a great deal of time pondering and praying about his special day. I wanted it to be unique and created just for Steven. After having such a powerful celebration for Christopher, I prayed that Steven's event would somehow hold the same wonder for us all.

That prayer was answered.

THE SPECIAL DAY ARRIVES

What an incredible joy it was for me when Steven's celebration day finally arrived. His event was unique and yet built upon some traditions begun three years earlier when Christopher was the guest of honor. On his special day, Steven and I had a fine dinner with Grandpa Hayes and then made our way to the same hotel room that had been so wonderfully filled with God's presence at the first celebration. This time, the celebrated son knew exactly what was coming, and he could hardly wait!

Steven and I actually arrived at the hotel before any of the other guests and were able to greet the men as they entered the room. Once again Kathy had done a great job of decorating and had placed a beautiful cake on a table near the door. This time the inscription read, *This is my beloved son, in whom I am well pleased.*

Once all the men had arrived, we opened the celebration with a greeting and simple prayer. We followed that by singing a chorus of "Holy Spirit, Thou Art Welcome in This Place." I marveled at the fact that while not one man in the room possessed a particularly good singing voice, together we made beautiful harmony.

Two skits about emotions and the choices that men make in life followed our song. These were patterned after the lessons taught during Christopher's celebration. Next, Pastor James Glenn gave us a mini-teaching on the impact of a man's words on others. He taught us to use words to build up and never to tear down. As they were at Christopher's gathering, the messages were simple and yet profound.

Following this, we began to share our letters and gifts with Steven. Once again, I read the letters from his grandfathers and those from men far away. I must have set a record for taking the longest time to read a letter when I attempted to share my own with my son. I did quite well for a while, but when I looked up to see his face, I began to weep. I was hit with waves of wonderful thoughts about Steven, his future, his potential, and how inadequate I felt at capturing my love for him on paper.

The morning after his celebration, I reflected on the importance of a father's communicating his deepest thoughts to his son at this special time. We often don't take time to say how we really feel, and the celebration provides the perfect opportunity to bless our sons with words. Below, I have included my letter to Steven to give you some ideas about the kinds of things you may want to write to your special young man.

To my beloved son, Steven David Molitor,
in whom I am well pleased...

Dear Steven,

Congratulations on this special night and time of transition into manhood! During the past few years we have talked about this night, and it has finally arrived. Everything that has been done here has been done for only one purpose—to bless and support you.

The men in this room, and those who have sent greetings from far away, know how important it is for just one man to succeed in life. Their prayers and support have been with you and will continue to be with you as you walk the path of maturity.

As your father, I wanted to put some things in writing so that you would always have them. First, it's important for you to know how much I love you and how proud I am to be called your dad. As a son, you may sometimes wonder about this, especially when I get on your case about something. Rest assured, when I speak with you about anything it is to help build you into the man that God has ordained for you to become.

It has been my great pleasure to watch you grow and develop in so many areas of life. Athletics, schoolwork, music, friendships, humor, and work are all aspects of your life that impress others and me. God has given you an engineering mind that truly amazes me. You can see a project from start to finish before the first nail has been driven or shovel of dirt has been moved. When it comes time to go to work, you are on the top of my list of companions to have by my side.

God has given you a unique role to play in our family. You are often the one who gets us all going in a new direction. Your ideas are fresh, and your intensity inspires others to get involved. At times your wonderful sense of humor has turned a dull day into a complete riot. Often God has used you to lift my spirits with your fun-loving ways.

On this special night, I reflect back nearly fourteen years, to the time when your mother and I were in the greatest battle of our lives. You see, our precious son Steven was impatient and wanted to get on with his life right then. The problem was that he needed to stay in the womb for another six months! That was a time of incredible spiritual warfare, spiritual blessing, faith building, prayer, and weeping. Son, more than once it looked as if we would lose you and never have the joy of your presence in our lives. It was in those times that I cried out to the Lord Jesus, who answered faithfully and brought you safely through.

I knew then that you would be a fighter in this life. I knew then that God had given you an extra measure of vitality, intensity, and zeal that few others had. God has given you these qualities to change the lives of others in positive ways. In the coming years you will see how important your words are to others. You will see that a kind word from you can lift another up, while a harsh word from you can crush like a brick. Together we will continue to learn how to handle this kind of power in a way that pleases God.

From early on I also knew that God had made you a leader. This too is a quality that must be yielded to the lordship of Jesus or you will simply lead people the wrong way. I am certain that, by God's grace, you will lead many into the kingdom of God, into righteousness, and into the fullness of their own callings.

One of your many gifts is found in music. You are a talented musician, but more important, you are an anointed one. Be careful not to allow your gift to be used by anyone other than God. God has given a similar gift to many rock musicians, rappers, and heavy metal performers—they just don't realize it and therefore allow their gifts to be perverted. That will not happen to you. I want to encourage you to write songs that glorify God and also touch people with the beauty of life. I believe that as time passes, people throughout this land will know of your songs.

I am certain that God has written a wonderful plan for your life. It is a plan that includes honor, prosperity, family, and countless opportunities to serve him. As such, please fight against distractions and things that would steal your precious time. Time is a gift from God, and it must not be wasted. It takes hard work to live out God's calling on your life, but you can do it.

In closing, let me say that despite all of your wonderful gifts, talents, and abilities, I love you for only one reason. That is because you are my beloved son. Nothing you can do would make me love you more—or less. I am totally committed to see you through. I will never withdraw my commitment or love from you.

Son, you are about to enter into a new phase of life, one that will require stamina and courage. Both are within you. As you run this new race, you will sometimes have the wind at your back and the crowd cheering you on. At other times you will feel like you can barely run another step and that everyone is against you. At those times just keep running, son. Never give up, and never quit.

As you run, I promise that you will hear one voice cheering you on from the crowd, a voice that is different from all the rest. In that voice you will hear pride, joy, and love. Steven David, know that that voice belongs to your father.

Love,
Dad

As we had done years before, the other men then read their letters, told their stories, and blessed Steven with their gifts. Once again the range of presents and life lessons was amazing. Steven received books, a wooden puzzle, a blessings jar, a prayer journal, a symbolic candle, and many other gifts that he will treasure for a lifetime.

Once again men sacrificed and gave away prized possessions to seal what God wanted to do in a young man's heart. A beautifully designed shirt that Pastor James had brought back from a trip to Ghana became Steven's that evening. One precious brother, Teal, had recently returned from a trip to the Holy Land and gave my son a beautiful ram's-horn *shofar* that was over three feet long. Teal placed the horn to his lips and blew a blast that shook the room with the sound that the warriors of old heard when it was time for battle. It was that same sound that told

David, Gideon, and so many others that there was an enemy on the prowl, trying to take what was not theirs to take. The men in the room got the wonderfully chilling message.

As my friend blew that trumpet, I envisioned men all over the world awakening from their slumber and arming themselves for battle. As the trumpet sounded again, I could feel the war cry rising in the heart of every man. *No longer will we allow an enemy to take our sons without a fight.* Warriors were awakened that night. We will never be caught asleep again.

When our time of letters and gifts came to a close, we brought Steven up to the front to pray blessings over him. As with Christopher, I had some of the most senior men gather around him to pray. We asked God to protect, guide, and counsel this fine young man. We spoke words over Steven that every young man must hear. He heard us loudly proclaim that he is valued. He is loved. He is respected. He is accepted.

After the others had prayed, I took my place in front of my son, laid my hands upon his precious head, and proclaimed the essence of what the night was all about: "You are my beloved son, in whom I am well pleased."

Following this, we brought our celebration to a close and said good-bye to the many faithful men who, as others before them, had given up three hours of their night to bless my son for a lifetime. Kathy was waiting up for us when we arrived home, and Steven excitedly shared his experience with her. It was well into Sunday morning when the lights finally went out in our home.

DAD LEARNS HIS LESSONS TOO

Steven wasn't the only one to be blessed on that night, of course. And he certainly wasn't the only one to learn something new. In fact, I learned a couple of new lessons from the celebration for my second son. I used them to plan for my daughter's celebration two years later. I hope these simple lessons will assist you as well if you have more than one young person to celebrate.

Be Ready for the Inevitable Comparisons

Sibling rivalry is alive and well in most homes that are inhabited by more than one child. My home has been no exception, and Kathy and I work very hard to ensure that none of our four offspring feels slighted, overlooked, or less valued than his or her siblings. Since the time of celebration is a time of powerful imprinting, it's vital that the celebration for a second or third son be of comparable size and scope to your first one.

Rest assured that your sons will compare notes about their respective celebrations, and there should be no glaring differences between them that could someday harm their relationship. Simply put, you would not want to host one celebration in a fancy hotel and the other in a garage.

Determine the Role of the Older Brother(s)

I knew it was important for Christopher to attend his younger brother's celebration and hoped it would be a wonderful time of bonding between the two brothers who sometimes viewed each other as competitors or even adversaries. Christopher wrote his own letter for Steven prior to the celebration and let me review it before the actual event. His note was filled with a combination of sound advice, sincere support, and humor. When he read it during the celebration, Chris had us all laughing by pointing out that if this special event for his brother were being held in eastern Africa, we would be gathering for his circumcision. Christopher then brought the house down when he produced his gift for his brother—a razor-sharp fillet knife!

It was such a blessing to hear my oldest son read his letter to Steven and then speak to him straight from his heart. Christopher's voice was much deeper, and his words were weightier than those I had heard him utter three years earlier in this same room. His growth and maturity were evident. It made me proud to see him play such an important role in the maturing of his younger brother.

Since Chris knew about the importance and sanctity of the event, he did nothing to trivialize the celebration in any way. During our time of prayer for Steven, Christopher came forward, placed his hands on his brother's shoulders, and prayed a beautiful prayer of blessing, reconciliation, and commitment for the future. I am certain that God used that time for cleansing and strengthening the relationship between two fine young men.

THE AFTERMATH

When the celebration ended, Steven and I made the long drive home and talked about the event. He was clearly moved by the men's generosity, love, and commitment, which had made his celebration so special. As his brother had done three years earlier, Steven laid his head back, closed his eyes, and quietly recounted his favorite parts of the evening. As I had done three years earlier, I wiped tears from my eyes and thanked God for giving me a family to love.

In the days following his celebration, Steven showed signs that the event had truly changed his approach to some very important aspects of life. Interestingly, he grew much closer to Daniel, his younger brother. While the two of them had been fairly close before, Steven had sometimes been antagonistic toward Daniel. Following the celebration I watched this negative aspect of their relationship melt away. Immediately Steven was much more inclined to invite Daniel into his world and began to take on a mentor's role. Soon the two of them were engaged in work, play, and even homework projects. As a father, one of my greatest thrills is seeing my children in unity.

This changed relationship between Steven and his brother has been wonderful to watch, but that relationship was not the only one to be altered. I continue to see a similar positive change in Steven's relationships with his other siblings as well.

Another powerful result of the celebration came when Steven made a choice to stand up for what is right under some very difficult circumstances. Several weeks after the event, he faced a tough situation at school. Several of his friends became involved in some very unhealthy activities. Rather than join in, Steven confronted his peers about their actions, knowing that it could cost him their companionship. I would like to report that his friends immediately saw the error of their ways, thanked Steven, and lived happily ever after, but I can't. Instead, Steven's friends withdrew and kept him out of their lives for quite a while. I was concerned that the negative peer pressure might cause him to change his mind or soften his stand. It didn't. Without question, Steven was emboldened by the lessons taught in the skits and strengthened by the affirmations of the men that night at his celebration. He still has no regrets about taking his stand for righteousness despite the cost to him. I call that maturity.

A NEW SEASON BEGINS

Steven's celebration took place in late summer. Soon thereafter the woods behind our home exploded into the wonderful colors of autumn and the air began to chill. For four generations of Molitors, this has been God's way of announcing something very important. Hunting season was just ahead! This meant that it was time to sight in our rifles and to build blinds for the deer-hunting season that was soon to come.

Steven had shown a keen interest in hunting that year, and I confess that I let him skip one day of school so that he could build his own blind in a spot he selected. I will never forget the wonderful time we had trimming branches, hauling materials, planning, measuring, cutting, and eventually nailing boards together, watching the blind take shape. As we worked, I told my son stories about his ancestors' hunting adventures in northern Michigan. Steven was especially eager to learn more about his great-grandfather Henry, since my son seemed to inherit his grandfather's love for the outdoors.

As the day in the woods drew to a close, we put the finishing touches on our creation and then took several moments to rest inside the blind. Steven's face was beaming as he looked at the forest glowing in all its fall brilliance. In his mind were images of a huge ten-point buck that he hoped would appear on opening day. Overhead, flocks of geese loudly announced that they were making their own passage to a warmer climate.

I was soon lost in my own thoughts about the incredible beauty of God's creation and the joy of having this fine young man sit next to me in the middle of the woods. That day two men, one young and the other not so young, had worked together and built something that would last. Through the process, we laughed together, planned together, made mistakes together, and finally, as the shadows lengthened, succeeded together. At that moment, there was nowhere else on earth that I would rather have been and no one else I would rather have had for my companion. It occurred to me that the celebration for my second son had changed my heart once again and made me a better dad.

Soon it was time to walk the winding trail back to our house. The sights, sounds, and smells of the forest surrounded us as we slowly moved toward the welcoming lights of home. Neither of us hurried or spoke much along the way. This was a day to be remembered. I had spent it with my son—my beloved son in whom I am well pleased.

13

NEW LIFE FOR
A PRODIGAL SON

I AM OFTEN ASKED whether parents should hold a celebration for a son who is currently rebellious or involved with alcohol, other drugs, sex, violence, gangs, and so on. My response is unquestionably *yes!* A plan of intentional blessing capped off with a customized rite of passage will help get many of our wayward boys back on the right path.

This chapter is all about restoration and reconciliation of our wayward boys to their parents and to their Creator. This is achievable; however, first we need to understand the type of boy we're talking about. As we do so, we will find ways to look beyond his rebellion and find what is often missing in these situations—hope.

WHO OR WHAT IS TO BLAME?

The term *wayward* is an old-fashioned one, but it still accurately describes many young males today. According to Webster, *wayward* means: "insistent on having one's own way, contrary to others' advice, wishes, or commands; headstrong, disobedient. Conforming to no fixed rule, or pattern; unpredictable."

All too often, young men today insist on going their own way, despite the advice of those in authority. Many troubled youths have grown up without proper supervision. Others have had fathers abandon them, leaving no positive male role model to follow. However, while it is easy to see why such homes can foster rebellion in young people, there are also many troubled, disobedient, and unpredictable teenagers today who were raised by loving parents in "good" homes.

Whenever a child chooses the wrong path, it is common for someone to ask, what went wrong? In other words, who is to blame? In my view this is irrelevant. In fact, pursuing the issue of blame is foolish, given the complex host of potential causes.

Our children are bombarded each day with conflicting messages about life, manhood, sexuality, morality, and a host of other issues. Raging hormones and bouncing brain chemistry yield massive mood swings in even the most stable teenagers. Love lost and broken hearts cause many teens to do things they will regret years later. Peer pressure pumps our sons full of ideas that seem right in the short term but yield long-term pain and embarrassment. Drug- and alcohol-related problems, speeding tickets, fights, sexually transmitted diseases, children out of wedlock, and nights in jail are all possible for today's young men. Parents of children caught in any of these traps are victimized by the inevitable fallout of grief, guilt, shame, fear, embarrassment, and legal woes that come with the territory. As a parent, I realize that I have made many mistakes in raising my children. Things I should have said, I didn't. Things I should not have said, I did. I could have spent more time with each child, and I should not have worked so much when they were young, and I should have—. You get the message here. Of course, we *all* could have done better raising our children. However, none of us was perfect. This is why our sons still need a heavenly Father, so that he can make up for our shortcomings.

In writing this, I hope to remove the unnecessary guilt that some parents carry. Those whose sons have wandered away or gotten into trouble should rest in the very real possibility that they did nothing seriously wrong to cause the rebellion. Remember, young people make choices in life, just as we do. If they make good choices, their chances of having a good life increase. If they make bad choices, their chances increase for having a bad life. One of the greatest tragedies for families occurs when a child chooses the wrong path and the parent(s) involved waste years paralyzed by guilt and condemnation. We all make mistakes as parents, but none of our mistakes justifies or excuses poor choices on the part of our children.

Prodigal sons and daughters even come from homes where the parents did all they could to create the ideal setting for their offspring. God himself knows a little something about that. Consider the account of Creation, in which our heavenly Father designs a wonderful world for his first son, Adam, to live in. This firstborn had it made, right? Perfect weather, no conflicts, daily walks with God, and a wife who was hand picked by his Creator. All this, and yet Adam dropped the ball. He stepped smack into the middle of the only mess available on earth at the time. (Does that sound like any teenager you know?)

The bottom line is this: don't allow condemnation to overtake you when it comes to your children and how they are doing at this moment. Whether your son is in trouble, in rebellion, or in prison, there is still hope as long as you stay engaged in the process. For some parents whose children have made bad choices, it is time to cast aside the guilt and move forward. As long as the child is still alive, you can influence him with your renewed commitment to love him, pray for him, and bless him. Just as God did with Adam, we can cover them to the best of our ability and do our best to make a way for them to succeed, even after they have fallen away. Our heavenly Father never gave up on Adam, so don't you give up on your son either. If you have been sitting around worrying, regretting, or mourning over his mistakes, please realize that there is a time for grief, but there is also a time to move forward with a new plan. If you have been stymied by self-doubt and second-guessing about decisions that you made, then realize that the only reason to mentally revisit a mistake is so that you can learn and avoid making it again in the future. Any time spent reflecting beyond that is a waste. Right now, it is time to get up and dust yourself off. There is work to do!

LESSONS FROM A WAYWARD SON

In Luke 15:11–32 we read a fascinating story involving a father and his two sons. The older son is a real gem. We learn from the account that he is obedient and respectful of his father. He seems to have a real sense of purpose for his life, and he diligently stays at home to take care of the family business, which someday he will inherit.

His younger brother is exactly the opposite. Brash, shortsighted, and demanding, this rebellious son prematurely takes his share of the father's estate and heads off to a distant country, where he squanders both his money and his self-respect. Son number two enjoys the temporary pleasures of sin in the company of prostitutes but soon ends up at his life's lowest point.

Eventually this wayward son comes to his senses and chooses to return home, where his father holds a wonderful celebration in his honor. The father proudly announces the reason for the celebration to those in attendance: his son was dead and now is alive, his son was lost and now is found! To any father, this is a great reason to celebrate!

As I study this ancient passage, it is clear that its primary message is about the unconditional love that our heavenly Father has for lost souls. However, I'm also amazed at its many implications for the rite-of-passage concept today if we view the account simply as a story about an earthly father and his two sons. Seen from this perspective, we learn:

Modern-Day Teen Rebellion Is Nothing New

Young males have been making bad decisions with their lives for generations. Also, it is clear that the traps for our young people today are no different than they were back then. Substance abuse, rebellion against authority, and sexual immorality are still high on the list of common snares for unsuspecting young men.

Teen Rebellion Has a Wide Impact

Another interesting aspect of the account is that not only are the traps the same, but so is the impact of teen rebellion on everyone involved. Parents of wayward sons are devastated and distracted from the other aspects of their own lives. Siblings are torn; they love their brothers but also harbor resentment over what seems like unfair tolerance of their poor behavior.

Teen Rebellion Hurts…Teens

We tend to forget that the worst impact of the rebellion is always inflicted upon the teens themselves. They suffer spiritually, physically, financially, mentally, emotionally, and relationally as wild living robs their vitality and their zeal for life. By getting what they think they want, these wayward souls actually lose what they so desperately need—structure, family unity, boundaries, purpose, and direction. They pay a heavy price for gaining too much freedom too soon.

Yet all is not lost. We can approach the wayward son from a hopeful perspective by learning to look at him in a new way.

Look Past the Rebellion

The good news about this story is that it reminds us that despite all of our youthful mistakes, there comes a time when even the most rebellious young man comes to his senses and wants to return to home base for another try at life. This should give hope to many parents whose boys have chosen the wayward road. Please don't give up. Like the father in the story, keep watching down the road for their return.

Also, keep in mind that there are two key people involved in the reconciliation process: the father *and* the son. When the dad saw his son, he seemingly had every right to go down the road and angrily berate him with several years' worth of "I told you this would happen!" He did not do this. Instead, he saw his wayward son while he was *still far away* and ran to him, kissed him, and honored him with a robe and a special ring of authority. This is a model for all of us to follow. Can you picture how the boy looked after his long time of wild living, poverty, and filth? Can you imagine how the boy smelled after literally living with pigs? And yet the father ran to him and kissed him.

Clearly, the father saw what others missed when they looked at this wayward son. As only a parent can, this father *looked past the filth and saw all of the potential,* the promise, the gifts, and the calling that a sovereign God had placed within his flesh and blood. After all, this was still his precious son. With sadness the father saw the lines around his young man's eyes and the wounds on his body that inevitably come from a hard life on the road. However, despite the scars, he knew that there was once again hope for this young man's future. This was well worth celebrating!

Recognize the Impact on the Rest of the Family

It is difficult to imagine the emotional highs and lows experienced by the father that day. Shortly after the thrill of seeing his younger son return, the father found himself confronted by a very angry older son, who told him, "Look! All these years I've been slaving for you and never disobeyed your orders... But when this son of yours who has squandered your property with prostitutes comes home, you kill the fattened calf for him!" (Luke 15:29–30). The wayward son's rebellion had an impact on the rest of the family that couldn't be ignored.

At first glance, the older son's words seem to indicate a resentment of his sibling's party. I have heard numerous well-meaning preachers condemn the older brother's response as jealous and envious. They seem to ignore that the older brother did have plenty of reasons to be upset—they didn't even come to get him when the party started!

It is important to read the actual words spoken by brother number one. In fact he never said that his younger sibling's return should be ignored or that his homecoming was not a legitimate cause for celebration. The older son simply spoke his mind about his father's lack of celebration of *his* life. Perhaps the events of the day helped identify what had quietly troubled the older brother for years. His underlying message to his father is, "Dad, for years now you have watched me grow, trusted me with the family fortune, and prepared me to rule over this estate. All this, and yet you failed to acknowledge my accomplishments, manhood, and maturity with even a modest celebration. That hurts!"

I find it fascinating that while the older brother had everything money could buy, including houses, lands, servants, and livestock, he was troubled by what he did *not* have—a celebration initiated by his father. Imagine the impact on this family if the story had been written something like this:

> A man had two sons. When his older son came of age, the father decided to hold a special celebration to acknowledge his manhood, clarify his identity, and launch him on the journey to maturity.
>
> While the younger son was still at home, the father ran to him and hugged him. He then called his servants and friends together for a celebration in his son's honor, just as he had done for his elder son several years earlier.
>
> For the celebration, the father had a feast prepared that included all his son's favorite foods. After the dinner he placed

a handsome cloak over this son's shoulders to signify that a new mantle of manhood had arrived. He then placed a special ring of authority on his son's finger.

During the celebration the father shared with his son about the many wonderful opportunities that awaited him in life. Also, he encouraged his son to demonstrate increasing maturity as he waited to receive his full inheritance. Then some of the men in attendance told the young man of their tragic journeys to distant lands that had beckoned them with promises of sexual pleasures, lavish parties, and the lure of unlimited freedom.

They told the young man of the dangers of following this path and how they themselves eventually returned home muddied and bloodied, having to start over again. These wise mentors told the boy of a better path, one that would leave him safe and satisfied. Others told him of the blessings of obedience, patience, and self-control.

The father and his friends then blessed the son with many prayers, gifts, and affirmations of his true identity. After their time of celebration ended, the father and his two sons went about their lives until it was time to celebrate the coming of age of their next generation.

As much as I honor the inspired biblical account about our heavenly Father's compassion for the spiritually lost, I like to envision the story with an earthly father and his two sons played out in the manner above. While the endings seem much the same, the second account eliminates all doubt about the father's love and the devastating effects of waywardness on everyone involved. When we learn to mentor, bless, and celebrate our sons *before* they head off to distant lands, we will all benefit greatly. This is a lesson for every parent whose son is still living at home. Don't wait!

KEEP HOPE ALIVE!

Of course, many parents have sons who have already departed, either physically or emotionally. Often, parents of these wayward ones feel that all they can do is wait passively for their son to reappear. While these seem like the bleakest times, there are several reasons to remain hopeful.

First, your heavenly Father loves your son more than you do. Your son is first and foremost a creation of God, and therefore, despite his waywardness, the young man will always have his heavenly Father's attention.

Second, even if your son has gone to a distant land, you can still reach him with prayer. "Watch and pray" is a much better strategy than "fret and worry." Sooner or later you will see him coming down the road. Don't stop watching, and don't stop praying.

Third, each of us was created with a desire to know who we are, where we are from, and why we are here. No one ever found his true identity in wayward living, and no one ever puts down lasting roots in a pigpen. Eventually, like the younger sibling in the parable, your son will desire to reconnect with his family. When—not if—this happens, don't ask questions. Just run to him, hug him, and plan his celebration.

Remember, the father in the biblical account held the celebration for his son when his boy was still filthy and before there was any proof that he had truly changed. If you wait to hold a celebration for your son until he has his life totally together, you will never hold one. So again, there is no reason to wait.

Without question, a transitional celebration itself is the key to much of your son's future. Perhaps for the first time in his life, he will be honored just for being a man. With his harsh life experiences as a backdrop, a wayward son is able to understand the two basic paths that every man has before him. One path leads toward maturity, responsibility, and lasting satisfaction. The other leads toward further immaturity, irresponsibility, temporary pleasures, and lasting regret. He will appreciate another chance to pursue the proper path.

If you are able to contact your son, then go to him. Attempt to reconcile the differences you may have and begin to rebuild your relationship. Forgive him now for whatever grief or embarrassment he has caused you. Our society has made it easy to divorce our spouses, but thankfully it has not yet figured out a way for us to "divorce" our children. He is still your son! As a father you must remember and accept that God gave your son to you and no amount of family conflict will ever change that. If out-of-sight becomes out-of-mind, your mind is on too many other things that are not nearly as important as your son.

Please don't think I'm being insensitive to the nearly unbearable grief that our sons can bring into our lives with wrong choices. Also, I realize that many brokenhearted parents of wayward sons and daughters have tried unsuccessfully to reach out and reconnect with their children. Their best efforts have been refused by insensitive, selfish children who seem bent on self-destruction. Over the years, I have worked in prisons and with programs for troubled youth and have heard nearly every imaginable horror story about family breakdown. I have held far too many parents in my arms as they wept for their wayward sons. These were not sons who simply ran away from home. Many were sons who cursed, mocked, stole from, shamed, and physically hurt their parents. Often these young men ended up in jails, prisons, or other detention programs, seemingly out of reach. However, I am certain that our heavenly Father is able to touch a son in the darkest place on earth and break through to even the hardest heart. The bond that holds fathers and sons together is never broken to the point where God cannot reconstruct it.

Here is the good news. Just as I have seen the many family tragedies, I have also seen a large number of miracles where seemingly hopeless young men were reconciled to God, family, and their destinies.

As expected, there is a pattern to this process of restoration and reconciliation. Prayer is the foundation, and unconditional love is the motive. You must love your son despite what he has done. This never means that you love his sin but rather that his sin has not caused you to stop loving *him*. Forgiveness is essential. Without it, you will simply remain a ticking time bomb, waiting to explode about your son's past transgressions at the worst possible time.

Finally, you'll need to be patient if you're to avoid countless sleepless nights. Remember the father who watched for his son to come down the road and saw him when he was far off. My guess is the father looked in the daylight and slept at night. Keep the rest of your life moving forward as you patiently wait. Keep watching, praying, and loving. Pour out your love and attention on the family members who remain under your roof. If you have some extra time, then get involved in a men's ministry to youth in your church or community. Your interaction with other families in need will release the compassion in you and bring great comfort to them. Then, when your son does come back, *immediately* make your plans for the celebration that will restart him on his journey to mature manhood.

PRACTICAL SUGGESTIONS

Here are some thoughts and suggestions to help you plan a celebration for a prodigal son.

Recognize How Much Your Son Has Already Changed

Understand that a young man who has lived waywardly for any length of time is quite different now. Sadly, he is not the same little boy he was before. Like Adam after the fall, his eyes may have been opened to things that he was never created to see. His mind may be filled with what was previously unthinkable. Drug abuse, sexual encounters, drunkenness, crime, rejection, and violence all cut deeply into a young man's soul. They may cloud his view of even the most sincere efforts to help him regain his spiritual and relational footing, so remember to be patient.

These changes mean that you may not get the reaction you are looking for when you begin the process of reconnecting with him. The concepts of intentional blessing and rites of passage will be foreign to the young man, and it will naturally take time for him to adjust to them. Remember, mentoring, blessing, and hosting a celebration for the young man is the right thing to do, regardless of his initial reaction.

The wayward son may also reject initial efforts to mentor him, since he has made many of his own decisions up to that point. Words of blessing and affirmation may feel disingenuous to a young man unraveling the chains of guilt and shame. That's all right. Keep blessing him. On the evening of his celebration, a prodigal may look uninterested in the letters and gifts that are brought to him and may lack the social graces to thank the attendees. Again, keep your expectations realistic and your own emotions in check. As time passes, the plan for his maturity will work, and before it is all over, your son will look back fondly on his celebration. The letters and gifts will become treasured keepsakes that God will use to encourage him when no one else is looking.

Avoid a Big Surprise

I would not recommend that you surprise a wayward son with a celebration. My inclination is to let him know well beforehand that you have a gathering planned in his honor so he can adjust to the concept. He will probably think long and hard about it. A surprise may be too much for him to handle emotionally and could make him feel very uncomfortable.

Invite Just the Right Men

When planning a celebration for a wayward son, I would also prayerfully consider whom to invite and, just as important, whom *not* to invite. You do not need a friend or relative using the celebration as an opportunity to "set your boy straight."

Quite frankly, the celebration isn't the time to push hard for your son's conversion to an active life of faith or to drag him back into the mainstream of society. Instead it is a time to demonstrate your love for him and to show that a different way of life exists. It is a time to tell him truths about his own manhood, show that a positive path still lies ahead, and lovingly encourage him that God and you are cheering him on. The celebration is a time to confirm and affirm that he is a man. It is also a time for other men to talk about some of their own mistakes in the past and share how God helped get them back on track. This will help your son overcome the guilt and shame. It will also let him know that his situation is not unique and that he has not gone beyond the point of redemption.

Recall the Good Times

The celebration for a wayward son is also a time to rekindle good memories from the past. I realize that you may have to go back years to remember a time when your relationship consisted of more than shouting matches and slamming doors. However, nearly every family has some special moments from the past that can unlock even the hardest hearts. Perhaps it was a fishing trip or vacation that occurred more than a decade earlier. Or it may be reflections of quiet moments spent together on a couch. The boy's first hit in baseball or his first basket may be a milestone worth revisiting. Your son's particular talents—as a carpenter, artist, or singer, for instance—are positive things to be remembered. An old videotape or photo album of his childhood could be brought out and utilized as points of fond reflection. These mile markers from the past will help him realize that his life has not been all bad; he once knew happier times.

Regardless of what your son has experienced during his time of waywardness, know that God has made sure that some good memories are safely stored inside his mind and will reappear with just a gentle nudge. Your job is to lovingly wake him from the temporary "amnesia" that seems to afflict so many wayward boys. No amount of shouting, threatening, or intimidation has ever helped someone regain his or her footing or sense of true identity. Instead, that is accomplished by love, patience, and a series of gentle reminders of who the person truly is.

Establish Hope

One of the most vital messages for your son to hear is that God is willing and able to create a new beginning for any man who has the courage to ask him for it. No one has gone too far for God to restore. God has promised that nothing will separate his children from his love, and with God all things are possible. You must give your son sufficient hope to overcome the feelings of loss, shame, guilt, and despair that often walk alongside a boy returning home from his time of waywardness.

Make the Format a Good Fit

I'd be careful not to do skits or dramas that could be interpreted as condemning any of your son's previous mistakes. In fact, skits should be designed to focus on the positive aspects of life and the benefits of mature manhood. If some appropriate humor can be added to keep things relaxed, that would be good—as long as it does not trivialize the event.

One of the most important aspects of the celebration, especially for a wayward son, is for you to pray and speak blessings over him. Wayward boys have heard plenty of curses. They need to hear blessings! They need to hear words of hope and a future. You can provide these life-giving words.

Also, your son needs to hear you and the other men in attendance say that he is unconditionally accepted, no matter how wayward he has been. It is vital that you communicate that the God who created him to do great things is always waiting for the slightest sign that the boy is coming home—just like the father in the biblical account.

Keep an Open Mind about the Response

I want to encourage you to prepare for and host your son's celebration without prejudging how he, or you, will respond. Let's start with you. Be prepared for some emotions to be stirred and some tears to flow. If you are angry with your son, then get prayer or counseling before the celebration so that you are able to truly be a blessing to him at this crucial time.

It is difficult to predict how your son will react on the day of his celebration. He may seem upbeat and happy, or he may appear sullen, depressed, or uninterested.

It may seem simplistic to say that every wayward son will respond either very positively or very negatively to his celebration. But remember, these young men have been living a life of extremes. Some of them may become angry because the celebration is showing them what they've been missing. If they feel too "dirty" to accept the unconditional love offered, they may aggressively reject all the attention. Others may think it's too late for their lives to change. For example, the young man who is in a gang may feel that he will put his family in danger if he leaves the gang, so he feels trapped in his destructive lifestyle. Be mentally and emotionally prepared for any of these responses.

It is good to keep in mind that a celebration is simply the door to maturity, not the final destination. Some boys may respond positively to the celebration—perhaps breaking down in tears—but have no idea how to go about changing. They may need many more months or years of your support, mentoring, and blessing before they can fully incorporate the message of the celebration into their lives.

Regardless of the initial emotions your son displays during his celebration, his life will probably move in one of two directions. The first possibility is that he will immediately recognize a better way to live, run to you, and ask for forgiveness, and you will move on with life together. The celebration will be the key to returning him to his family, society, and the path that God has for his life. If that happens, it will be wonderful, and I have no doubt that many families will see this occur.

However, it is also possible that it will take time for your son to pull away from the bad habits of his past. There may not be an instant rekindling of love between father and son either. Please remember that the cycle of sin, guilt, and shame often causes boys to bury their emotions so that no one sees inside them. If this happens, don't despair or accept the lie that your renewed commitment to mentoring and blessing or the celebration itself has somehow failed. You have planted some wonderful seeds that will grow within your son. In time, they will bring forth a harvest of maturity and restored relationships.

Remember, even if some aspects of your son's behavior seem to worsen after the celebration, you still have released the incredible power of a blessing into his life. The celebration will remain an unmistakable sign of your devotion to your son that can never be taken away. God will cause the event to act like a wonderful flower that grows in your son's soul and blooms at just the right time.

Regardless of which immediate reaction you get from your son, you will have done the right thing for the right reason. Following the event, if you must wait a little longer for your son to completely return to his senses, this will make your wait much easier. The only way that a celebration of blessing for your son will fail is if you fail to host one!

14

CELEBRATIONS FOR ALL FAMILY STRUCTURES

NOT EVERY CHILD GROWS UP in a home with both a mother and a father. Divorce, absentee parents, and various forms of abuse are sad realities of the age. Death of parents has been a sad fact in every age.

Concerned sociologists, counselors, and psychologists put forth a steady stream of theories on how to help children grow up in homes where one or both biological parents are absent. While many books have been written on this subject, there is one aspect that has been largely overlooked: the transition of our young people into adulthood.

CELEBRATIONS IN CHAOS?

When divorce or a parent's death occurs during the first ten to fifteen years of marriage, young children or teenagers are often involved.

In the case of divorce, children must deal with divided loyalties and often bitter battles for affection from their parents. Both the mother and father also face new struggles. Each must adjust to changes in his or her finances, responsibilities, and schedules, and at least one of them has to find a new place to live. Their social circumstances change as well. They may begin dating again. Potential new partners appear on the scene and must be factored into family life. As all of this change swirls around single parents, most do their best to make sure that their children have the essentials they need—food, shelter, education, and as much emotional support as the restrictions of the new life will allow. For all involved, life moves rapidly into uncertain new realities.

In the instance of a parent's death, the tumultuous impact on the surviving spouse and children can be much the same. A host of emotions strike everyone involved. Disbelief, anger, fear, anxiety, and depression can, and often do, take up residence in homes where a parent has died. The sudden void upsets family order, finances, and even the accomplishment of simple household chores.

Somewhere in the blur of chaotic change, there is one constant. The children involved are growing, one day at a time, toward their own adulthood. Sadly, this fact is often overlooked, resulting in serious consequences. Granted, single parents dealing with added responsibilities and a heavy weight of grief do their best to watch for signs of trouble in their children. As is true of all homes, these parents obviously do the best they can with overt problems but often mistakenly believe that if their child shows no outward sign of trouble, then he or she is fine on the inside as well. This may be a faulty assumption.

Thankfully, all parents, single and otherwise, can create and implement plans of mentoring, blessing, and rites of passage for the children under their care. When they do, even the most wounded child will have an excellent opportunity to be healed and headed on the path of success.

SINGLE-PARENT CELEBRATIONS

A single parent can be either a mom or a dad. In terms of a celebration, the single dad will have fewer modifications to make in the planning process than a single mother. A single father can essentially follow the same pattern outlined in this book, while the single mother will need to make some modifications as described later in this chapter. Here are some ideas to help with planning a single-parent celebration.

If the single parent instigating the celebration has never talked about the divorce or the death of the other parent with the son, then he or she should do so prior to the celebration.

I must be clear here. If divorce is involved, the purpose of the sharing is not to discredit the other partner or to point out his or her faults.

It is not a time to criticize or scandalize in-laws, lawyers, or other outsiders. Instead, it is time to talk about the pain of divorce and the problems it causes for every member of a family. Remember, whatever we grow up with is "normal." If a boy grows up in a divided home, then for him that is the pattern for a "family." Prior to the celebration, the parent in charge of the celebration should discuss God's lifelong plan for marriage, family, and childrearing so that the son understands that there is an optimal model for healthy families.

Once your son understands God's ideal plan for marriage and how easy it is for us to fall short, it may be appropriate to share some aspects of what went wrong to cause the breakup of his own family. Perhaps later, parent and son can discuss details of what happened, but for now the boy simply needs to know that he does not have to follow the same pattern that more than 50 percent of couples do when it comes to marriage and childrearing. The conversations that happen just before, during, and after the celebration will stick with your son for a lifetime, so choose your words carefully.

If the boy's other parent still has some connection with the family, it is important that he or she be kept informed about the celebration plans for two reasons. First, so that the other parent does not schedule a conflicting event on the same date as your son's rite of passage. Second, and more important, so that he or she has the option of being part of the process.

This is a time for some real humility and personal sacrifice for moms and dads who have gone their separate ways. When a relationship is broken, of course feelings are hurt. Divorce often results in bitterness, resentment, and a "get even" mentality. However, if there was ever a time for a man and a woman to set these negatives aside and work together, it is now. Their son's future is worth far more than either parent's ego and will be greatly influenced by the cooperation, or lack thereof, that he sees during this special time.

THOUGHTS FOR SINGLE MOMS

Single moms can and must oversee rites of passage for their sons. In the past few years, my wife and I have worked with many single mothers as they carefully crafted plans for mentoring and rites of passage for their sons. There is really only one significant difference between a single mom and a single dad when it comes to rites of passage for a son:

mom must not be the one to host her son's celebration. As we will explore, there are many ways in which she can support her son during his time of transition, and she has the huge responsibility of finding the appropriate adult male to assist with her son's rite of passage. The idea of not hosting the celebration herself can be hard for some moms to accept, especially for those who have lovingly served their sons as both father and mother. Many women have sacrificially worked both inside and outside the home just to make ends meet. In many instances mom has provided strength, nurturing, love, and discipline for her son without much help from anyone else. However, despite all of these wonderful acts of love, service, and sacrifice, there is one thing that she can never be: a model of manhood.

It is for this reason that I strongly recommend that single moms resist the temptation to host the celebration themselves. This is a time when a mother must make a transition concerning her son. She must be willing to let go of her boy temporarily and allow him to become a man in the presence of other men. An intrinsic part of moving into manhood is a youth's establishing new relationships with his mother and other women in his life. This is assisted by a rite of passage in which mom steps away from her accustomed role in her son's life, both symbolically and literally, making way for a new one. While this new relationship involves a momentary separation from mom, it will result in a lifetime of respect and admiration for her many acts of kindness and sacrifice on his behalf.

Kathy and I believe that the proper way forward is for a single mother to enlist at least one adult male whom she respects and trusts as the overseer of the celebration. This may be her pastor, priest, male relative, or another appropriate man from her local church, her son's scout group, or another organization. It is important to find a mature, godly man to work with mom on the design of the ceremony and then to serve as the host of the special evening. Ideally, the man selected will be someone known and respected by her son and someone who can have ongoing contact with him both before and after the celebration.

Important Words of Caution

Predictably, I have some warnings here. In order to prevent any tragedies with the celebration, allow me to be straightforward about two issues:

Issue #1: No temporary boyfriends. I need to underscore that the man called upon to host the celebration should not be mom's temporary boyfriend, who may not be around in a few months. It is a fact of life that men and women begin dating again after a divorce or the death of a spouse. Obviously, this complicated process does not go unnoticed by the children.

To be fair, sometimes mom's serious boyfriend (or dad's serious girlfriend) can bring much needed support and stability to the family that has survived an abusive spouse or other tragedy. However, children of divorce often initially view the new people as competition for their parent's affection, as the cause of the divorce itself, or at least as a stumbling block to their parents' reconciliation. In such instances, it would be a huge mistake for a single mom to expect her new boyfriend to successfully host a celebration for her son.

One idea would be for the boyfriend to write a letter to the son and give it to him after the celebration has concluded. This way, if the man becomes a permanent part of the son's life, he will have had a tangential role in the celebration. On the other hand, if the boyfriend eventually departs from the scene, no lasting harm will have been done.

Issue #2: Check on backgrounds. For some single moms there will be one obvious choice to assist with her son's rite of passage. This may be her own father, an uncle, a brother, or her pastor. In cases where there is no obvious choice, she can enlist the help of her relatives, members of her congregation, or her coworkers to search for an adult male to assist with her son's celebration. Hopefully this will result in multiple candidates from which she can choose. However, when she has narrowed down the list of volunteers for the celebration, she must carefully check these men out to determine their motives and their backgrounds.

It is a sad commentary on today's society that some sick men join certain organizations just so that they can get close to young males. Under no circumstances should a mother automatically assume that because someone came forth to volunteer, he is the right man for the job. Check the person's background. Get character references from someone you know well. Ask questions.

Don't worry about offending the man. Be assured that the right man will not have a problem with your efforts to protect your son. If a prospective host does object to your inquisitions, cross him off your list and move on. If for any reason you are not completely convinced that you have found a suitable candidate to host your son's celebration, then simply wait, watch, and pray until the right person comes forth. It is better to delay the event for a few weeks or even months than to open the door to more heartache.

Selecting a Spiritual Man

One of the most vital considerations for deciding which man to select involves the issue of spirituality. In a society filled with so many different ideas about religion, a mom must really understand a prospective host's views on the subject.

Don't assume that someone shares your faith, even if he attends the same church you do. Make sure! This is vital in today's bizarre world where what was once considered lunacy has now become the norm.

Select a man whose approach to spirituality is acceptable to you and in line with your approach to your faith. In other words, make sure that the individual has found answers to his own questions about God before you put him in charge of your son's transitional event. The last thing a boy needs on his special night is for his host to send confusing signals about faith and spirituality.

If the man is not a close family member, a good approach here is for the mother to meet at church or another public place with the prospective host for an initial discussion. If the man was recommended by a friend or relative, then he or she should attend the initial meeting as well. During the meeting, talk about the celebration process and have a frank discussion of what you want to have communicated about spirituality. Again, if you are uncomfortable with the man's approach, continue your search until you find a suitable host. One will become available if you do not give up!

God has blessed men throughout the world with a true father's anointing. These are not men who would schedule your son's special event as if it were just another meeting. Instead the right man will prayerfully prepare for the celebration as if it were one of the most important days of his *own* life. These men will realize that it is an honor to be chosen to help a young person transition into adulthood. When you find a man who understands this truth, sign him up. Not only will he do a complete job of planning and hosting the event, but also he will be the proper man to pray over your son at the conclusion.

Once the right man is located, and when he agrees to accept responsibility for overseeing the event, the mom can then assist him in all phases of the preparation. This will include selecting the right place for the event and providing a list of grandfathers, uncles, brothers, family friends, and other possible attendees, along with their contact information.

As the planning process moves forward, the mother can again meet with the host and give him some background about her son. This includes her son's vision, passion, favorite activities, fears, and greatest challenges in life. Armed with this information, the host can focus on the most important issues and avoid any highly sensitive subjects.

Once the single mom has made a "handoff" to a qualified host, she can prayerfully wait for her son's special day to arrive. During this time she can counsel her son about the changes that are coming and assure him that her love for him will never fade, even after he has become a man.

CELEBRATIONS HOSTED BY GRANDPARENTS

In the past few months, I've had the bittersweet pleasure of helping two grandfathers design unique celebrations for their teenaged grandsons. Each of them did so under heartbreaking circumstances. In the first situation, the boy's father had murdered his mother and was sent to prison for life. In a split second the boy had lost both parents. In the second situation, the boy's father had committed suicide, leaving the boy and his mother to face the challenges of life alone. The grandfathers decided to intervene and create powerful celebrations for their grief-stricken grandsons. In both cases the impact of the celebrations on the boys was profound. According to the grandfathers, it was as if the rites of passage created walls of protection between the boys and the tragedies of their recent pasts.

Today it has become commonplace for grandparents to serve as fathers and mothers for their own grandchildren who come to live with them. In such instances the grandparents mentor, bless, and host rites of passage for the children just as if they were the birth parents.

Concerned grandparents can create and host celebrations for their grandsons by following the steps outlined in this book. They must remember that it is never appropriate to criticize another family member at a celebration. Further, it would be wrong to belittle an absentee or unfit parent in front of the young man. This means that no matter how angry you are at a deadbeat son-in-law or runaway daughter-in-law, you must not vent any of that anger during your grandson's special event. Remember, the focus of the celebration is on his future, not your past.

I am convinced that grandparents are extremely effective hosts for celebrations, even when the parents involved are less-than-ideal role models for the children.

I have seen instances where a boy's parents are still part of his life, but sadly, they don't want to participate in a rite of passage for their child. When that happens, the grandfather can still ask for permission to host the event and, once given permission by the parents, can have a profound impact on his grandson. The dedicated grandfather can use the event to bestow powerful blessings upon his heritage and launch the boy on his journey to mature manhood.

CELEBRATIONS FOR YOUNG MEN
OUTSIDE YOUR FAMILY

In 1999 I hosted a unique celebration for a wonderful young African American man named Brian Pruitt. This rite of passage was unique for two reasons. First, it was held for a nonfamily member; second, the honoree was nearly thirty years old at the time.

I first met Brian when he began to attend my church in the mid-1990s. At the time, we used to invite many of the college-age students to our house for home-cooked meals and informal Bible studies. Over time, Kathy, our children, and I came to view Brian as part of our own family.

Since the day I first met Brian, I had been amazed at all he had going for him. An incredible athlete, Brian played football at Central Michigan University until he graduated in 1994. In his senior year he was the second leading rusher in the nation and was named a first-team all-American. As a result, the young man was on the Bob Hope college football television special and played in numerous college bowl games. The story of his accomplishments made headlines throughout the country. Those were exciting days! However, what the headlines did not tell was that one of Brian's greatest victories was surviving his boyhood on the streets of Saginaw, Michigan, without a father. It was only by God's grace and the loving support of his mother and some coaches that Brian made it through his turbulent childhood and began to excel in athletics.

During his college years, Brian spent many hours at my home playing with my children, eating at our table, and talking with us about his life. During those times I could see that despite all the awards and adulation, something was missing, but I was unsure of exactly what it was. After I held the celebration for my son Christopher, I knew that I had found the missing ingredient. I immediately became burdened with the need to help put back what life without a full-time father had taken from Brian Pruitt.

Soon it became clear what to do. One fall day in 1999 I invited about a dozen men to come to my home to celebrate Brian Pruitt's life and to affirm his manhood. At the time of his celebration, Brian was married to his beautiful wife, Dede, and was serving as a youth pastor in a church in Detroit. My concerns that the celebration concept would somehow not work under these conditions soon disappeared. The celebration was a powerful time that resulted in a tremendous blessing for all of us—especially for Brian.

I am always amazed at the wonderful presence of God that fills the room whenever men gather to celebrate, affirm, and bless another man's identity. Brian's event was no exception. The rest of us assembled in my home prior to Brian's arrival and readied ourselves for the event. Here were twelve men sitting around my family room talking about the weather, the football scores, and many other topics unrelated to the celebration. As soon as Brian arrived, we turned our attention to him and could literally feel a wonderful change in the room. The men got very quiet as someone said an opening prayer. Then, as with my sons' celebrations, some amazing things began to happen.

The first activity was to pass around a piece of paper with Brian's name at the top. We asked the attendees to write down the first two words that came to their minds when they thought about the guest of honor. The paper quickly made the rounds and returned to me. I slowly read the words that captured the essence of this fine young man: "Leader...Friend...Man of God...Integrity...Courageous." By the time I finished reading the last word, tears had begun to flow from our eyes.

Next we read letters that the men had prayerfully composed for Brian. Life lessons, personal victories, and deep heartaches all poured forth with great power. Brian sat very still as he listened to his friends talk about their lives, their families, and their God.

One young man, a pastor's son, was only sixteen at the time of the celebration for Brian. Over the previous few years he had gotten to know Brian through various church activities and youth retreats. It was clear that this young man had watched with admiration as Brian handled all of the pressures of stardom and still maintained his integrity and his faith. The young man was facing slightly away from Brian when it came time to share his letter. As he began to read, the teenager turned to glance at Brian. As soon as their eyes met, the young man burst into tears. His letter dropped to the floor, and through profound tears, he testified of the tremendous respect that he had for Brian. It was an amazing and touching testimony of the impact one man's life can have on another.

We finished our celebration with Brian by praying a blessing over him and sending him home with many gifts and symbols of our love for him. It was a thrill for me to lay my hands on his head and utter the same words to Brian as I did for my naturally born children: "You are my beloved son, in whom I am well pleased." You see, the power of the blessing and celebration transcends race, color, and age. The fact that Brian's skin is black and mine is white is irrelevant in God's kingdom. What matters is that by God's wonderful design, Brian Pruitt became my son, and I became a father to him. He calls me often for advice and for prayer about important matters, just as a son should. What a joy for me as a father to see God add to my family such a wonderful son as Brian.

You probably know young men in your own life who were raised under tough circumstances. Divorce, absentee parents, death, abuse. The list goes on. Whether the path they are currently on seems good or bad, it will get infinitely better when someone takes the initiative to celebrate the seeds of greatness residing within them. The time and effort that it takes are insignificant when compared with the incredible benefits that will be realized when you celebrate the life of another. As you've read this chapter, has anyone come to mind? If so, don't wait. Get planning now!

THE UNIVERSAL CALL

Regardless of your current family structure, it is very likely that there are young people in your life who need mentoring, blessing, and ultimately, a rite of passage. The call to bless and support the next generation goes out to all adults, whether married, divorced, single, or widowed. Those who answer the call will be challenged to find the time, patience, and energy to pour blessing into the young lives around them. They will wonder if their investment will pay off in the long run. I can tell you that I have looked into the eyes of many young men as they sat at their rites of passage surrounded by those who love them. In some of those eyes I saw hope kindled for the very first time. In others I saw the realization dawn that the young man was truly loved and valued. In yet others I witnessed a healthy sense of self-worth take root and begin to grow.

When you choose to take on the task of champion for the next generation, you, too, will look into young eyes and be forever changed. So come on. Regardless of who you are and what state your family is currently in, open your heart and then give it to the next generation.

15

RITES OF PASSAGE IN OUR CHURCHES

TODAY'S WORLD IS FILLED with thousands of differing religious practices. They range all the way from the mundane to the bizarre. Even within the Christian church, there is a wide variety of religious expression and doctrine. One group dances with rattlesnakes to prove their faith while another concludes that a single hand raised in praise is decidedly *un*religious.

With these differing practices in mind, I am glad that the Bible speaks in plain terms about the foundations of true religion. Reading James 1:27 should bring us back to our senses—at least for a moment: "Religion that God our Father accepts as pure and faultless [or undefiled] is this: to look after orphans and widows in their distress and to keep oneself from being polluted by the world." This is an extremely powerful verse, and the idea of looking after orphans has strong implications for the celebration of manhood.

CARING FOR THE FATHERLESS

To better understand James 1:27, we need to investigate the full meaning of the words and phrases that have been translated into modern-day

English. To begin with, in the original Greek language of the New Testament, the phrase "to look after" comes from the word *episkeptomai*. It is used in the active sense and means "to look upon something with mercy and favor; to take care of; to go and visit." Also, the word used for orphan is *orphanos,* meaning "comfortless" and "fatherless."

Now, if you will allow me to put these concepts together and focus on the issue of orphans, the passage could accurately read like this: "Religious practices that God our Father accepts as pure and faultless are these: to look with mercy and favor upon the fatherless children who are currently without comfort. Also, not only to look upon them but to go and visit them and to take care of them as a loving father would."

The implications of this passage for Christian men are staggering. It convicts me of having a mind-set about church and ministry that is completely opposite from God's. How many times have I hurried past the Sunday-school classrooms filled with young people, never once stopping to consider their needs? I was in too much of a hurry to get into the service (think about the word *service* for a moment) so that I could let God know how much I love him. Amazingly, God tells us that if we want to show him that we love him, we are to look after the fatherless.

There are two types of fatherless youth in our churches today. The first literally have no father in the home. Dad has either died or departed. The other category of fatherless children have a male who lives under the same roof but either abuses or neglects his children.

In recent years many different groups have established programs to help meet the needs of the fatherless. Government agencies, public schools, and privately funded organizations have done what they could to touch our troubled youth. Many churches have also made youth services a vital part of their ministries. These innovative churches often have bus or van ministries that send vehicles into their communities to pick up young people who otherwise would not be able to attend services. After the service (there is that word again!) is over, the youth are driven home, back to the same environment they left a few hours before. A week later, the cycle repeats itself.

These few hours each week give these "orphans" hope that there are people who care about them and that life has a few ups to accompany the downs. The church is the ideal place for these young people not only to receive spiritual instruction but also to find surrogate fathers to celebrate them into manhood.

God himself has put together the church to do more than sing hymns and build buildings. Within each local church exists both parts of the equation needed to rebuild an entire community, nation, and world. In one room sit hungry, hurting youth, waiting for someone to show them the way forward. In another room sit older men who are successfully making their way through the minefield of life. The young males want to be mentored, blessed, and celebrated. These older men want God to use them but are unsure what to do. The elders may or may not have official church titles, such as pastor or deacon; however, they are specially equipped to serve the young people who are so dear to God's heart.

IT'S A MATTER OF SERVICE

I've asked you to think about the word *service.* The point is this: I strongly suggest that each church revisit its mission and honestly evaluate its effectiveness in serving its youth. It may be time to try something radically different. What would happen if all the adult males in a congregation decided to band together to bless and mentor all the fatherless children in their congregation? Then, what if those same men chose to take responsibility for an entire neighborhood? What if church leaders set aside programs of all sorts and focused on religious practices that God himself declared to be pure and faultless? What if...? In reality, this could easily be accomplished. It is a relatively simple matter of aligning a church's vision with one of God's clearly stated purposes and then connecting hurting youth with loving father figures to care for, look after, and comfort them. Pure and faultless.

I believe that each church should implement a mentoring-relationship program among its men and the young people it serves. The program can be as simple as assigning each interested man one or two young people whom he greets and prays for each week. It could then progress into a mentoring relationship in which the young man is invited to participate in some of his mentor's family events. Over time, trusting relationships between the men and the young people will develop. As these youth come of age, a celebration can be planned for each of them and implemented at the church or at the mentor's home.

The impact on the young people, the mentor, the church, and society will be life-changing.

Obviously, every attempt should be made to involve the young person's natural family members if they are willing. Another great door of ministry, to the boy's family, will open up as his mentor calls or visits the boy's home. Chances are good that those at home have never experienced someone showing unconditional love and concern for them. Their initial reaction may be one of skepticism, but given enough time, such attitudes will turn to gratitude.

The men of the church can help one another host celebrations for their young protégés by following the guidelines in this book. In time, some of the same young men who were initially mentored will take their places as mentors to the next generation of "orphans."

I realize that some pastors, especially youth pastors, may read about this concept with some frustration. They often don't have enough men in their congregations to go around, or sadly, the men who are available simply won't commit to this type of service. If this is the case, there are still some powerful ways to bless the young people in the church.

Ideally the pastor will hold a celebration for each fatherless youth who attends his church. This does involve a lot of work, but what other investment offers a better return than time and energy poured into the lives of our young people? If the boy's mother or guardian is open to the idea, the pastor can make all the necessary arrangements to host the event right at the church. He can then invite members of the staff to attend, along with a few other men from the congregation, and help the event succeed.

If a lot of young people attend the church, or if time is a limiting factor, the pastor could host a celebration for more than one young man simultaneously. The main components of the celebration will still be very similar to the one described in this book. Perhaps the primary difference is that adult attendees would need to bring multiple letters and gifts. Done in this manner, the celebration may take a bit longer to complete, but it will still be time well spent. An additional benefit of this approach is that some deep bonding will take place among the honorees as they enter into manhood together.

With all of the possible variations, there are many ways to put a celebration together. Recently I was invited to help design and participate in an interesting church-sponsored celebration. An internationally known evangelist came to minister in our area and brought his family with him. For years this man had dedicated his life to missionary out- reaches in third-world countries. My private conversation with him revealed that he was often torn between the needs of his family and the demands of his ministry. As he shared from his heart, he told of his great love for his teenage son, who often accompanied him on his trips abroad. His son was going to turn sixteen during the week that he was in our area, and the man knew that he needed to do something special for him. He just wasn't sure what it should be.

When a friend and I shared the celebration concept with him, the evangelist was overjoyed. The challenge was that he and his son would be in town only a few more days. After a mad scramble of phone calls, room reservations, skit creation, and invitations to prospective male attendees, we had the basics pulled together.

Two nights later twelve men were assembled in the downstairs fel- lowship hall of the church, waiting for the evangelist to finish his min- istry in the sanctuary. At about nine o'clock he led his son downstairs under the guise of getting some refreshments. The young man's eyes grew wide when he saw the men assembled and learned that the cele- bration was in his honor. After an opening prayer, we presented several skits about integrity, manhood, and the need for a man to leave behind childish things as he pursues maturity. Some of the skits were very solemn and others were hilarious. All the skits were well received by the young man and his father, who sat through most of the event with the most wonderful look of joy on his face.

We closed the celebration with a time of prayer for the son and then spent nearly an hour having refreshments and talking about the need for men throughout the world to bless our priceless young people. The following day we put the two men on a plane to Zimbabwe to carry on with God's design for their lives.

TIME FOR A PRIORITY CHECK?

In light of the crisis we face with our young people today, I want to encourage each pastor, youth leader, and member of a men's ministry to reevaluate their priorities. Please take time to think through your mis- sion and goals for the coming years.

For you pastors, youth pastors, and men's ministry leaders whose hearts are broken for the youth, please don't be offended by my challenging questions here. I applaud you, pray for you, and cheer you on. So that you understand I am not painting all ministers with the same brush, let me explain that the goal of this chapter is twofold. First, I want to equip those dedicated servants who have been seeking concrete ways with which to bless the young men and women under their care. Second, I hope to wake those ministers who are asleep or are caught up in activities that are insignificant in light of the plight of our youth. With that, allow me to respectfully ask a couple of questions.

Pastors, are you preoccupied with plans to build buildings and increase your church membership? Those are not bad things by any means; however, they are not what is closest to the Father's heart.

Youth pastors, are your thoughts consumed by ways to attract more "kids" to your services—and once you get them there, to figure out how to compete with secular entertainment to hold them there? Again, these are not bad things to consider. But the reality is, you can never outdo the world's glitz and glitter, so why try? You have something so much more meaningful to offer in mentoring, blessing, and rites of passage.

Men involved in men's ministries, are you going to spend another year trying to get your own lives more together? Of course we all need to strive to be more Christlike. But if you wait until you have perfected your walk of faith before you move into mentoring, you will have allowed countless youths to fall by the wayside.

We all need to awaken to the fact that we have a sacred responsibility to accomplish all that God has for us to do. Yes, we should build new buildings when they are needed. Yes, we should find innovative ways to attract new people to our services. Yes, we should continue to get rid of our own bad habits. However, if our pursuit of these activities leaves us without time, energy, or other resources to invest in our young people, then our priorities are out of balance. Men serving in any of these capacities may need to reprioritize and redirect their efforts to where they will do the most good for the kingdom of God. This means that we must add "looking after the fatherless young people" to the top of our list. Otherwise we may drift into self-centered activities that only give the illusion of progress but miss the will of God by a mile.

To illustrate, I am reminded of the evangelist who was asked about the success of his previous evening's crusade. When questioned about the number of converts, the evangelist mysteriously replied that two and a *half* people were converted to the faith. His answer momentarily shocked his listener. Regaining his composure, the inquirer then nodded his head knowingly, smiled, and gave his interpretation of the riddle.

"Oh, I get it," said the man. "You mean that you had two adults and one child come to the Lord. Hey, that's great! Why just last week we had…"

The evangelist raised his palm and shocked the listener again.

"No, you don't get it," he said quietly. "Last night there were two children and one adult responding to the call. I consider the adult as a half because he has only half his life to live for the Lord. In contrast I count each young person as a whole; they have their whole lives before them for serving God and others."

Of course God can do amazing things in and through us no matter what age we are; he is always seeking us and loving us. Yet if there was ever a time to prepare and release this next generation, it is now. This generation will soon be the leaders of this world. They will make the laws. They will decide what is right and what is wrong. They will accept or reject God's ways in their homes, communities, and nations. The world is ready to be changed by their ideas, vitality, and faith. Our churches are filled with countless young people with their whole lives to give. The question is, what will your church do to make the young people's lives whole?

16

HEALING
A FATHER'S
HEART

🌿 I AM SO THANKFUL that you have gotten this far in the book. Your presence here means that your heart is turning to the next generation and you are beginning to walk in the promise of Malachi 4:6. In order to help you succeed, we need to look into something that few of us want to examine: our own hearts. Together, let's take some time to explore the conditions of our hearts and allow God to bring healing where it is needed.

I am convinced that every man has been wounded in this life and every man's heart has been broken at one point or another. Each of us, in our own way, copes with the pain and moves on to the best of our ability. Generally we are doing well enough to get by. That would be the end of the story—except for one simple fact: we men are responsible for leading the next generation of young people into the fulfillment of their own destinies.

At times our own wounds limit our effectiveness in mentoring and blessing our sons and daughters. Left to fester, these wounds caused by rejection, abuse, abandonment, and fear cloud our judgment about who we are and why we are here. They also cause us to withdraw, lash out, criticize, and even reject the precious young ones God has given us to protect. When we acknowledge our pain and allow God to heal us, then the hearts that we turn toward our children will be pure, whole, and full of love for them. This will take courage to accomplish.

In addition, we must become transparent with each other in order to be healed. This may sound a bit scary, but I promise you that it is worth the risk. Let's do it together.

THE WOUNDED WARRIOR

Barely alive, the soldier was dragged into the makeshift hospital and laid on a faded green stretcher. His hair, graying at the temples, was matted with blood. His painful attempts to draw life-giving air into his lungs filled the room with a rasping sound.

Half-healed scars crisscrossed his chest bearing silent witness to the soldier's many battles. The enemy always aimed for the heart.

Sounds of the fighting nearby shattered the relative quiet of the sanctuary. The incessant bombardment caused the soldier to close his tired eyes and wish for peace. However, he knew that his fight was far from over—only the dead were excused from battle. All others were patched up and sent back to the front lines to slow the onslaught of the enemy.

He slowly raised himself up to look at his companions strewn around the hospital. Some were white, some black; others had brown, red, or yellow skin. Some were in their seventies and others were barely eighteen. All were in great pain, but few even uttered a sound, choosing instead to suffer in silence.

Sounds of surgeons at work soon mixed with his quiet meditations on the war. Healing hands cleaned, stitched, and soothed his broken body and damaged soul. In a dark vision, the soldier replayed parts of his past. Mistakes made. Harsh words from his superiors. Abandonment by those closest to him. The leering face of the enemy closing in for the kill. Fear—always fear.

Mercifully, sleep came and brought rest to his troubled mind. Then all too soon he heard a familiar voice. The voice of his commander. Immediately, the soldier struggled to rise from his creaking cot.

"Soldier?"

The voice was a mixture of compassion and urgency.

"Soldier, can you stand?"

"Yes, sir," the wounded warrior painfully replied.

"Soldier, things are not going too well up at the front. We have lost many good men, and I need you to get back to the fight. Can you do it?"

"Well, sir, I am pretty beat up and could use some rest," the seasoned soldier responded. "It's my heart, sir. I've been wounded pretty bad and could use some time to heal."

"I understand, soldier," the commander said quietly, "but we have a group of new recruits that just arrived. Without your leadership many of them are going to die. You have been up there, and you know what it is like. Without you, I have to send them up to face the enemy alone."

The commander's words hit with the power of a hollow point. *Alone.* The veteran remembered what it was like to be alone. No one had been there for him during those first fierce battles. Many of his companions had been killed or maimed within weeks of being on their own. More than one had taken his final breath cradled in the arms of this broken warrior. Their names were lost to him, but he could never forget the anguished looks on the faces of the young as they slipped into eternity

"Now," continued the commander, "with your wounds, no one would blame you if you had enough...but I—no—*they* need you, soldier."

Without another word, the hero slowly, painfully, pulled on his uniform, now clean and pressed, and struggled toward the door. The young recruits outside snapped to attention when he first appeared. Their eyes filled with amazement at the sight of the veteran. They could not see his scars, now hidden from view, nor could they feel his pain. Instead they simply drew comfort from one simple fact: he had been there before.

Stepping into the sunlight of a new day, he stretched his hands toward the heavens and noticed that his pain was subsiding; his wounds were healing. The loving doctors and nurses had worked their wonders once again. Now alert, the veteran surveyed the new troops and quickly concluded that they were of good stock. *Potential*, he thought. *A lot of potential. With a little training and encouragement, they will do well in battle.*

He then turned his face toward the fight and gave the orders the young ones had waited all their lives to hear.

"All right," he said, "follow me."

Do you recognize the soldier? He looks a lot like you and me. This unlikely hero is just an ordinary man born into ordinary circumstances. Consider his condition. Does it sound familiar? A wounded heart. Deep scars that others may not even see. Memories of betrayal and abandonment. The pressure of endless responsibilities. Fear. To some degree, all men have been scarred by these afflictions. Some are well on their way to wholeness, and others have just begun the healing process. Amazingly, still others deny that they carry any pain from the past. Deep in denial, these men limp their way through life's race, wondering why they can never quite catch up.

While the natural tendency for anyone in pain is to want to stop and rest, we fathers cannot afford to be absent without leave just as the next generation takes the field. Only the dead are excused from battle. Therein lies the paradox and one of our greatest challenges as men. We need healing ourselves, but if we wait until we are completely whole, then we lose the opportunity to lead countless young people into their destinies.

The solution is simple but certainly not easy: we must do both simultaneously. We must begin the healing process for ourselves and, at the same time, provide leadership, support, and loving guidance for the new recruits coming behind us. It can be done. It must be done.

MAN'S UNIVERSAL BATTLE

Virtually every man has been wounded during life's incessant battles. Some wounds came early in childhood. Harsh words and criticism from a parent. Rejection from classmates. Disappointments from a thousand possible origins. High school is another prime time for painful wounds and scars. Often this is the time when young people first fall in love, only to be rejected by the object of their affection. The pecking order is established whereby the biggest and strongest students often dominate others, doing damage to the fragile psyches of teenagers. Peer pressure causes young people to do things that they later regret. Illegal drug use, alcohol abuse, and loss of virginity often happen during this turbulent time.

Other wounds happen later in life but cut just as deeply. Disappointments in college. The breakup of a marriage. The loss of a child.

The death of a parent. Abuse from a superior at work. For some the deepest cuts from life are received at age forty, fifty, or beyond, when the reality of what was hoped for is eclipsed by what life truly has become.

At times we can even believe that God himself has wounded us. I felt this very deeply when my beloved grandfather died many years ago. For nearly two decades I was angry at God, thinking that he had some-how taken my hero away from me. I now realize that God did not cause my grandfather's death but instead his love sustained me through that dark time and will continue to undergird me all the days of my life. However, despite the fact that God is love personified, many of us still mistakenly believe that God has somehow let us down. When this occurs, we often do the worst possible thing: we run away from God instead of running *to* him.

Our responses to all this pain are widely varied. Some actually seem to continue to function well, despite the pain. Others sink into dis-couragement and depression. Many drown their sorrows in a variety of substances that numb the mind and suppress the soul. Still others look for ways to disengage from the responsibilities of life, hiding behind desks, computers, or blaring televisions sets. They often try to dull the pain by working long hours, as if a promotion or more money will somehow heal their damaged hearts. Still others, like vicious dogs abused by cruel owners, lash out at those closest to them, becoming abusive to spouses and children alike. Sadly, for some the pain is so great that they do the unthinkable and abandon their homes. This begins a new cycle of wounds that bleed the vitality from the next generation.

Clearly, there is no shortage of pain carried by the men of the past few generations. What has been in short supply are answers on how to deal with it. We can blame others for our hurts, or we can ignore them and hope things get better. Either of these two options will cause us and those around us to suffer needlessly for years. A better option is to acknowledge that some pain has been inflicted and then find ways to be healed.

THE CHALLENGE

Unfortunately—or perhaps by divine design—a man must face the demons that plague him before he can successfully serve the next gen-eration. Is this overstated? Hardly. If I fail to deal with my own issues of pain, rejection, abuse, and abandonment, I then struggle to help the

next generation with theirs. If I fail to find my own God-given identity, then I will likely force my sons and daughters into a distorted
sense of identity for themselves.

The Bible makes it clear that we all were made in *God's* own image.
Therefore, we should strive to help our children become godlier in their
actions, motives, and character. However, when our *own* self-image is
faulty or damaged, we tend to push our sons and daughters, consciously
or unconsciously, into our image of what they should look and act like.

A classic example of this is repeated countless times each day when
men tell their sons who are crying over some physical or emotional
hurt, "big boys don't cry." Now, no parent wants his or her son to be
labeled by his peers as a crybaby or sissy, and therefore every young
male benefits from teaching on how to handle physical pain, disappointments, and emotional wounds. *However,* the motivation for a man's
comments to his weeping son may come more from the man's own discomfort and wounds from his own past than out of concern for his son's
development.

I am convinced that when we men wrestle with feelings of weakness or fear, we become hypersensitive to any signs of "weakness" in our
sons. We think that an absence of tears is somehow an indicator of
strength in our young men. However, we must ask ourselves how that
view lines up with the truth that man (and the sons of man) is made in
God's image. The shortest verse in the Bible makes it quite clear. In
John 11:35 Jesus was surrounded by friends grieving over the loss of
their brother and friend. In response, Jesus did a very manly thing—he
wept. Filled with compassion, he cried because he felt the pain of his
friends. His tears were not a sign of emotional instability or weakness.
On the contrary, they were a sign of wholeness for a man of God.
According to the Bible, big boys *do* cry and lose nothing of their manhood when they do so. We must remember that our children were created in *God's image,* not ours, and certainly not in the distorted image
of our society. Unless we are willing to be healed of our own wounds,
we will likely push our own sons into an ungodly image of manhood.
If Jesus is *our* role model, then he must also be the model for our sons.

THE EMOTIONAL LIMP

When our bodies are injured, our brains react instantly to minimize the
pain and prevent additional trauma. Unfortunately I have had numerous

opportunities in my life to test this. My athletic career was laced with various injuries, including torn muscles in my shoulder, broken ribs, and countless sprains. My left ankle was most susceptible to sprains over the years. Each time it was injured, the process of healing and restoration was the same. First I had to realize and acknowledge that I was injured. The intense pain made that part simple. Next came complete rest for the ankle in order to begin the healing process. This generally meant lying on the couch with the foot elevated for several days. Once I was finally able to put some weight on the ankle, out would come the crutches and I would use them instead of putting my weight on the ankle. Finally the crutches were laid aside, and I began to "walk" again. Those first few steps were always uncertain and scary. Pain has a way of staying with us. However, I realized that eventually I would need to walk so that I could then run, so that I could then get back into the game. Therefore, when faced with the option of staying on the couch, I pushed past the pain and did my best to walk once again. The "walk" after the injury was always slow and accompanied by a noticeable limp. There was just too much pain for me to walk without favoring the ankle. Eventually the injury was healed, and I was completely whole once more.

It is much the same with emotional pain in our lives. Whatever the cause, it always results in an emotional limp that stays with us until we are healed. For example, men with broken hearts often withdraw from life or become calloused so that they can avoid additional pain. These are both forms of emotional limps. A man who has known a great deal of rejection no longer cares to venture out into the world, where he may face more rejection. People who have been criticized all their lives learn that the best way to avoid more wounds is simply to limp along without trying anything new. Life lived this way soon loses the vibrant colors created by God and devolves into a sullen rainy gray. We know that the game is still going on around us, but we are afraid to jump back in. The risk of more pain is just too great until we are healed.

An emotional limp remains even if we have an appearance of success in a variety of areas. Big house. Good job. High-visibility ministry. Busy times two. Are these all signs of health and wellness in a man? Perhaps. However, what others often fail to see are the wounds that we carry—and hide—just under the surface. The busyness, the fast pace, the endless activities may actually be symptoms of a man's limp. For too many men, they are just different ways to hide, and hide from, their own wounds. Remember, without healing a wounded man limps forever.

There are some easy-to-spot signs of wounds in men if you know where to look. For example, wounded men often wrestle with decision making—too risky. Wounded men fight against showing too much affection—sign of weakness. When wounded, we struggle to say simple things like "I love you" to those closest to us—might be rejected. I am convinced that much of our anger, discouragement, rage, depression, anxiety, and fear is rooted in past wounds rather than in current challenges. Those of us who choose to stay in the fight may appear to be strong, but the reality is, unless we have sought healing for the wounds of the past, an emotional limp always slows our progress or shows up when we least expect it.

To be sure, the wounds received in life do much more than just impede our forward motion. They change our very self-image. Words of undue criticism, condemnation, failure, and shame all distort the way in which we see ourselves. This is even true of born-again believers. Over the years I have encountered countless people of faith who wrestled with self-image, self-worth, and self-esteem. Despite all that God says about their being new creations, these troubled souls still hear the haunting voices of fathers, mothers, and others declaring them to be worthless, wounded, and weak. Words from long ago have turned into slowly festering wounds that are evident to all but themselves.

Is this an exaggeration? Could there be that much power in just a few careless words? Without question. I remember an instance where my own self-image was markedly changed by just a few words from my father. It happened at age nine on a Saturday afternoon in our backyard. My dad had bought a secondhand set of barbells, and they had drawn a crowd of neighborhood kids. Naturally, each boy tried his hardest to outlift all the others. One boy had sneaked his mother's tape measure out of his house, and each boy took a turn measuring his arms, legs, and any other muscle that he thought would impress his peers. Since I was the youngest in the group, I sat with my dad until it was finally my turn to try to lift the bar, which, of course, I could not. After a vain attempt, I walked back to my father and took my turn wrapping that accursed measuring tape around parts of my undeveloped body. After doing my best to measure up to the older boys, I shared an observation with my dad.

"Hey, Dad," I said innocently. "My forearm is the same size as my upper arm—"

Without much thought, my dad replied, "That's too bad. Your biceps are supposed to be bigger."

Unfortunately the rest of the Schwarzenegger hopefuls were standing close by and heard our brief exchange. Much laughter followed at my expense, but I barely heard it. You see, my mind was working overtime to process this new revelation. At such a young age, I was shocked to learn that I was not built the way I should be. Something was wrong. I was deficient, less than the others. What else could I conclude? After all, my dad had said it, and for a nine-year-old boy, that was the final word.

For years after that summer day, I continued to see myself as skinny and comparatively weak. Even though I grew to be well over six feet tall and one hundred eighty pounds in high school, I still struggled with my physical status as a man. As I look back, I can see that this same concern followed me for years beyond high school and was the catalyst for numerous decisions that I made, all aimed at proving that I did measure up. College basketball, semiprofessional football, and other violent activities all were ways to prove to myself that I wasn't weak and that I was as good as, strong as, and tough as any other man.

It is almost laughable when I consider that at age thirty, I chose to play semiprofessional football. At a time when I should have been focused on faith, family, work, and ministry, I was running around with a bunch of other guys, all of us trying our best to knock someone else down in order to lift ourselves up.

To be fair, a number of good things came from that experience, such as camaraderie, lessons in advanced teamwork, and the thrill of winning championships. And I hope that I never lose my desire to compete and to be very good at whatever I do. However, I do regret the fact that my motivation was so skewed and that the experience did nothing to change my perceptions of who I was. Here is what I mean.

During one playoff game, I heard the then-satisfying sounds of another player's ribs breaking as I hit him. Standing over the fallen man who was writhing in pain on the ground, I scarcely noticed my excited teammates celebrating my macabre accomplishment. In their eyes, I was tough, mean, and someone to be respected or, in the extreme, feared. I remember walking into the locker room after the game, taking off my pads, and heading to the showers. As I passed the locker-room mirror, I perceived that I was still somewhat weak and secretly wished that I could add a little more weight. The odd thing about that scenario is this: at the time I was six feet four and weighed two hundred thirty pounds.

It was many years later, while I was in prayer, that God gently took me back to that day in the backyard, when a few careless words seared my thinking about myself as a man. God then showed me the root of the wounds that had so distorted my view of myself and brought healing to that once troubled area of my life. As soon as I understood what had happened, I was able to forgive my dad for his words, ask God for a proper self-image, and move forward.

SITUATIONS THAT WOUND

At times we can be wounded by situations that were not anyone's fault but which we were simply not prepared to handle properly. I recall a time when I attended a Cub Scout function held at the annual county fair in our community. My group of scouts went there to participate in a model-car race called the Pine Wood Derby. For this event, fathers and sons assembled small wooden cars and then raced them on a twenty-foot track. This was pretty exciting stuff for a bunch of elementary-school kids.

On the day of the race, my family and I packed up the car and drove across town to the fair. Once there, we had to walk through all the mayhem associated with a county fair to get to the small building that housed the race. Blaring music, whirling rides, noisy barkers trying to entice passersby to play their games, and the smells of livestock waiting to be judged all combined for a sensory overload. Especially for a youngster struggling to keep up with his parents as we moved through the crowds. We finally arrived at our destination and proceeded to enjoy the friendly competition with other fathers and sons. When our time to race came, my dad and I put our car on the track and then watched it fly down to the finish. I do not recall if we won that day, but it was great just to be part of the race.

After our turn was over, my folks said that they needed to run a couple of errands and told me to wait in the building for their return. This seemed all right to me at the time, since I knew some of the other fathers and, in my estimation, "a couple of errands" could not possibly take more than ten or fifteen minutes. So I watched my parents walk away into the noisy crowd and then went back to observe the remaining races. For a while it was fun and kind of exciting to be there by myself. The first ten or fifteen minutes went by smoothly.

Then, as fifteen minutes turned into thirty, some things began to change. The other men and their sons from my scout group finished with their races and began to leave the building. As scheduled, other people then came in to use the track, and at some point I realized that I was completely alone among strangers. I want to be clear that these men and their sons were harmless and I was never in any actual danger. However, to a small boy it felt as if I had been completely abandoned. It also seemed as if I had no options. There was no way I could navigate through the madness of the midway, and I was miserable where I was. At that point, I found a metal folding chair near the door, sat down, and closed my eyes, hoping my parents would return before I completely lost what little composure I had left. Exactly how long I sat there is lost to me now. Perhaps an hour or just a bit more. When my mom and dad finally came back, I burst into tears and sobbed uncontrollably for a long time.

Looking back, I imagine that they were shocked at my outburst. After all, they had done what they had promised—run a couple of errands and returned. While it would take smarter men than I to sort it all out, I only know one thing: as a very young boy, I believed that I had been abandoned. The result was fear, anxiety, and an unwillingness to be separated from the comforts of the familiar. Did I ever get over it? Sure—sort of. You see, as I stated earlier, I am convinced that situations like that cause wounds in our hearts. The resulting injury causes us to limp through life and make decisions that protect ourselves from further pain. Upon reflection I can see that it took me a long while before I wanted to be separated from my parents in any sort of crowded place. Even years later, when I traveled the world as an international business consultant, I occasionally had to fight a subtle fear of being alone in faraway places. While I cannot prove it, I believe that I was feeling some residual impact from the unintentional wounds that I received as a small child. The pattern for healing this wound was easy to follow. Share the situation with trusted friends, take it to God in prayer, forgive my folks for their unintentional error, move on. It is amazing how it works.

HEALING: A WAY OF LIFE

Once I began to realize that my current attitudes, actions, and words were influenced, at least to some degree, by things that happened in my past, I became much more reflective. This was especially true when I acted in a way that was contrary to my core values. For example, if I was unkind to my wife, impatient with my children, anxious or fearful about an upcoming event, or unforgiving toward another person who had wronged me, I would take time to look back in my past to see if I could find some underlying cause. As with all men, I had no shortage of wounds caused by others. Over the years I have discovered wounds that came from various people, including, for example, childhood friends who one day became enemies, fickle high-school girlfriends who left for greener pastures, self-serving athletic coaches who played one teammate against another. I also found that some wounds came when I realized that life is often simply not "fair." Loved ones you thought would live forever suddenly died. Pets ran away. People stole items that belonged to you. Summer vacations were canceled because your dad had to work. The list goes on.

I want to underscore that the reason for reflecting upon the past is not so that you have someone to blame for your current misery. Nor is it so that you can justify living your life in the gutter or sooth your conscience if you are knowingly doing something wrong. Instead, there are two primary reasons for looking back to discover the cause of your wounds. First, you should look back to help understand your reactions to life's challenges today. Anger, jealousy, fear, pride, and other negative emotions had to originate somewhere. Once you know their sources, it is much easier to deal with them. Second, you should look back so you can better understand those who hurt you and then forgive them so you can be healed. Once you begin the healing process, you are then free to lead the next generation with a purer heart and a clearer conscience.

THERE ARE NO PERFECT PARENTS

It is important to understand that often the people who hurt us had no clue that their words or deeds did us any harm. My father never meant to cause me any grief with his backyard comments. He just said what came to his mind at the time and never gave it another thought. Likewise, my parents had no idea that leaving me alone for an hour at the county fair would damage my soul in any way. They had things to do and simply misjudged the time it would take to get them done. (For the record, my folks are still alive and we get along just fine.)

In reality, there are no perfect parents, nor are there perfect siblings, or in-laws, or teachers, or coaches, or pastors, or girlfriends, or friends. They—no, *we*—are all capable of wounding those around us, intentionally or unintentionally. As a grown man, I find this truth easy to accept. However, it can be extremely difficult for children to comprehend that dad or mom is flawed in any way. Parents appear much like God to small children. After all, dad and mom provide children with shelter, clothing, food, comfort, and protection from day one. Children cry and we hold them. They get hungry and we feed them. They make a mess and we clean it up, and so on. Imagine the shock when we first learn that our father or mother is less than perfect. It really rocks a young person's world. For many, whatever dad or mom said was absolutely true and irrefutable. In the eyes of a child, mom and dad know all. Therein lies the problem for some men whose parents' words were used to wound, embarrass, or reject them. In these all too common situations, it takes the work of God and the support of trusted friends to bind up the wounds that have occurred.

At some point we must all accept the fact that we were raised by mere mortals who did their best but often fell short of the goal. Once this truth is internalized, forgiveness can be extended, healing can come, and we can live life at a much higher level.

Even those of us who study this subject drop the ball at times. Here is a sad example of one parent's words and the wounds they caused—in my own family.

When he was eleven, my youngest son, Daniel, had an aversion to certain bugs. We live in the country, where there is no shortage of bees, wasps, and hornets, so I assumed that it was a childhood sting that caused my son's fears. At one point I asked him to explain why he was so troubled by these winged tormentors and was surprised at what he said. Daniel quietly told me about one hot summer day when we were all out at the back pond getting ready for a swim. As a joke, one of his older brothers had sneaked up behind Dan and placed a large bug on his back. The insect, trying to avoid falling, did what bugs do. He dug into Dan's skin and held on. My young son recounted how his siblings laughed at his anxious attempts to be rid of the bug and how frustrated—and scared—Dan had become.

As he told the story, I found myself getting angry at my older boys for playing that sort of trick on Daniel. I mentally prepared to give them a lecture once we got together again to straighten them out. To think that my sons were capable of that type of insensitivity really bothered me. Why had they not considered the consequences of their actions? Had they not realized the damage their behavior could have done to such a young boy's psyche?

I was preoccupied with building my case against the heartlessness of my older sons when I suddenly realized that Daniel was still telling his story. He had more to say about the situation that had left a wound in his tender heart that day. After he told of his frantic attempts to dislodge the bug and the laughter from his brothers, Danny finished the story with words that I will never forget.

"And, Dad, when all that was going on," he said quietly, "you just stood there."

When my son said that, I was shocked, crushed, and deeply saddened. After all, I would gladly give my life for him, and yet I had stood idly by instead of coming to his rescue when he needed me the most. I immediately asked Daniel to forgive me and continue to pray that God will heal the wound I unknowingly caused my precious son one hot summer day.

There are no perfect parents. It is easy to wound those entrusted to our care without even knowing that we did so. My dad did it to me, and I did it to my own son. Okay. That's my confession. Now it is your turn. Who wounded you? And how has the wound caused you to limp? Are you ready to be healed? If so, stick with me. God is up to something here.

HEALING A FATHER'S HEART

Thankfully, for those of us willing to acknowledge that we have been wounded, there is some very good news. God is able to bring healing to each of us, regardless of who or what has wounded us. Let me repeat that for you personally. *God is willing and able to heal and restore you!*

The process for this healing is simple and can begin immediately. It can be summed up in this short phrase: *Look in, look back, look forward, and look up.* By this I mean that in order to be healed, we must first *look inside* to see where we have been wounded. Next we must *look back* to identify where the wounds came from. Then we *look forward* to envision a life free from bitterness and full of compassion, especially for the next generation. Finally we *look up* to God, offer forgiveness to those who have wounded us, and move on with our lives. Here is some more detail on how the process works.

Look In

We must acknowledge that we all carry some pain from the past. The key is to take time to do an inventory of your life and then honestly identify areas where the painful words and deeds of other people have wounded you. If you are not sure about the exact nature of your wounds, I suggest that you simply look for your limp. In other words, where are you trying to unduly protect yourself? What issues are you overly sensitive about? How do you see yourself? Are you afraid to make mistakes? Are you anxious, fearful, and discouraged? Do you work too much? Can you show affection to those around you? Can you tell your family that you love them? Do you have any problem praying to God? These questions can help you identify your wounds.

Look Back

Next we look for the origins of our wounds. It is especially helpful to recall the kind of home environment in which you were raised. Did your parents or other adults focus on strengthening your sense of a healthy identity? Was your life filled with mentoring, words of blessing, healing touch, and a rite-of-passage celebration? If it was, you are in a tiny minority and are very fortunate indeed. For most people raised during the past few generations, life was a wild mix of good, bad, and ugly, so know that you are not alone.

Now, here are some more questions to help you look back. Who or what were you afraid of while growing up? What memories haunt you? What makes you mad? Are you oversensitive about anything? Are there people in your life, past or present, whom you find it hard to forgive?

Are you still trying to prove anything to anybody? If in doubt about any of these questions, you can simply pray and ask God to show you things that wounded you. They will be keys to your healing as you move forward.

As we reflect upon our early years, one very healthy conclusion to reach is that those who raised us did their very best and chances are that those who wounded us were wounded themselves. Alcoholic fathers, abusive mothers, twisted relatives, and mean-spirited peers all did and said what seemed right to them at the time, regardless of how idiotic it seems to us now. Jesus provided a great model for us when, on the cross, he looked at his tormentors and asked his heavenly Father to "forgive them, for they don't understand what they are doing." It also often helps to realize that we are not alone in our pain and that the wounds we suffered are common all over the world.

Because we live in such a "blame someone else for my problems" society, I want to repeat one very important thing here. The point in looking back and identifying the sources of our wounds is *not* so that we can excuse our own poor choices and negative behavior. Nor is it to place the responsibility for our errors on someone other than ourselves. There is way too much of that occurring in our world today. The old excuse that "my dad abused me, so I now abuse my own children" does not fly in the light of the gospel and God's amazing power to transform us, and our behavior, from darkness to light. The whole point in looking in and looking back is to help us understand *why* we think and do certain things. Once this is discovered, we then move quickly ahead with the healing process.

Look Forward

We have looked in to find our wounds and looked back to understand where they came from. Now it is time to gather the strength and motivation to keep moving forward. We learn from the Scriptures that Jesus endured the pain of the cross *because of the joy set before him.* And what was that joy? What could possibly make it possible for Jesus to make such a sacrifice? The joy of Jesus came from the fact that his sacrifice made a way for all humanity to be reconciled to our heavenly Father. In other words, he chose to endure humiliation, pain, and suffering so that the generations that followed could be whole.

In much the same way, we must make a choice. We can play it safe, limp along, and hope our sons and daughters somehow turn out all right. Or we can endure the temporary pain of the healing process so that we can effectively lead those who follow.

In Malachi 4:6 God clearly called us to turn our hearts toward the next generation, and countless men are answering that life-changing call. However, we must be certain that the hearts we turn are as pure and whole as possible. Our sons and daughters carry enough pain of their own. They do not need ours dumped on them as well. We simply need to make a choice to do what it takes to receive healing for our wounded hearts and then turn those refurbished hearts to the next generation.

We must remember that there are two sets of hearts—fathers' and children's—that turn in Malachi 4:6. The order in which this passage is written is the order in which it happens. First a father's heart turns toward his children, and then, in response, the children's hearts turn back to the father.

In the fall of 2003 I was eyewitness to the power of this principle. It happened at what may seem like an unlikely place and time, during an elk hunt in Colorado. Two of my close friends and hunting partners, Harry Marcus and Scott Moore, had traveled to a wonderful hunting camp north of Durango. There we met our hosts and a dozen other men from around the country. The lodge was absolutely perfect from our perspective. Knotty-pine interior. Walls covered with mounted heads of huge bull elk, cougars, bears, and other animals that we potentially could see during our treks to the mountains. The terrain was rough, and with the elevation over ten thousand feet above sea level, we were pushed to our physical limits throughout the week. In the evenings we would sit around with the other men to review the details of the day's hunt and have a short Bible study. I underscore short here because by the time we got back from the hunt and had dinner, our bodies and minds were exhausted and our sleeping bags looked extremely inviting.

On the fourth day of our hunt, Harry and I decided to take the morning off and visit the rustic mountain town of Silverton. As we were getting ready to depart, another one of the hunters, Jeff, asked if he could go with us. Soon we all jumped into our vehicle and headed north up the scariest road I have ever experienced (but that is another story). As we traveled, we briefly talked about the breathtaking scenery and the joys of elk hunting in such a rugged location.

Then it was as if God suddenly redirected our conversation onto matters of much more importance. Our companion suddenly began to pour out his heart about his life, church, work, and family. It soon became clear that his heart was greatly troubled about his twenty-year-old son's struggles with his faith and purpose in life. During the long trip to and from Silverton, Jeff then told us how his relationship with this precious son had been strained and how much he longed for reconciliation. When we finally arrived back at the lodge, none of us could imagine that within twenty-four hours, God would show us all the power of Malachi 4:6.

Later that evening, during our time of sharing, the host asked me to talk about the Malachi Global Foundation, our men's retreats, and healing fathers' hearts and to recount the story of my children's rites of passage. As we sat around on wonderfully worn couches and chairs, I simply spoke about God's wonderful plan for men and the next generation. When I finished sharing, I asked if any of the men wanted prayer. Now, keep in mind that these guys were elk hunters, some of the roughest characters I have ever come across. As I looked around the room, I noticed that many of them had tears in their eyes as God slowly opened their hearts to his plan. One man stepped forward immediately and had us gather around him for prayer. A few others followed, and God wonderfully touched them through the loving prayer of men like Harry Marcus.

At one point, I looked to see where Jeff was and found him sitting very quietly on the edge of a couch. I motioned for him to join us in the middle of the room, and at first he hesitated. Then he slowly stood, came forward, and asked us to pray for him to be healed from hurts from his past. Harry led us in prayer and was soon followed by other men who had gathered around Jeff and gently laid their hands on him. As soon as the men began to pray, God began to answer. Jeff seemed to fight the inevitable for a short while and held back his emotions. However, within moments the dam holding back his emotions gave way, and he began to weep. Feeling his pain, other men shed a few tears as well. For me it was a marvelous picture of what men, whole men, can be. Here we were, a bunch of rough-and-tumble, modern-day mountain men willing to let our Creator heal the part of us that our children need the most—our hearts. Our time of prayer that night lasted well over an hour, with many of the men coming forth as Jeff did, asking God to heal them, forgive them, and bless their children. No one complained about the lateness of the hour when we finally all slid into our bunks.

The next morning took us all back out to the mountains to hike, hunt, and enjoy God's wonderful creation. After a full day, we all arrived back at the lodge for dinner and then gathered for another time of sharing. We had just begun to reflect on how God had moved the previous evening when a phone call came into the lodge—a phone call for Jeff. After a short conversation, Jeff returned to our group with the most marvelous look on his face. It was somewhere between disbelief and bliss. He told us that the call had come from his wife, who had just returned from an evening meeting at their church. It seems that just before she left for the meeting, their son had asked if he could go along. This shocked Jeff's wife, but she knew better than to let it show and simply took their son with her. At the meeting, an evangelist shared about God's love and purpose for each person on earth. At the end of the message, the minister invited people to come forward and receive Christ. The first one to the front was Jeff's son.

Once again, high in the mountains, this group of men laughed and cried together at how quickly the heart of a son turned in response to his father. What makes this so amazing to me is that the son was over a thousand miles away when his father's heart was healed and turned. Like prayer, the message of Malachi is not hindered by distance or geography. When we allow God to heal our hearts and then turn those hearts to our children, we can anticipate that our sons and daughters, no matter how far away they may be, will turn their hearts to God and to us.

When compared with the joy of seeing our sons and daughters succeed, the price we pay for our own healing is next to nothing.

Look Up

Once we accept the fact that we have been wounded and understand the importance of our role in leading the next generation, we can begin the healing process. We receive our healing in two essential ways. First, we look up to our God for the deliverance and healing that only he can bring. There is no substitute for prayer to our all-powerful heavenly Father. He is willing and able to take the heaviest burden from the shoulders of a sincere man. Second, we share our burdens, wounds, and shortcomings with trusted friends. Powerful healing occurs when men bring their dark fears and wounds into the light of trusted counsel.

We read in James 5:16 that we are to confess our faults, errors, and transgressions with one another *so that we may be healed*. God certainly was speaking to men in particular when that passage was written. How do I know this? Well, as a man, I know how reluctant I am to share my problems with others. My shortcomings often seem either too petty to bother with or too personal to share. The obstacles of pride, fear, and isolation have been around a long time, and they constantly try to keep us from what we truly need: an open and honest relationship with God and with our fellow men.

As we move forward on the path of healing, we are inevitably confronted with two concepts: forgiveness and repentance. Not only are they foundational elements of biblical Christianity, but they are also absolute essentials for all men wanting to be whole.

Forgiveness. Men often struggle with the concept of forgiveness for a variety of reasons. Some men believe that they have done such terrible things that God could never forgive them. It will be comforting for them to know that God himself said that *all* have sinned and come short of his glory. Since everyone has made a mess of things at one point or another, this truth helps explain the sorry state of the world around us. Thankfully, it should also help individuals who struggle with guilt or shame over the misdeeds of their past. Remember, your particular brand of sin is nothing new; it was just new to you. If you, like so many others, believe the lie that you have gone too far for a loving God to reach and forgive, then you will never feel qualified or called to reach the next generation. Receiving God's forgiveness for yourself will begin the process of you forgiving others. Without it, you will never start.

Repentance. Repentance completes the picture of God's forgiveness. Scripture is very clear in saying that we are forgiven of all our sins *and* that once this happens, we are admonished to sin no more. This does not mean we live perfect lives by any means. However, neither does it mean the opposite, that we willfully continue to do things we know are wrong. Biblical repentance means to turn and go in the opposite direction.

In practical terms, this means that if you at one time were abusive to your family, you can approach God, ask for forgiveness, and receive a brand-new start. Further, it means that once you get the new start, you are never again to do things that hurt your family. This principle works for countless other scenarios where we have fallen short in the past. Internet pornography, drunkenness, and childish disregard for the well-being of one's family are all forgivable acts as long as the man involved truly repents and begins to act in a proper manner.

There is a time to weep and grieve over our sins of the past. Men who fail to do so carry backbreaking burdens unnecessarily. There is also a time to truly repent of our misdeeds and begin life anew. This means doing whatever is needed to avoid a relapse. If Internet pornography is an obstacle, then unplug your computer. If you spend each weekend golfing instead of spending time with your children, then sell your clubs. If you need some professional counseling to overcome bad habits, then find a good counselor and get your life back. Do whatever it takes to truly repent and go in a new direction.

A Word on Unforgiveness

There is another aspect of forgiveness that is common to many of us. This occurs when men willingly accept God's forgiveness for *themselves* but are reluctant to offer that same forgiveness *to others*. This leads to a very self-centered, delusional mind-set where a man's blackest deeds are miraculously forgiven by God but even the slightest sin by others condemns the offender to eternal damnation. Sorry, that pick-and-choose approach to forgiveness is not in the Book. God promised to *forgive us our trespasses as we forgive those who trespass against us.* Failure to forgive does incredible damage to the one holding on to the anger and rage that often accompany this wretched condition.

In addition, unforgiveness binds us to those who hurt us. It forges unseen chains that link our souls, thoughts—conscious and subconscious—and actions. As long as those chains remain intact, we drag a host of bad memories and bitterness around wherever we go. What a terrible way to live.

I remember some years ago when I was deeply wounded by a supposed friend whom I helped out of deep financial troubles. My kindness and the loan of many thousands of dollars saved him and his family from ruin. However, once his immediate crisis was averted, he repaid me by failing to repay my money and breaking off the "friendship." I confess that I burned with anger and bitterness over that situation for quite a few months. I knew the biblical mandate to forgive, and in all honesty, I simply did not want to do it! After all, this man knowingly cheated me, and he deserved to be punished.

For quite a long time, I held my feelings in. At least I thought I did. In reality I was slowly pouring out my anger on those around me. I snapped at my wife and snarled at my children when they had done little or nothing wrong. My belly was often tied in painful knots that only diminished when I slept. During that painful period, I rarely smiled and spent a great deal of time preoccupied with thoughts of revenge, retribution, and reprisal.

Eventually I swallowed my pride and shared my pain with some trusted friends, who did what needed to be done. They got me to see that my original motives in helping the man were good—even if my judgment was lousy—and that God would somehow make the situation right. They finally got me to pray a prayer of forgiveness for the man and to put him into the hands of a fair and just God to receive his "reward" for his actions.

After praying, I initially felt nothing change. The tormenting thoughts still tried to invade my mind for several days after I prayed the prayer of forgiveness. However, before long, I noticed that the constant bombardment of angry thoughts had ceased. I even began to pray for the man and his family. Now that was a switch! Eventually I moved from simply being angry to a place where I could grow from the whole painful experience. Clearly, I had been too trusting and had failed to listen to others who counseled me against helping this man who had cheated others in the past. Today I am happy to say that while I still regret the situation, I am no longer bound to it by bitterness. God will deal with him. I have forgiven. I have moved on. You can too.

Remember, whether your wounds are large or small, new or ancient, you still need to come to the place where you forgive those who inflicted them, so that *you* can be free.

It is important to realize that your forgiveness of someone who wronged you does *not* justify the other person's actions in any way. Nor does it remove the other person's guilt or responsibility to offer an apology or make restitution or, in extreme cases, face criminal charges. Instead your forgiveness does two simple things that will change the course of *your* life. First, it puts you back into right standing with God. In the Lord's Prayer, we are encouraged to ask God to "forgive us our trespasses *as we forgive those who trespass against us.*" Forgive so that God forgives you. The second thing that forgiveness does is it sets us free from entangling chains of bitterness, anger, and a whole host of other negative emotions. Once our hearts are clear, we can be filled with the true substance of God's kingdom, which is righteousness, peace, and joy.

I suppose that I could have gone on with life without extending forgiveness toward this man and the host of other folks who took more than they gave during our time together on this earth. However, had I failed to forgive and not gotten the chains of bitterness off my mind, there is one thing that I am sure of. My limp would be much more pronounced than it now is. I would see others through a filter of mistrust, and my soul would have been forever troubled. As a result, my ability to love, mentor, and bless my own children and to properly love my wife would have been crippled. Failure to forgive and move on would have caused my own "issues" to cloud my thinking, distort my personality, and generate untold amounts of anger waiting to invade my home without warning.

As I said before, all of us carry wounds from the past, and it is imperative that we take time to work through them. Please don't think that this applies to everyone other than you or that you are somehow immune to life's afflictions. Sadly, in the years since I hosted the celebration for my first son, I have witnessed the spiritual and relational meltdown of no fewer than six men who were in attendance. Please understand, these were men of deep faith and strong family ties. At the time I thought enough of them to invite their participation in my son's rite of passage. Outwardly, there were no indications that anything was wrong, and yet each of them ended up in affairs, divorce, or other unthinkable situations. One of these men, a formerly trusted church counselor, left his wife and ran off with a seventeen-year-old young woman he had been "counseling."

Isn't that amazing? Not really. I am convinced that these men simply failed to deal with old hurts, wounds, and the pain that led them into such childish, thoughtless behaviors. They failed to work through issues of their own identities and to share openly about their struggles with sexuality, lust, anger, and negative emotions. Wounded people wound others. Children, no matter how old they are, act like children. However, it does not have to be that way. God has made it possible for us to walk with integrity while on this earth. While it is not easy, I am convinced that it can be done. Moreover, if we are to effectively lead this next generation, then it must be done.

HEALED AND HOPEFUL

So look up. God is able to listen to, understand, and deal with every situation that you have ever been through. As you look up, you will also notice that there is one (or more) trustworthy man with whom you can share your hurts, frustrations, anger, and temptations before they explode into scandal and ruin. Those individuals may be family members, pastors or priests, neighbors, coworkers, or part of your local men's ministry. Keep in mind that your transparency about wounds and weaknesses will not shock others. Instead it will simply confirm that someone else has been through tough times and survived. The men around you will be blessed by your openness, and in return, you will be blessed by their acceptance and support.

Epilogue

ONE BOY
AT A TIME

THE BLACK CAR SLOWED TO A STOP at the railroad cross-ing near the edge of town; its passengers were startled to see a young man walking down the middle of the train tracks. Storm clouds approached, goaded on by a cruel north wind. *Where would someone be going on such a heartless night?*

Rain came in a whisper, then with an angry roar, soaking the young man as he shuffled down the tracks. With his hands thrust in his pock-ets and head down, it was hard to tell much about him. His race and age were concealed by the night. The men heard the distant sound of an approaching train. The young man didn't seem to notice, although he was in harm's way if he stayed his course.

The driver put down his window and shouted, "Hey, kid! Where you going? Hey! What's the matter with you?" Without a backward glance, the young man continued to walk down the track. His lack of response angered the driver. "Hey! Get off those tracks! There's a train coming! Don't be stupid! Hey, kid, grow up!"

The man in the passenger seat tried to calm the driver. "Easy, man. It's nothing to get upset about. You know young people today just don't listen. If he really wanted help, he'd ask for it. I'm sure he'll move before the train gets here." He glanced at his watch. "Come on, let's get going. We've already missed the start of the game. Hey, maybe at half-time we could call some agency or something. You know, somebody who gets paid to handle situations like this…"

The young man's thin figure was nearly hidden by the night's blackness as each step took him farther from the men. Only an occasional flash of lightning gave proof that he was still there. From the backseat came the third man's quiet voice. "We can't just leave him."

"What can we do?" snarled the driver. "We tried to help him, and it didn't do any good!"

"We can't just leave him," the quiet man responded. "He's headed the wrong way. I'm getting out."

"Now, don't rush into this," soothed the man in the front passenger seat. "He's just one kid. You know, he could be dangerous, too. Let's drive on. If you want, we can come back later."

"No," said the quiet man as he stepped out of the car and into the stormy night. "I've got to reach him."

"You're a fool!" fumed the driver. "I've got better things to do than wait for some dumb kid who hasn't got enough sense to get out of the rain. We're outta here!"

The black car sped away, leaving the quiet man alone in the storm. In the distance, he could barely see the young man. Doubts assaulted his mind. *Did I do the right thing? What if he is dangerous? What if he won't listen? What if…?*

The quiet man's questions were cut short by another blast of the train whistle. Beneath his feet, he could feel the rumble of the train as it approached. Adrenaline surged through his body as he began to run down the tracks, realizing that this was truly a matter of life or death. A warrior's prayer exploded through his clenched teeth. "Oh, God, please help me reach him in time!"

His flying feet soon closed the gap between them, and he was within shouting distance. "Hey, hold up!"

The train rounded the bend and screamed straight toward them. The young man's frame was silhouetted in the headlight of the giant engine.

"Hey! Turn around! *Please!*"

These words seemed to break the spell that had clouded the young man's thinking. He suddenly stopped and turned to face the man pursuing him in the storm. In his young eyes were confusion, fear, and something that had been dormant for months—hope. Someone really *did* care!

His silent celebration came to an abrupt halt as he realized the train was just yards away. Its whistle screamed, and the metal wheels roared out their final warning. Surely he had made a fatal mistake with his life. The young man shut his eyes and braced himself for the crushing impact.

But instead of jagged metal, he felt a strong hand grab his jacket and throw him out of the way of the train. Both men tumbled to a stop in the wet grass. The train flew past and mindlessly continued down the track. Soon the steel nightmare was out of sight.

Badly shaken, the young man spoke first. "Uh, thanks. I don't know what else to say."

The quiet man slowly responded. "You're welcome, friend. But that was a little too close for comfort."

After several moments, the young man spoke again. "Mister, I sure hated walking down that track. I just didn't know where else to go. It seemed better to go the wrong way than to go nowhere." His eyes pleaded for the quiet man to understand. "I don't suppose that makes any sense to you, does it?"

The quiet man smiled and tried to catch his breath. "Yes, son, it does. Not too many years ago I walked down these same tracks. But I found a better way, God's way. If you want, I'll show it to you."

It didn't take long for the young man to respond. "When?"

"How about right now?"

They picked themselves up off the muddy ground and began slowly walking together toward town.

"What's your name, son?" the quiet man asked.

The young man hesitated for a moment and then replied, "My name's Jason."

Far in the distance a train whistle screams out its warning once again. Someone else is on the tracks. Whose son is it this time? Is he mine? Is he yours? Will someone reach him before it's too late? Will someone care enough to even try to reach him?

Only one of these questions has a sure answer. *You* can be the one who cares enough to try. Throughout the world countless young people walk down tracks that lead them the wrong way. These youth come in all different shapes, sizes, and colors. Some of them are rich; others are poor. In each case there is a train of destruction hurtling toward them. Cynicism, despair, drugs, alcohol, HIV, gang violence, or perhaps suicide will destroy many of these precious young people if we don't intervene.

Some boys will live through these dangerous encounters and may even prosper later in life. However, many will die in their youth without ever reaching their potential. Others will be physically or emotionally crippled for life. Still others will drift from track to track without clear purpose or direction. These are the orphans spoken of in James 1:27. These are the fatherless ones without comfort. Can the lack of a father or father figure really have that big of an impact? If you are still not sure, here are some statistics from the National Fatherhood Initiative to help you decide:

- In the U.S.A., 24 million children live without their biological fathers.
- An amazing 82 percent of girls who get pregnant as teenagers come from families where no father is present.
- In the year 2000 approximately 1.35 million births occurred out of wedlock.
- About 40 percent of the children in absent-father homes have not seen their father at all during the past year, and 50 percent of children whose fathers are absent have never set foot in their father's "home."
- Children whose biological fathers are absent are, on average, at least two to three times more likely to be poor, to use drugs, to experience educational, health, emotional, and behavioral problems, to be victims of child abuse, and to engage in criminal behavior than those who live with their married, biological [or adoptive] parents.
- Children with involved, loving fathers are significantly more likely to do well in school, have healthy self-esteem, exhibit empathy and prosocial behavior, and avoid high-risk behaviors, such as drug use, truancy, and criminal activity, compared to children who have uninvolved fathers.

These data should be sufficient for us to realize the importance of healthy fathers being involved in the lives of the next generation. And now that the solution to these problems has so clearly been identified, this bleak picture can be changed. The destruction of our youth can end. This will happen, however, only when we men come forth and lead our young counterparts along the proper path to maturity. One on one. Generation after generation. Our young men don't need famous figures they can worship. They need father figures they can love. Though our sons naturally grow in *masculinity,* they must learn how to become men of *maturity.*

The sacrificial act of mentoring our youth will change not only individual lives but also our entire society. The logic is undeniable. The foundational building block of a godly society is the family—a husband and wife together doing their best to raise godly children. It is painfully obvious that the departure from this model threatens to tear down our nations. Thankfully, it is just as obvious that this trend does not have to continue.

When just one man, Jonah, walked through the city of Nineveh with a message of change, the city repented of its wicked ways. Imagine what will happen when thousands of godly men and women walk through our society with a message of positive change. When the older men encourage the younger men to follow them, when rites of passage, intentional blessing, and mentoring of the younger men become a way of life for your home, your church, your neighborhood—then strength will return to our cities and our nations.

Without question there is a movement of God upon the earth today to restore things that have been lost or stolen. Good things. Family. Faith. Fatherhood. Mentoring. It is God's desire that the hearts of the fathers be turned to their children and the hearts of the children be turned to their fathers (see Malachi 4:6). This is achievable in our time.

The new millennium has seen a reawakening of men's spirits throughout the world. Near the turn of the century, over one million men gathered at large-scale men's events to learn about their vital roles in changing our world. This was followed by the launch of countless men's ministries and new men's groups centered in local churches. Here is the vision that drives me each day: if each of these men commits to mentor, bless, and celebrate just two boys in his lifetime and teaches them to repeat the process, the results will be incredible. When men catch the vision, we can turn around entire nations within one generation. Only one thing can stop us: failing to start.

Therefore I solemnly challenge you to turn off the television this week—no, *today*—put away your business planner, and prayerfully find at least one young man who needs someone to help him enter into manhood. If you have a son, start there. If your sons are grown and you have grandsons, work with the parents and start there. If you don't have either, then search until you find a nephew, young cousin, or any other boy who needs a man in his life.

Once you find him, begin to listen to, love, and lead that young man. Pray for and with him. Speak words of blessing into his life. Host a celebration in his honor. Affirm his journey to mature manhood. Take him places with you. Teach him the value of work, rest, and play. Help him to laugh. Answer his questions. Hug him when he hurts. Show him the love of his heavenly Father. Teach him the Scriptures. You get the idea.

When you consider the impact that mentoring, intentional blessing, and a celebration can have on the future of a young man who has no affirming father, you will realize that it is one of the best investments you can make in life.

Our opportunity to change the direction of an entire generation is very real. Consider that just one or two men can positively change the course of their church simply by blessing the young men in the congregation. A small handful of men can redirect the course of their community by hosting celebrations and mentoring the young men from their neighborhood. It just takes a few men to accept their God-given calling as mentors. It just takes *you* to do it.

We need to set aside the incessant demands of the day in order to secure something of eternal value for the young men around us. We need to accept the mentor's mantle. Today, choose to do for other young men what you wish someone had done for you when you were a boy. Choose to turn a generation of boys into godly men, one boy at a time.

ACKNOWLEDGMENTS

THERE ARE MANY PEOPLE I want to thank for their support, encouragement, contributions, wise counsel, and prayers.

Thanks to my wife, Kathleen, and our children, Christopher, Steven, Jenifer, and Daniel. Your love, support, and patience bring out the very best in me. You have captured my heart and taught me the meaning of *home*.

A special thanks to both sets of grandparents in our family: Bob and Jinny Molitor and Jim and Betty Hayes. God used your love and guidance to bless our marriage and the next generation that bears your likeness. Now that we are parents, Kathy and I finally understand the sacrifices you made for your children. You have our gratitude, love, and devotion forever.

Thanks to our team here at Molitor International. You have been so supportive during this project. At the top of the list are John and Ann Bennett, Scott Moore, Andrew Forester, Karen Spickerman, Jan Clarkson, Burnett Kelly, Harry Marcus, Ric Suitor, and Linda Neuman. Thanks to Ric Olson and Trevor Knoeson, my partners in IBICC. You have all enriched my life and held up my arms more than you know.

I am so grateful for the many old and new friends who caught the vision of this book. They include Bradley Stuart, Ron Ives, John Trent, Jim Weidmann, and Ron Williams. I am also thankful for Warren Walsh and the people at Emerald who worked so hard to bring this project to completion. Marit, your thoughtful editing was outstanding!

A special thanks to Don Pape for his heartfelt support for this project and his unselfish approach to the business of publishing.

I want to say a special thanks to James Glenn, a precious friend who truly sticks closer than a brother. James, God has sent us halfway around the world together more than once, and each time it was a grand adventure. Isn't it just like God to take a black man from the streets of Detroit and a white man from the woods of northern Michigan and make them an inseparable team? James, thank you for standing with me through all the spiritual battles that have come. At times your buddy was wounded, tired, and about to give up when you came along, broke through the enemy's ranks, and pulled him out. Thanks, brother.

Thanks to all the men who attended the celebrations for my sons. Your zeal and commitment to the next generation of young men lit a fire within me that God turned into this book.

ABOUT THE AUTHOR
AND MALACHI GLOBAL
MEN'S RETREATS

BRIAN D. MOLITOR is the founder of the Malachi Global Foundation. This organization is dedicated to the fulfillment of Malachi 4:6 and seeks to turn the hearts of the fathers to the children around the world. The Malachi Global Foundation works closely with churches and men's ministries to host weekend retreats for men. It also produces a wide range of teaching materials in audio and video formats to help men implement strategies of lifelong mentoring, intentional blessing, and rites of passage for the children in their lives.

Brian is also the chief executive officer of Molitor International. His company specializes in consulting and training in interpersonal relationships, organizational development, team building, problem solving, and leadership coaching. He has produced and hosted numerous television programs on various topics, including family building. He writes business columns for several magazines and produces numerous training manuals, videos, and audiotapes that are used by people in business, ministry, government, and by families throughout the world. Molitor is also the author of *The Power of Agreement.*

Before his present career, Molitor worked as director of a residential camp for troubled youth and was the director of a statewide men's prison ministry, ministering to young men in particular. He and his wife, Kathleen, are the parents of four children: Christopher, Steven, Jenifer, and Daniel. As a dad, Molitor enjoys coaching a number of sports, including his sons' basketball and junior-league football teams. He and his family live in Michigan.

For more information on the Malachi Global Retreats for your church or men's group, or to contact Brian, please use any of the following methods:

Web site: www.malachiglobal.org
E-mail: info@malachiglobal.org
Toll-free telephone: 1-877-MALACHI
Fax: (989) 698-0469